DATE DUE

DEMCO 38-296

WONDER BOY

· WONDER ·
· BOY ·

Barry Minkow—The Kid Who Swindled Wall Street

by

Daniel Akst

CHARLES SCRIBNER'S SONS
New York

Charles Scribner's Sons
Macmillan Publishing Company
866 Third Avenue, New York, NY 10022
Collier Macmillan Canada, Inc.

Library of Congress Cataloging-in-Publication Data
Akst, Daniel.
Wonder boy : Barry Minkow, the kid who swindled Wall Street / by
Daniel Akst.
p.   cm.
Includes index.
ISBN 0-684-18988-7
1. Minkow, Barry.   2. Businessmen—United States—Biography.
3. Success in business—United States.   4. Fraud—United States.
5. Wall Street.   I. Title.
HC102.5.M5A65   1990   89-10240   CIP
364.1′68—dc20
[B]

Macmillan books are available at special discounts for bulk purchases
for sales promotions, premiums, fund-raising, or educational use.
For details, contact:

Special Sales Director
Macmillan Publishing Company
866 Third Avenue
New York, N.Y. 10022

10   9   8   7   6   5   4   3   2   1
Printed in the United States of America

"For what is genius, I ask you, but the capacity to be obsessed?"
—*Steven Millhauser*

Cast of Characters

Barry J. Minkow, who founded ZZZZ Best Co. in Reseda, California, as the vehicle for his own fantasies.

Mark L. Morze, ZZZZ Best vice-president and detail man who helped Barry's wild imaginings become real. His brother **Brian** helped, too.

Thomas G. Padgett, owner and operator of Interstate Appraisal Services, which helped make Barry's vehicle look roadworthy.

Mark M. Roddy, the Ultimate White Man, who helped Padgett.

Norman Rothberg, an accountant at Interstate Appraisal.

Daniel Krowpman Sr., who helped Barry get started and supported him along the way.

Jack M. Catain Jr., the local gangster who met his match in a teenager.

Maurice Rind, a stock swindler before financial fraud was fashionable.

Richard Schulman, a more ham-handed criminal than his boyhood pal Rind.

Robert Victor, born Viggiano and known that way to law-enforcement computers everywhere. Schulman's friend from prison.

Mark R. Moskowitz, a partner in the blue-blood law firm of Hughes Hubbard & Reed who represented ZZZZ Best.

Robert Grossmann, a stockbroker who helps companies like ZZZZ Best fulfill their potential.

Faith Griffin, an investment banker with Rooney, Pace Group Inc., who tried to do the right thing.

Jeri Carr, Barry's public relations woman.

Charles B. "Chip" Arrington III, Barry's flunky and ZZZZ Best's chief operating officer.

Jack and **Jerry Polevoi**, Barry's friends who cleaned the money.

Mike Brambles, a Los Angeles Police organized-crime detective.

Rose Schindler, a lawyer with the Securities and Exchange Commission.

James Asperger and **Gordon Greenberg**, Assistant U.S. Attorneys.

1

A nn Randall is still a beautiful woman. She used to be a
singer, and although she is blessed in many ways, fate hasn't
always been kind to her. Two marriages ended in divorce,
and her health has sometimes flagged. Ann Randall lived
through these travails without losing her sunny outlook or her faith
in people. She is no longer young, but she has led a full life, and
Southern California is a pleasant place to retire. Newhall, where she
lives, is warm and dry, farm country that is fast sprouting new sub-
urbs, but still a quiet place where sunshine and fruit trees can be had
for comfortable prices. Money wasn't going to be much of a problem.
Besides any pension or Social Security income she might have in the
years ahead, Ann Randall had put aside $150,000 in cash. Not long
ago she even had a little excitement come into her life. That was when
she met a charismatic young businessman named Barry Minkow. For
Ann it was love at first sight, in a motherly sort of way, and it was
exciting too to think that he could help her lead a better life by making
her savings grow. Barry was lively, gentle and kind. He was also
completely persuasive. He had helped a friend of Ann's make a lot
of money, and now he would help Ann too.

Sharon Elowsky is a ferocious skeptic, a New Yorker by birth and
a lawyer by training who is so careful that she wouldn't serve on the
board of her co-operative apartment building until she had read the
insurance policy guarding board members against liability. Elowsky
was thirty years old and single when she met Barry Minkow, and she
was fascinated by him. An executive at Prudential-Bache Securities
near Manhattan's South Street Seaport, Elowsky had an MBA and

ran a lending program in which rich entrepreneurs like Barry could borrow millions of dollars to buy securities. She didn't much like her job, but Barry added spice to her life. As a customer, he had a $5 million line of credit from Elowsky's department. As a suitor, he sent her flowers and talked seductively on the telephone. Elowsky knew her friend was a kid in some ways—Barry was only twenty-one and sometimes acted younger—but he was an interesting one, and twice she accepted his invitations to visit Los Angeles. His exuberance contrasted vividly with the conformity she saw in the financial district or at home in Brooklyn Heights. Barry combined innocence, ardor and financial sophistication, and he was also good business. Shari Elowsky cautiously let him borrow some cash from his line of credit. After all, what was $2 million to Barry Minkow?

Tom Padgett seemed born to follow. He flirted with radical politics in college and joined the Army twice, eventually falling into the white supremacist movement in Southern California. Tom is the opposite of those ideologues who love mankind but can't stand people. Tom seems to like everyone he meets, yet his principles insist that he exclude whole swaths of humankind. Padgett met Barry Minkow when Barry was just fourteen, while both were spending a lot of time lifting weights at a low-rent gym in the sunbaked San Fernando Valley, which sprawls hot and recumbent across the hills from Los Angeles like the city's feverish hallucination of itself. Tom and Barry became great friends, and the older man tried to provide the kind of guidance he felt Barry needed. After a short time it became clear that their relationship wasn't what it seemed, and that by reversing roles they would be in a more natural position with respect to one another. Padgett had no money to give to Barry, so he gave himself. If Tom Padgett was born to follow, Barry Minkow was born to lead.

Barry was just a teenager, yet all kinds of people followed him, and nearly all lived to regret it. A few regretted it early, when they saw him for what he was, but many more regretted it too late, when his financial empire had collapsed and they found themselves bloodied or buried in the ruins. Barry himself must have regretted at least some of it during the gray dawn of January 15, 1988, the first time he ever had the sickening feeling of waking up behind bars for what might be a long time to come. The transition was difficult. Barry had grown used to the freedom and power that flow from great personal wealth. He could go wherever he wanted, by chartered jet if it pleased him, and he took orders from no one. Barry snapped his fingers and the people around him jumped.

His first twenty-four hours in prison made a stark contrast to the life he had led before. Instead of a mansion in a gated community where the guards worked for him, Barry was suddenly a prisoner. Instead of freedom, movement was painful. Prisoners were handcuffed and then shackled to one another, and instead of giving orders Barry was suddenly required to take them from his underpaid and contemptuous jailers.

It was morning, Barry's first in custody following the spectacular collapse of his ZZZZ Best Co., which had plummeted in a matter of weeks from a value exceeding $200 million on the stock market to a mere $62,000 at auction. Barry was subdued in jail, but he was still Barry. Reunited the next day with a group of ZZZZ Best colleagues seized separately the night before, he joked with his friends about the outlandish chain of events that had brought them there, and reminisced about the good times they had had. Barry seemed quietly confident that he could deny blame for what had happened. "I'm like the sun," he explained. "I point in all directions."

It was amazing to think that all of ZZZZ Best (pronounced "zee best") could be bought for $62,000. That wouldn't even cover Barry's bail, which was about to be set in a courtroom on the tenth floor of the federal courthouse in downtown Los Angeles. But it was still early, and there was no action there yet. Barry hadn't arrived. The hubbub instead was in a briefing room downstairs.

There some men in dark-blue suits stood shoulder to natural shoulder, holding their own hands and staring out into the rabble of camera crews and reporters, as they announced that Barry and ten others had just been indicted on a litany of federal charges so long it could put some of them away for a lifetime or two, if a judge and jury were so inclined. Really, the list was impressive. There were several kinds of fraud, racketeering, money laundering, tax evasion, filing false documents with the Securities and Exchange Commission, aiding and abetting and so forth. Phones and mails were used, state lines were crossed and in general everything that federal criminal law is so prickly about took place. Four defendants faced more than 100 years in prison; Barry himself was looking at 350. "It's a good thing he's young," someone joked.

It was almost as if the federal prosecutors had had trouble finding enough charges to encompass the scope of perfidy that actually occurred. And in a sense they hadn't, because Barry and his friends hadn't merely hoodwinked banks and investors out of millions of dollars; they'd snookered all the rest of us as well.

Barry Minkow was the twenty-one-year-old wunderkind, the entrepreneurial genius who made zillions in the carpet-cleaning business before he was old enough to buy a drink. Amazing Minkow stories abounded: hauling water in someone else's carpet-cleaning business at age ten, starting his own business at fifteen, the first million practically before he could drive, the weakling-to-hunk self-transformation, the charity, the antidrug slogan ("My act's clean, how's yours?"), etc. Barry was a hero for our times, some Reagan Administration dream of a young person, the other side of the same imagination that forever conjures welfare queens.

To this day, Barry Minkow (his name rhymes with ginkgo) amazes everyone he meets. Shameless and fearless, he can look a man in the eye, swear from the depths of his soul never to let him down, and simultaneously take from him everything he might cherish, including his self-respect. Most of the people Barry encountered have never met anyone like him. Most add bitterly that they hope never to meet his like again. Betrayal is a cruel emotion, and his victims' fondest wish is for Barry to stay in prison for a long, long time.

None of them ever thought they would feel this way. When questions about the financial condition of ZZZZ Best or about Barry's personal integrity had begun to be raised, local newspapers were inundated with letters attesting to his saintly virtues. He had seemed so honest and filial, he had produced such profits for his investors and put so many people to work, it was inconceivable that things could come to this, inconceivable and unreal.

But then, there was always an element of parody about Barry Minkow, who often seemed like a walking satire of the society around him, or a careless, mocking *golem* sprung full-blown from our own most ardent and idiotic wishes for ourselves.

Barry wasn't just a thief. He had mocked the very idea of business, for despite all outward appearances, a going concern was the one thing Barry never actually had for himself. ZZZZ Best Co. had lost money from its earliest days, and after a while it didn't even try for profit. All it did was persuade people to invest. It stole from customers, borrowed from individuals and banks, and finally raised millions from private investors and the public securities markets. Then it ran these funds around and around, emitting before long the dark smoke and oily smell of a true engine of commerce.

Barry succeeded in creating not a corporation but the hologram of one. He did this by branching out from his much-ballyhooed but secretly insolvent carpet-cleaning business, telling everyone that he had won enormous contracts to restore buildings damaged by water and fire. All he needed was the capital to pursue these jobs, and anyone wise enough to provide it would earn returns of 50 percent or more—often in a matter of weeks.

Many people were suspicious. Some thought Barry was arrogant, immature, a phony. Some even wondered how he'd made such a success of the damage-restoration business so fast. If the trade was so lucrative, why weren't others doing it?

But no one imagined the most important thing of all: that the jobs didn't exist. ZZZZ Best had no large insurance contracts, and in a sense there really was no ZZZZ Best. What there was, mainly, was the 3-D, Technicolor, Sensurround imagination of young Barry Minkow.

That was enough, even for the technical problems. For instance, how did Barry string along all those lenders and investors who had helped make ZZZZ Best a $200 million company? He relied on Peter and Paul—on the time-honored tradition of paying off old lenders and investors with money raised from new ones. He developed variations on this theme: some would be repaid with their own money, for example. Others would *think* they had been paid off, but would reinvest with Barry before ever cashing the rubber checks he handed them.

This is a hectic and implausible way to make a living, but Barry and his cohorts amazed even themselves with how far they were able to carry the scheme. Before long Barry was living in a small mansion, driving a Ferrari, and commanding legions of servile employees. Sometimes, at their regular strategy sessions to plot out the fraud, Barry and his men would dissolve in laughter, giggling like children at how ludicrous it was, how completely amazing that the thing was working.

"Did you hear about the Boston job?" one would say. "The city of Boston burned down, and we got the contract."

"How about the Empire State Building?" someone would shout back. "The water tank broke—we're gonna restore the whole building."

"But we gotta finish the Eiffel Tower first—"

"You mean we can't do the Taj Mahal?"

"No, but the White House job will have to wait."

All of this was amazing, but the most amazing thing is how incredibly close they came to getting away with it. Maybe that's what they were thinking when they woke up on the rainy Friday morning of

January 15, 1988, and found themselves the center of attention in the City of the Angels.

That morning the eyes and ears of Los Angeles—its reporters, microphones and camera crews—were concentrated at the city's fine old U.S. District Courthouse, an august if roach-infested Art Deco structure set amid gracious lawns, bird of paradise plants, and the many homeless who live downtown. The assembled media listened intently as the local U.S. Attorney, balding, jowly Robert C. Bonner, explained phlegmatically that what actually happened was "the most massive and elaborate securities fraud perpetrated on the West Coast in over a decade."

Barry and his friends had caused losses exceeding $100 million, the kind of figure that implies huge banks and investment houses to whom money is a series of electronic blips that can be translated into comfy homes and German automobiles. The facts of the Barry Minkow fraud are somewhat different.

Widows and orphans lost their money. Hardworking folks lost their jobs, or had their careers ruined, their lives stained, their hopes turned to ash. There was much humiliation; lots of people were taken in, and a few unlucky souls had their most private feelings smashed and put on display. For some reason it is not just embarrassing but also shocking to see how easily the malevolent—and the cleverly so—can prey upon the honest. Not the perfect, mind you, but the merely honest, and to say that you cannot fool an honest man is to value wit above veracity.

It was well known by the morning of January 15 that Minkow and his friends were crooks, but still there was an air of unreality about the whole thing, what with the klieg lights and the TV reporters, their thinning hair blow-dried over bald spots. "What about the drug money?" someone would boom theatrically above the din. "What about the mob?" a piercing alto would demand. "Where's Barry now?"

Robert Bonner wasn't answering many questions, but the last could be answered with certainty. Barry and his friends had been rounded up the night before, and so after the lawmen announced their charges (the Internal Revenue Service, the Federal Bureau of Investigation and the Los Angeles Police were all represented), the reporters and camera crews trooped upstairs to watch the bail hearing.

It was not, as the saying goes, a pretty sight. The defendants were heralded by the jingle-jangle of chains, and all of them walked in rubbing their wrists. Shackles were removed in the vestibule just outside the courtroom, and when everybody was inside, the pile of gleaming cuffs and chains in the corner looked like a vicious little snakepit.

Barry's motley co-defendants were brought in first, and then there was a gap in the proceedings before Barry turned up, so for a while everybody just waited while things got organized. I was working for *The Wall Street Journal* in those days, and suffering from a cold so bad that I carried a big box of Kleenex wherever I went. Woozy and infectious, I wasn't about to miss Barry's arraignment, since I cherished my haphazard role in both his giddy rise and sudden fall. As a reporter for the *Los Angeles Times*, I had helped Barry achieve entrepreneurial stardom with a feature story in 1985, and two years later I unwittingly triggered his downfall by exposing massive credit-card fraud at his company. I subsequently followed the much larger ZZZZ Best story for the *Journal*, culminating in a page-one piece about the wonder boy who had, and lost, it all.

My eustachian tubes in an uproar, I fell into a pew beside a willowy young woman with blonde hair arranged along the lines of Farah Fawcett's in the actress's heyday about ten years ago. She sat wide-eyed, with an unnatural smile playing occasionally across her face, and once or twice she said to the burly young man who accompanied her, "I don't know what I'm doing here."

"Who are you?" I asked.

"I'm Barry's girlfriend," she replied. Here was a woman without an identity crisis. Her name was Joyce Lipman, and in her lap she clutched a Bible and some Alcoholics Anonymous tracts.

Joyce had been through a lot, which didn't show right away because of the general airiness about her. It seemed strange that she didn't float. She said Barry was holding up well—"He's very strong"—and in retrospect the inspirational reading material wasn't surprising, since Barry had said in a television interview a few days earlier that "The Lord is my defense and my deliverance and I'll take it as it goes, one day at a time." This was a definite shift in such a self-reliant young man, just as it was a definite shift to hear his lawyers go around saying that Barry was just a kid—a mere callow youth—who couldn't possibly be blamed for the fiasco he seemed to have caused. It was the mobsters, the co-conspirators, and all the other grown-ups who were truly responsible.

Finally Barry appeared outside the courtroom, where he stood patiently as the handcuffs were removed. He looked rested and fit—almost rakish in a gray and red sweatshirt, black sweatpants, and sneakers—and inside, while waiting for the magistrate to make an entrance, he looked through the drawings of himself done by the news artists, who were present because cameras aren't allowed. "The nose is too small," he told one of his portraitists. This was a good joke; Barry's beak is enormous.

Despite his placid demeanor, it was clear this wasn't a great day for him. Perhaps the magistrate's black robes and dour mien were a reminder that the end was at hand, as if some judicial Grim Reaper now controlled his fate. Barry looked hulking and caught standing up there before her, and most of all older, as if some veneer of innocence had finally been rubbed away to reveal a far worldlier countenance than the public had ever seen before. The joking was over. Also gone was the frantic quality that was once his trademark, as much as the brashness and self-promotion. Barry wasn't frantic anymore; now he could relax.

To one way of thinking, Barry found himself in the courtroom of U.S. Magistrate Venetta S. Tassopulos on January 15, 1988, mainly because he could never have enough money. He wanted money because it was power, and no matter how much money or how much power he managed to amass, Barry could never quite stop feeling powerless. In court that day Tassopulos set bail at $2 million, fully secured, and Barry's worst fears were realized: he would remain powerless, because he didn't have enough money.

Outside, people kept asking Barry how all this had happened. His best response came earlier in the week, when he calmly explained to a TV interviewer that "I'm not mature enough to handle a company with fourteen hundred people. I wasn't then, and at least I have the ability without the ego and the pride to admit it now." Barry never used to claim such a thing. Instead he had always boasted of his accomplishments, insisted they were his own, and claimed they had come in the face of opposition from his elders. He'd even seemed genuinely hurt at the discrimination he faced. Just because he was a teenager, some old farts were reluctant to trust him with a few thousand dollars. Eventually, Barry overcame their inhibitions, and soon they were pushing millions at him. Soon they, like everyone else, were calling the kid "Mr. Minkow."

2

Happy birthday, Mr. Minkow, I'm your legal arm
With advice from me you'll come to no harm,
My fees may be high, but I'm not here from greed,
Happy birthday, Mr. Minkow,
From Hughes Hubbard & Reed.

Barry turned twenty-one on March 22, 1987, and it's hard to say which was a bigger hit at his party the night before: a rap video prepared by his friends, or the exaggerated account of his life delivered in a schmaltzy accent by comedienne Liz Giosa, who runs a service called Meshugah-Gram. Barry loved both, sitting on the couch convulsed with laughter. There was also a stripper brought in by one of his sisters, and the 140 or so guests included everyone who was anyone in the world of Barry Minkow. A parade of them appeared on the video, but few could top Mark R. Moskowitz's affectionate rapping about his role as Barry's lawyer. Barry's father also rapped out a lyric:

> *I'm your Pop, better known as Bob R.M.,*
> *Now I know I've raised me a gem,*
> *Happy birthday, son, you're twenty-one,*
> *And all the fun has just begun.*

So it seemed. By the time of his twenty-first birthday, Barry Minkow had already surpassed the wildest expectations most people could ever have for themselves. His birthday fell on a Sunday. The party was the day before, at Barry's house, where Giosa found him "very gracious, very humble. He wasn't arrogant at all." He might have been; just before the weekend, ZZZZ Best stock closed in national over-the-counter trading at $10.875, meaning that Barry's 5.9 million shares, which gave him a controlling stake in the company of 53 percent, were worth roughly $64 million. Barry also knew the stock was going up. Its rise was so steady and inexorable that he became millions of dollars richer virtually every day; in less than a month, his shares were worth $110 million.

Barry was living every boy's dream: He was rich and famous. He could have virtually anything he wanted. His whim was law. Women fell before his charms, and important men treated him with deference. Anyone who asked about Barry's parents got a snappy answer: "They work for me." He made his mother his senior vice president at $36,000 a year. His father was merely a "commercial representative," a salesman of ZZZZ Best services to restaurants, bowling alleys and so forth. He got $24,000 plus commissions.

Barry, who loved baseball and thought nothing of paying people to round out a softball team, was now talking seriously about making a $30 million bid for the Seattle Mariners.

And as his father suggested, Barry really did seem a gem. As a nineteen- or twenty-year-old kid with little education and no inherited wealth, he had worked hard, astonished all the doubters and made a part of the world his own. From nowhere and out of nothing Barry had created a great big company, one that the stock market—O ruthless and unbiased arbiter!—valued at more than $210 million, based on the number of ZZZZ Best shares multiplied by their price. Just think: almost a dollar for every man, woman and child in America. Barry put hundreds of people to work and received two official commendations from Los Angeles Mayor Tom Bradley, first for his success in business and later for his philanthropy. He had high-priced lawyers and accountants at his beck and call, and Wall Street in his pocket.

All were impressed by Barry himself as much as by the business he founded. Barry is one of those rare individuals who fills a room the minute he enters, whose energy and intelligence are so unbounded that they can't be harnessed to books, but whose mastery of his fellow men seems complete. Barry metabolizes people, situations and facts the way teenage boys metabolize food. His grasp of personalities and processes is instinctive and brilliant, and he makes a powerful—and generally positive—impression on everyone he meets. He is not altogether polished or by any means learned, but that's part of his charm.

His formal ignorance passes for innocence, and innocence was essential to Barry's mystique.

This radiant persona was amplified by his publicist, who cranked out press releases that helped make him a national hero. His own evident generosity helped as well. Barry donated more than $10,000 plus carpeting and services to the West Valley YMCA. He gave another $10,000 to a local drug-treatment program. He coached a girls' softball team, and when the ball field needed fixing, Barry spent more than $20,000 on sod, sprinklers and a new red-dirt diamond.

Barry was an inspiration. He funded an anti–drunk driving commercial and starred in another in which he pleaded powerfully with young people to avoid drugs. Barry increasingly made this cause his own, condemning the evils of narcotics at every opportunity and forcing drug tests on his own workers. Drug abuse became his personal crusade. He explained these really quite paltry charitable impulses by insisting that his own success couldn't have happened if not for the American free enterprise system. Barry simply felt obligated to give something back. Before he was twenty there was a completed autobiography called *Making It in America*, in which Barry eagerly shared his experiences with the world.

It is hard now, in retrospect, to convey the level of apotheosis Barry Minkow achieved. *Newsweek* carried an article on young entrepreneurs and led with Barry. *USA Today* loved him, of course; they might have invented him if he hadn't existed. Likewise the television stations; he was profiled adoringly—even repeatedly—on almost all the ones in Los Angeles. Barry was also written up in the *Los Angeles Times*, *The Washington Post*, and almost everything in between. A data-base search will turn up his name in Arkansas. He even made "The Oprah Winfrey Show." After all, Barry Minkow was a great story: the brash young businessman with the heart of gold, the one who fought drug abuse, who believed in The American Way. Barry worked so hard he got ulcers, and even his ulcers were the stuff of legends. It seemed only a matter of time before his parents' humble garage, in which he started ZZZZ Best, attained the status of a national shrine, visited by schoolchildren for a glimpse at what they could aspire to.

Barry was even scheduled to present the Israeli Knesset with an oil portrait of David Ben-Gurion, signed by world leaders including Ronald Reagan, Jimmy Carter, George Bush, Senator Edward Kennedy and Yitzhak Shamir. Something came up, and a stand-in went instead.

That was understandable, given Barry's hectic schedule. His young life was a maelstrom of meetings, phone calls and hated airplane travel, of which he was deathly afraid. Barry conquered his fear of flying, just as by dint of sheer will he seemed to conquer any other obstacles in his own personal flight path.

"I'm obsessed," he would say cheerfully, and indeed he was. Barry worked seven days a week, day and night. He rarely went to movies, and when he entertained, his guests were usually ZZZZ Best cronies or business contacts. He stole only a few hours a week to work out with weights and add more muscle to his beefy five-foot eleven-inch, 195-pound frame. Otherwise, ZZZZ Best consumed him.

Barry's birthday is a good place for a snapshot of his life, because he was at his peak then, and because his birthday is a reminder that this extraordinary person had only just reached the age of legal majority. The picture would show a muscular young man with thick black hair and huge, pouting lips parted just enough to reveal his crooked teeth, for which he had shunned the braces his parents bought when he was a child. Barry's dark, heavy-lidded eyes would be wide open but slightly off, slightly furtive, as if he were looking around to take in more than the camera or whoever stood with him in the picture. Barry's dark eyes are deeply sincere, but just a little too mobile. The shot might include Joyce, tall and pretty in a naïve, long-faced kind of way, and Barry's stance toward her would be familiar, complex, but not especially warm. He looks to be deflecting her somehow. His clothes would be casual and disheveled. Barry was sloppy in his personal habits, and such a slob at the table that people around him were put off their food. When his company was trying to sell stock to the public, his investment bankers arranged luncheons and then told Barry it was customary for the star—him—to eat in advance, so he'd be free to talk to everybody else. This was no custom. They just wanted to be sure people weren't nauseated. "He was a strange combination of little kid and experienced businessman," says Robert Grossmann, a stockbroker who once touted Barry and his company. "It was scary, because you never knew who you were talking to. It was like the movie *Big*."

This combination of innocence and sophistication was one of Barry's greatest charms, and played to a special susceptibility of his audience: Americans conditioned on the one hand to embrace the simple sage, whether youthful or rural, and on the other to expect the worldly child. Either way, we figure, kids say the darnedest things.

Barry's diet, which ran mainly to meat and potatoes, was an expression of this man-child duality. A culinary Jekyll-and-Hyde, he would stuff himself with pizza, Ding-Dongs, and barbecue one week and

guiltily shift to more abstemious fare the next. He always hated veg-
etables, and loved sugary breakfast cereals like Lucky Charms and
Crunch 'n' Berry. He especially relished eating Oreos and watching
James Garner in reruns of "The Rockford Files" while Joyce slept.
He never seemed to read a book.

His eating habits notwithstanding, Barry was always thick with
muscle from weight lifting, which he performed almost devotionally,
and he loved posing in a skin-tight tank top to show off his swollen
physique. This physique was the literal embodiment of Barry's amazing drive to bend himself and the world around him to his will. Barry
wasn't born big; he was responsible for his own physical transformation, and his build proclaimed his fanaticism to anyone he met.

"I have an interesting philosophy," Barry once said on television.
"Life is a movie. You're the actor, you're the director, you're the
writer. And if you don't like the way your life is going, you'd better
change the script, because it's your life and you have complete control
over it."

After his morning workout, Barry would get into his white BMW
or blazing-red Ferrari, or whatever it was he was driving lately, and
head over to the office, where he was treated gingerly by everyone.
Those who worked for ZZZZ Best knew how volatile their mercurial
chief executive could be.

Barry was temperamental, but he wasn't one of those grimly driven
workaholics who project the misery of enslavement. At the office
Barry and his fellow executives worked hard, but he also liked to have
a good time and wanted others in on the fun. He seemed to see ZZZZ
Best as one big party. The soda machine was free, for example. Barry
liked sick humor, and his favorite comedian was Sam Kinison, the
brooding, bellowing fat man known for his routine about starving
Ethiopians: "You live in a *desert*," he would scream. "Why don't you
go where the goddamn *food* is?" Always the showman, Barry loved
to play with the audio system. Sometimes he'd get on the horn and
imitate President Reagan, perhaps out of the same instinct that made
him enjoy talent shows as a boy, or the clowning he always did in
school. Barry loved to throw lavish parties—around holidays, for
example—and he was fond of giving out awards. He was still a kid
in so many ways. He even hired Sherrie Maloney, his childhood baby-
sitter and longtime surrogate mother, as his personal secretary.
Maloney, Barry's real mother and the other women in his inner circle
loved their boss and were intensely loyal to him.

Impressive as his life and accomplishments were, Barry promised that what had come before was only the beginning, and in the spring of 1987 it no longer seemed prudent to doubt him.

Shortly after his twenty-first birthday, he hired the investment banking firm of Drexel Burnham Lambert to help ZZZZ Best make a $25 million offer for Flagship Cleaning Services Inc. of Newtown Square, Pennsylvania, which did business as KeyServ Group and had the concession to do carpet-cleaning under the respected banner of Sears, Roebuck & Co. in most of the United States. The acquisition would have made ZZZZ Best a national company, and the dominant force in an industry consisting mainly of thousands of mom-and-pop operations. Just as Barry had predicted, his business was well on its way to becoming the General Motors of carpet cleaning.

When the two companies agreed to merge, Barry staged a lavish three-day conference at Los Angeles' Century Plaza Hotel, ostensibly to help blend the two firms into one. KeyServ's managers already thought it strange that their company would soon be run by someone young enough to be one of their sons. When they arrived at the Century Plaza, they found themselves at a macabre cult rally dedicated to the greater glory of Barry Minkow.

ZZZZ Best had pulled out all the stops, spending more than $750,000 on food, lodging and other expenses for about 600 guests. Barry ran the ceremonies with all the power and presence of a charismatic fundamentalist, a prancing, strutting preacher of God whose word was himself, and who inspired with the strength of his own magnetism as much as by his message of faith. In this case the faith was in material success. The message was that each of us can achieve it by following Barry Minkow.

Steve Storti found the whole thing chilling. KeyServ's sensible and articulate vice president for marketing was forced to attend in order to help facilitate the merger. He found himself stuck in a freezing-cold ballroom for hours on end, listening with hundreds of carpet cleaners to repetitive exhortations from Barry and others about the future of KeyServ and its people under the Minkow regime. Storti and his fellow guests were marched in and out to a recording of the *William Tell* Overture, and treated to a series of bite-sized presentations that Storti found insulting in their simpleminded assumptions about him and his colleagues.

Barry's mother testified embarrassingly about his early days and his struggle for success, and Barry himself performed a little skit in how *not* to be a carpet cleaner. Vera Hojecki, ZZZZ Best's grandmotherly vice-president for telemarketing, also got up and said a few words, but "she was just simply from another planet," Storti recalls.

He was particularly appalled by the way Barry leered at women onstage. Storti's marketing and advertising managers, both women, fretted that they'd be among the KeyServ people called upon to receive awards.

"It was one of the strangest spectacles I've ever seen," says Storti, who was thirty-seven at the time. "These adults were absolutely venerating Barry."

The rank and file carpet cleaners seemed especially vulnerable to his message. All through the three-day conference—its theme was "The Sky's the Limit"—Barry kept asking people if they were happy, if they were finding the events meaningful, and the yeses he received were often genuine. The carpet cleaners found Barry powerfully inspirational. Some actually got up onstage and told of how moved they were. Others wrote in, saying he had changed their lives.

Many people were sold on Barry outright, but many others who were uneasy about him—or even found him transparent—went along just as Storti did, holding their noses and doing what had to be done. For those who weren't mesmerized or greedy or both, it was just business.

David Marchese, for example, also thought there was something strange and even distasteful about the boy wonder. Marchese was an advertising man in his early forties whose firm had been hired to do commercials for ZZZZ Best. Weekly meetings with Barry were always at Barry's office, and always followed a pattern. First, Barry would switch the appointment around once or twice, often at the last minute. Then there was the wait; Barry kept almost everybody waiting. Once inside, Marchese would find Barry talking on the phone, his feet up on the desk. Everything in his manner broadcast disdain. Barry would be wearing sneakers and sweats, and now and then he'd shove his hand inside his pants and scratch his crotch. There were no business lunches or dinners, Marchese assumed because Barry's ulcers were so bad, and the boy genius even took medicine at times in the middle of a session. He also took countless phone calls, often using the speakerphone to show off, and allowed certain of his lieutenants to barge in and out, sometimes disappearing with them as the admen sat and fumed.

"He could be charming, sweet and soft in one second," Marchese recalls, "and in the next he could chew someone out, scream, curse, yell; he was a chameleon."

He was also a superb study. Marchese was astonished to find that

Barry could do any commercial perfectly in a single try: "I've been working with actors for years—renowned actors—who can't do it in one take."

Barry talked to accountants like an accountant, to bankers like a banker, and to an adman like an adman. Everything was coming together for him. He was opening new carpet-cleaning outlets all the time, and he was about to get the Sears business. "The guy was a wizard," says Marchese, shaking his head over coffee one morning in a San Fernando Valley diner. Marchese's elderly mother was impressed too. At some point she bought stock in Barry's company.

It's difficult to describe exactly what she bought stock in without an example, so picture this. The sun shines on San Diego as the long, black Lincoln Town Car eases up to a new office building. It is May 1987, and Barry Minkow is at the peak of his powers. The day is warm, but the car is air conditioned, which is good, because the man behind the wheel is enormously fat. The odd thing about him is that he is almost blind, yet has managed to pilot this automotive behemoth without incident all the way from Los Angeles, although the car is slightly battered from some previous mishaps. Perhaps today he's had help from his companion, although on second look that doesn't seem likely. The man with him, a husky guy in a dark three-piece suit and diamond-studded Rolex, is far too engrossed in a gun catalogue or mercenary magazine to help much with the driving. Possibly it was *Soldier of Fortune*, but more likely it was *Guns & Ammo*, and perhaps in accord with standard mercenary practice, there were similar publications strewn across the backseat. Perhaps the sun was glinting off the passenger's gold Nazi SS ring.

The passenger was Tom Padgett, an important man in this mess. The driver was Mark Roddy, his good friend, and why not? Padgett is an avowed white separatist, and who could be whiter than Roddy, a six-foot one-inch, 275-pound albino convicted on a cocaine charge? Padgett, who has a good deal of self-consciousness for a lunatic, called him the UWM—Ultimate White Man—to distinguish him from another Minkow lieutenant named Mark. Men like Padgett and Roddy weren't interviewed by the newspapers or talk-show hosts, but their activities were much closer to the truth of Barry Minkow. While the world was busy lionizing its favorite young entrepreneur, he was directing an unusual collection of flunkies in an effort to perpetuate the myth that ZZZZ Best was actually a legitimate business.

Besides the Nazi and the Ultimate White Man, Barry's supporting cast included a former UCLA fullback who had completed much of the course work for a doctorate in the history of science, a specialist in applied physics, a stock swindler who should audition for the role of Wolfsheim if yet another Gatsby movie gets made, a producer who should audition for the role of producer, a former Brooklyn holdup man, the world's most oleaginous attorney, and various cops, call girls, bankers, brokers and weight lifters.

None of this made the papers until it was too late to do any good. What the world saw as a burgeoning business empire was actually an insolvent little flimflam from the day it opened its doors. Barry's evident dynamism was actually desperation. His charity was self-promotion. His platitudes were the most cynical sort of manipulation. His whole life was a fiction.

It's tempting to say that the image of Roddy and Padgett—the blind leading the crazy—perfectly captures ZZZZ Best Co., the weirdly named enterprise that was the vehicle for Barry Minkow's larceny. But that would be to ignore Barry himself, who sent these strange and deluded men to San Diego in the first place. Barry may have been crazy, but he certainly wasn't blind. On the contrary, Barry Minkow was a visionary.

It takes vision to conceive something like ZZZZ Best and make everyone around you believe in it. The company's main business wasn't carpet cleaning or restoring damaged building-interiors. It was simply a giant, ongoing sting operation. Look at Roddy and Padgett. Their errand was to secure office space that Barry could use to fool his independent auditors into thinking ZZZZ Best was restoring a building. The idea was to stage a tour one weekend when no one else was around. It doesn't seem possible, but it worked. Supporting documents were forged. Dummy companies were founded. Large sums of money were spent to make it seem as if large sums were being made. For a while, Barry had a whole collection of different tax returns for different purposes. They were all fake; none had been filed with the IRS.

The breadth of Barry's accomplishments is hard to grasp, considering that for a while he fooled all of the people all the time. His fraud was an imaginative triumph, and in fact its success and sweep may be attributed to Barry's towering imagination, which dwarfed any of those around him. At one point ZZZZ Best had a chance at a genuine $5 million construction contract, right in Los Angeles. Barry turned it down. It was a mark of his genius: he recognized that the lie needed integrity, and that to pollute it by trying to perform some real work was dangerous.

"Successful people are not all fact people," Barry—or his ghost-writer—said in *Making It in America*, his 1985 self-published auto-biography. "They let their imaginations soar."

3

Barry Jay Minkow wasn't always a visionary. For a while he was just a baby. He was born in Los Angeles at 7:57 P.M. on March 22, 1966, the youngest of three children and the only son of Robert and Carole Minkow, who bring to mind critic Reyner Banham's comment that the Pacific Coast was "where the great waves of agrarian migration from Europe and the Middle West broke in a surf of fulfilled and frustrated hopes."

With roots reaching back across the country to European Jewry, the Minkows are both Depression babies whose hopes were often frustrated. Robert Irwin Minkow was born in 1931 and comes from South Bend, Indiana, where there are still some Minkows. At the age of nineteen he suffered a brain tumor, the removal of which left him "handicapped," Barry says. People who meet the elder Minkow typically describe him as kindly but slow. He's not stupid, just detached in some way, so that things don't seem to reach him at the same time they reach everyone else. A hearing impairment—Robert wears hearing aids in both ears—enhances this impression. Robert Minkow and his parents moved to California when he was twenty-one, and he continued to live at home with them, working in his father's menswear store, until he was twenty-eight.

In 1960 he married Carole Marie Winkelman, a dark, nervous woman from Philadelphia who had also come west. Born in 1933, she was "emotionally abused by her mother," who supposedly spanked her with a hairbrush and told her she was unwanted, according to a sentencing memo filed by Barry's lawyer. "For many years, Carole Minkow suffered from bouts of depression that have resulted in psychiatric hospitalizations on numerous occasions," the memo says, adding that she was hypersensitive to noise and alternately angry and sad. The memo, which is a public record, quotes Barry's oldest sister, Gail, as saying that her mother physically abused her, while Sherri, the middle child, played the role of "the good kid who vainly attempts to mediate the emotional and physical casualties around them." Barry was always closest to Sherri, who was nearest him in age.

The Minkows never had much money when Barry was growing up, and sometimes the financial strain was severe. Often the family depended on handouts from family and friends, the memo says. Robert held a variety of jobs, working as night watchman at one point, and Carole worked too to help make ends meet, often spending hours at home making cold calls for carpet-cleaning services. In Barry's early years, the family lived in Inglewood, California, a suburb south of Los Angeles, and then moved to Reseda, in the heart of the San Fernando Valley, when Barry was a boy.

From Los Angeles, you can reach the Valley by taking the San Diego Freeway north through the starkly beautiful Santa Monica Mountains, their hunched peaks crowding the highway until you feel surrounded by wilderness, the steep hillsides purple and green after a little rain. But then the implacable river of concrete pours out of the canyon and suddenly there is a vast, hazy basin spread below. At night, seen from the air, the effect is of technology writ large, the freeway a cable shuttling electrons back and forth between a pair of pulsing silicon chips. An Englishman, Banham found the Valley a confusing doppelgänger of the metropolis he had just departed, but if you keep driving you get a better feel for the place. The Valley is a hot, smoggy, sprawling mass of 1.8 million people living in tract homes and apartment buildings, all set between great empty boulevards that race off straight and flat among the overgrown palm trees and billboards and fast-food signs, until they run up against the rugged mountains that girdle the land all around. The Valley is the place of middle-class aspirations, the Long Island or New Jersey of urban Los Angeles. Despite Moon Unit Zappa and the Valley Girl mystique, the Valley hasn't been fashionable since it was covered with orange groves and Hollywood stars began buying ranches in it. Since World War II it has been a place where people like the Minkows could have their little piece of the American dream, with sunshine and fruit trees in the backyard. The homes are cheaper, the architecture and the air quality are mostly terrible, and like anyplace that doesn't predate the primacy of the automobile, the Valley would have a no-there-there problem if not for its Siamese embrace of Los Angeles, part of the same city that many Valley dwellers regard as a sink of traffic and sin over the hills.

The Valley is a landmark in the path we have taken in our collective flight from one another, and Reseda is one of the places we have mostly left behind. Sections of the Valley down around Ventura Boulevard—the leafy, pricey sections close to the Westside of Los Angeles—literally look down on neighborhoods like Reseda, further out into the deep, dusty heartland of the place. At one time downtown Reseda was a shopping district that drew people from all around, but as Barry grew up it was eclipsed by surrounding malls. Yet Reseda has character, and Barry's hometown really wasn't so bad, even if he does try to portray himself as the product of a log cabin. Sherman Way and Reseda Boulevard function as old-fashioned Main Streets, and their intersection is more or less the center of the neighborhood, which is legally a part of Los Angeles. Secondhand bookstores, thrift shops, Army-Navy–type outlets, sweaty gyms devoid of yuppie socializing, and cheap-eats joints serving weird agglomerations of pastrami and tortillas stand chockablock on the main thoroughfares and spill onto some of the side streets. Lots of places sell boating equipment, trailers, parakeets and the like, as if residential Reseda housed a fair number of folks living lives depicted by Booth cartoons in *The New Yorker*. It's not Paris, but neither is it Rodeo Drive or some artificial, climate-controlled shopping mall. There is an endearing authenticity about Reseda, which is a community that actually looks lived in. Reseda is just a little ragged; not so much that it's unpleasant, but enough so that it's real.

The Minkows still live in the house Barry grew up in. The place is a fine specimen of 1950s Southern California bungalow, with a low sloping roof, a backyard swimming pool, and high-powered air conditioning. The house has three bedrooms, two baths and a fireplace, all on one level. Back east it would be called a ranch-style home, although at 1,250 square feet it's hardly sprawling. The decor is Sears colonial: a plaid, burnt-orange sofa with ornate oak arms and matching recliners, all set on the most amazing mustard-colored shag carpet, which surely played a seminal role in Barry's later life. When I saw it I thought this might be Barry Minkow's first rug, an exciting prospect to contemplate that later proved untrue. The dinette area is dominated by an enormous portrait of the Minkow children, itself dominated by Barry. The background is sky-blue, and there are touches of cloudlike white around his head in a kind of halo effect. The image is sadly ironic. Robert Minkow must have been thrilled to get a son, especially one who proved such a fast learner. But Barry was difficult to handle almost from the outset, and seemed to lack a moral compass even as a child. Unruly and opportunistic, his energetic misbehavior finally drove his parents to seek professional help.

As a little boy Barry was diagnosed as hyperactive, and at age six he was placed on daily doses of Ritalin, a little-understood stimulant that somehow seems to help such children. It was given to Barry until he was twelve. Hyperactivity is a brain disorder that afflicts one out of ten boys to a varying extent, and is found much less frequently in girls. Its causes are not clearly established, but there is some evidence that heredity plays an important role. Hyperactive children are somewhat more often found in families with other hyperactives, with alcoholic men, and with hysterically neurotic women.

In general, seriously hyperactive children are always in motion to no particular purpose. They are chronically inattentive, impulsive and take unnecessary risks. They can drive parents and teachers crazy with their incessant demands for attention, violent temper tantrums and classroom disruptions. "They act like a windup person," says a clinician who treats these children. Although hyperactive kids are often charming and vivacious, their parents are sometimes so embarrassed, annoyed and frustrated that they can end up disliking their own offspring.

Hyperactivity can be difficult to diagnose. The list of symptoms for Attention Deficit Disorder with Hyperactivity—the new formal name—in the American Psychiatric Association's *Diagnostic and Statistical Manual of Mental Disorders* reads like a list of the characteristics of childhood itself: squirming, fidgeting and distractibility, for example. But the list is long, and the association says a child who exhibits eight of the symptoms before the age of seven probably has the disorder. Barry's childhood included virtually all of them; indeed, the list seemed to apply even while he was running ZZZZ Best. He always had trouble sitting still, for example, and was unnaturally energetic even for a healthy young man.

Hyperactivity is most pronounced up to age nine, after which the overt physical symptoms tend to diminish. But many hyperactive young people still suffer from "conduct disorders," in which they frequently lie, steal, cheat, cut school, behave cruelly toward animals, provoke fights and hurt people on purpose. Barry had some of these problems in adolescence, if not before the age of fifteen, then certainly afterward.

There are also signs that such antisocial behavior persists into adulthood, and researchers have found higher-than-average rates of criminality and mental instability in adults who were hyperactive children. For example, in a study of 110 such adolescents published in *The American Journal of Psychiatry* in 1982, Dr. James H. Satterfield and two colleagues found that, depending on socioeconomic level, 36 to 58 percent of hyperactive subjects were arrested at least once for a serious offense, compared with 2 to 11 percent for a group of 88 closely matched normal youths. Incarceration rates were similarly skewed.

Ritalin wasn't the Minkows' sole response to their son's problem. "Carole and I and his sisters went to meetings with a psychiatrist to learn how to help him," Robert recalls. Told that "hyperkinetic kids don't have coordination," the elder Minkow went out and taught Barry to play baseball and basketball when the kid was eight or nine years old. Barry went on to star in Little League and Pop Warner sports, his father says proudly.

Robert is a plump, jovial-looking man with gold-rimmed eyeglasses that darken in sunlight, a potbelly, and gray hair combed across his shiny, balding pate. He seems like a nice fellow and a loving father, but feckless somehow, and so thoughtfully detached that he seems almost wry. He is articulate and frank, but better at talking than listening, and during an impromptu interview at his house one Sunday afternoon, he was friendly and cooperative. Carole Minkow stayed in another room, emerging occasionally to see if I was still there. After about an hour she threw me out.

Of himself, Robert says amiably from one of the orange plaid chairs, "I'm pretty much doing the same thing I've always been doing since before Barry got his tit in a wringer."

What the elder Minkow used to do is sell real estate, but in 1967 he took a relatively cushy job downtown as a property manager in the real estate trust department of a bank. "I only intended to go to the bank for a year," he says now. "But for the first time in my life I found myself able to interface with my wife and children on weekends, go to the beach, and so forth. I said, 'this is the life.' "

The new job (which lasted until Barry was nine) gave Robert a chance to get to know his son. So what was Barry like as a young man? "He was never a young man," Robert replies. "He was always a kid." This is one of the central paradoxes of Barry Minkow: he was always a kid, but "he never had a childhood. He started in the garage at fourteen or fifteen years old; before that he was out hustling newspapers or getting whatever job he could. He'd lie about his age—he got one job at some little hot dog stand on Reseda Boulevard and they made him an assistant manager after three weeks. Then they had to fire him when they found out how old he was."

Some of the neighbors remember Barry as "a brat" who always had to have his own way, and the Minkows warned his baby-sitter not to say no to him. But Barry could also be polite and extremely charming, using social skills developed far beyond his years. He would buy candy for his friends sometimes when the older girls among them didn't want to play with Sherri's kid brother, and once when he was nine or ten years old he knocked on a neighbor's door and solemnly asked if he could take the little girl who lived there to the local Thrifty for an ice-cream cone. Her mother said yes, and Barry disappeared. A few minutes later he was back in a suit and tie, ready to pick up his date.

Robert blames Barry's hyperactivity for a lot of his son's troubles. For example, Barry had an almost obsessive need to be in the spotlight, and as a boy he used his considerable talents to capture it. "He had a flair for the theatrical, and for showmanship," Robert says. "As a kid he would do a Groucho Marx routine, and then he started doing Ronald Reagan. I'd take him around to amateur shows."

Although the family often had to scrape to make a buck, Robert Minkow insists that money wasn't Barry's main motivation.

"He was driven more by his hyperkinetic tendencies," says Robert. "He was driven to be number one. He had to be the best in everything he did. He did it to get attention. A hyperkinetic kid is driven to do something without thinking. They have to be the center of attention. If a teacher asked the class a question, Barry didn't raise his hand—he just blurted out the answer. They also have a fear of being closed up in a room alone"—when we talked, Barry was awaiting trial in solitary confinement, which must have given his father special sorrow—"and of pain and getting hurt."

Barry had other fears. He was afraid of the ocean and terrified of flying. He especially hated being alone. Yet school was a problem; Barry had a quick mind but was often disruptive. Rosalie Van Rosenbergh, a neighbor since Barry was five years old, says he was never much interested in school, and that from early on he wanted to make lots of money because his parents had had so little.

The Minkows were not particularly religious Jews, but were observant enough so that when Barry was thirteen he had a bar mitzvah, just as Sherri had been bas mitzvah before him. "Barry was a young child growing up in the congregation. He grew up with Temple Judea in Tarzana," recalls Rabbi Steven Jacobs. In the mid-1980s, when the rabbi left the synagogue to form a new congregation, Barry's parents came along.

The stresses in the Minkow household began to show on Barry and Sherri during their adolescence. Sherri became anorexic and bulimic; her eating disorders were bad enough to require hospitalization. Barry would soon take the opposite tack. If Sherri tried to achieve perfection by diminishing herself, Barry would strive for superiority through bulk. Meanwhile he became increasingly resentful of their father. As a child he had struggled to please his dad, but as a teenager Barry competed furiously with him.

Barry's father seemed weak from lack of money, and Barry recognized early on that money could be power. Instead of comparing himself to the elder Minkow, realizing it was no contest, and deciding to emulate the man, Barry saw his father as inadequate and defeated him while still a teenager, gradually assuming the mantle of breadwinner. Robert Minkow was soon reduced to working for his son, who regularly promised to fire him if he didn't pull his weight. But Barry probably never stopped identifying with his father, and never felt secure in his victory. Perhaps as a result, he spent a good deal of time locating paternal substitutes and sooner or later emasculating them, often by taking their money. He repeated this ritual with a whole series of older men until finally it landed him in jail.

"As a young man Barry always wanted to compete with me," Robert affirmed back in 1985, when I first talked to him. "That edge of competition stayed with him. He always wanted to do more." Robert also said at the time: "I knew he'd be a success, but to what degree I had no idea."

Barry also continued to be disruptive in school. "I was at the principal's office every week," his father says with a fond laugh. Figuring the kid needed discipline, he wanted to send Barry to a military academy, but couldn't afford it. Finally he got a job at a Beverly Hills real estate concern, helping to liquidate a large land trust, and was made a partner on the commissions. Barry was promptly dispatched to the toney Ridgewood School, a military academy in nearby Woodland Hills where the tuition was about $1,200 a year. Barry spent seventh and eighth grades there.

Ridgewood was located on the site of a five-acre estate once owned by Mae West. A former speakeasy and later a motel, it was purchased and turned into a private school in 1943 by a determined émigré from the Guatemalan upper crust who was herself educated in Northern

California. The place was hardly Parris Island; the military was just a modest "structure of discipline around which the curriculum was built," says the founder's son, Rudy Berger (pronounced ber-ghay), who spent twenty-five years there. The school is closed now, but Berger is happy to reminisce about it. He says alumni include the children of William Holden, Mary Astor and Roy Rogers. The boys and girls pictured in Barry's eighth grade yearbook—the school's last—look happy and healthy.

Berger remembers Barry as short and skinny for his age, a bright student who never got into trouble. But Robert Minkow says his son didn't have a pleasant time of it. He was always cutting up, and his antics were frowned upon in a military academy. As it turned out, the academic authorities were the least of his troubles.

"By the time he was fourteen years old he was getting the shit beat out of him at military school," says Robert. "He had a big mouth and a big nose."

Barry's family was also among the poorest at Ridgewood, and that must have added to his sense of inferiority. But his stay there didn't last. After two years, he graduated from the school's last class and was headed for public high school. That, his father assured him, would be *really* tough. Grover Cleveland High School was being integrated, Robert Minkow warned, and Barry would have to do something to hold his own with those tough inner-city kids.

At this point Robert likes to show a couple of pictures. One is of a cute, skinny little kid in an oversized Army cap and uniform. The other, taken about two years later, is of a young Charles Atlas flexing his right bicep for the camera. The transformation is stunning. Barry accomplished it by joining a gym.

The Valley Gym in downtown Reseda was no place for dabblers interested in carrot cocktails and conversation. Founded by a friendly ex-New Yorker, it was a sweaty establishment where strong people went to pump iron seriously. Barry was fourteen when he joined in the summer of 1980, and he threw himself into weight lifting unreservedly, pumping for four hours a day on Tuesday, Thursday, Saturday and Sunday. Unable to afford the fees, he scrubbed the showers Saturday and Sunday mornings in return for use of the facilities.

At the gym Barry continued to prove himself adept at gaining attention from grown-up men. For instance, Dan Krowpman lifted on some of the same days that Barry did. Krowpman's boy, Danny Jr., was a friend of Barry's, and they had played on opposing Little

League baseball teams. The elder Krowpman was an amiable bear of a man, a regular at the gym who could bench-press well over 400 pounds, according to Barry.

"He was my idol . . . He had money, he had build, he had everything I didn't have," Barry said subsequently on the witness stand. "He used to come into the gym and have money and was nice to me, and he was like the father I never had. I loved him."

Barry couldn't help contrasting powerful, affluent Dan Krowpman with weak, poor Robert Minkow. Barry's father was always broke. Once the phone was turned off because the Minkows hadn't paid the bill. Even the water was turned off briefly. Barry says that Krowpman, on the other hand, walked around with large sums of money on him. He also paid attention to Barry, who felt he could talk to the older man about his troubles and aspirations. Barry even cleaned his carpets once. Dark-haired, with wide nostrils and a small tattoo on one wrist, Krowpman looks shy but has brawled occasionally, and enjoys making a bet. He ran a small business selling tools door-to-door to various San Fernando Valley service stations, and sometimes he took Barry with him on his rounds. He liked Barry and was good to him. Before long he was treating Barry like one of his own sons, which Barry encouraged in every way possible.

Tom Padgett was another of the men at Valley Gym who found in Barry an eager young admirer. It was the fall of 1980, not long after Padgett's second tour in the Army, and he was working out in the gym with a friend, with whom he'd persuaded the owner to postpone payment. Padgett had just finished a punishing round of squats when a nerdy, gangling kid said admiringly, "You work out like an animal." The next time Padgett came to the gym, he wore a T-shirt with some kind of animal on it, and Barry began working out with him.

Though Barry was only fourteen, the man and the boy were soon friends; occasionally they'd go to the movies or get some burgers together. Possessed of a strong didactic streak and without siblings of his own, Padgett liked the role of older brother, and nobody could have been more interested or willing to learn than Barry. He was sympathetic, too. Padgett was in the insurance business but was also doing a little amateur boxing on the side. He would get the daylights beat out of him and then find himself ridiculed at the gym by everyone except Barry.

"Hey," Barry would say, "at least Tom got in the ring and fought."

At a diner in Reseda one day, Padgett pointed to the ketchup bottle on the table. He complained to Barry that the vast majority of Americans—Gentiles and nonpracticing Jews alike—must pay more for things like ketchup because such products carry a kosher seal of approval, just to make them palatable to a handful of observant Jews.

Born in 1950, Thomas George Padgett was one of Barry's early father figures, but he didn't have a lot in common with Ward Cleaver, the friendly Dad on "Leave It to Beaver." A self-proclaimed "white separatist," Padgett is a husky, dark-haired Vietnam veteran who loves talking about manly things like guns and warfare and the psychology of conflict. He tells some people he used to be a mercenary.

Actually, Padgett is another of those faintly hyperactive types who seemed especially drawn to Barry, and he can be almost as captivating, his rage untempered by his very real self-consciousness or his quite substantial schooling. Padgett would have made a great actor: he's articulate and loves to talk, and when he warms to his subject he bellows, whispers, gestures wildly and slips in and out of voices, performing with gusto until his blue eyes bulge eerily and he gives the impression of one poised near the edge of some Mephistophelian outburst. ZZZZ Best is one of his favorite subjects. "I don't know how familiar you are with the National Socialist hierarchy," he will say sometimes, and then go on to explain who in the conspiracy corresponded to Goering, Himmler and so forth. Barry was always Hitler.

"He had the same gift as Adolf Hitler," Padgett says. "He could simplify a problem. Hitler cut through the bullshit."

But Padgett insists this is just an analogy. "I'm not a Nazi," he says. "I think National Socialism is dead and buried." Still, the Third Reich does come up in conversation quite a bit with Padgett. He's fond of talking about where the Führer went wrong. ("He never should have attacked Russia, there are too many white people," Padgett says. "He had no business attacking Britain, but then we could argue who declared war on who.") References to heredity and eugenics regularly slip into his speech. Padgett likes to refer to his Viking blood (he is actually an Irishman from Akron, Ohio) and he calls Barry "a little half-Jew kid from Reseda."

Padgett's very real affection for Barry illustrates the odd dichotomy in his personality. Padgett seems genuinely to like people, and even tries to judge them individually, whatever he might think of their race or ethnicity. He vehemently denies being a white supremacist. Yet he defends Hitler, brawled with the Jewish Defense League, and appeared on an insidious cable television show called "Race and

Reason" with Tom Metzger, a notorious white supremacist and former California Ku Klux Klan leader. Padgett even dated Metzger's daughter.

Later he would stick to Barry like gum on shoeleather, playing the good soldier to the younger man's general. But early on, Padgett just took pity and wanted to help his scrawny young friend become a man. He overlooked Barry's lack of Viking blood and respected his determination to improve himself. In some ways Padgett was probably a good influence. He urged Barry to stay in school, for example.

"You're cheating yourself, Barry," he would say. "You've got to know some history, some classic literature, some basic science. You'll see when you get older, money isn't everything."

Having just come back from mercenary school, he tried to get Barry interested in combat, rifles and so forth. "They'd go up and watch 'Twilight Zones' together, and Padgett would show Barry his gun collection," says one fellow weight lifter.

Guns never meant much to Barry, who was more interested in increasing his physical strength. But he was frustrated. For all his weight lifting, for all the hours and hours of sweat and toil, Barry felt he wasn't putting on muscle fast enough.

That was when he began taking anabolic steroids: Dianabol at first, and then Anavar and Anadrol-50 at various times. He said later, on the witness stand, that he started in 1982 and never stopped for more than two weeks at a time from then on. The steroids worked: Barry transformed himself into a hulk virtually overnight. At his peak he could bench-press 415 pounds.

Anabolic steroids are synthetic variations of testosterone, the male sex hormone, and in massive doses they yield stunning gains in muscle mass for athletes who have already reached a personal plateau in their workouts. Developed in the 1930s to build body tissue in the ailing, their first "nonclinical" use may have occurred during World War II, when steroids reportedly were administered to Nazi troops to increase their aggressiveness. During the 1950s, the Soviets used testosterone to boost their performance in international athletic competition; according to the Food and Drug Administration, American athletes began taking steroids soon afterward. Today they are widely used by body builders, football players and others despite the spread of drug tests. Occasionally users get caught: Canadian sprinter Ben Johnson was stripped of his 1988 Olympic gold medal after tests showed he had taken steroids.

Steroids can occasionally have serious side-effects, including acne, hair loss, jaundice, cancer, cardiovascular disorders, sterility and altered sex characteristics: women get hairy, deep-voiced and masculine, while men can develop breasts and minor testicular atrophy. Some athletes report vomiting or urinating blood, muscle spasms and terrifying panic attacks. There is also a substantial increase in sex drive.

But these physical side-effects are often outweighed by the psychological ones. Major mood swings are common, and psychotic symptoms—paranoia, hallucinations, delusions of grandeur, and violence—have been found in a significant portion of steroid-using body builders who never before experienced such things. Increased irritability and aggression are widespread among steroid users, and " 'roid rages" are well known around the locker room and the home.

Giving Barry Minkow anabolic steroids was like throwing gasoline on a raging housefire, since they would tend to exaggerate all his worst traits. Steroids heighten aggressiveness, and they can also induce euphoria, manic episodes and feelings of invincibility. When two Harvard Medical School researchers, Drs. Harrison Pope and David Katz, discovered a high incidence of psychotic episodes among steroid users (none of whom reported such incidents before taking the drugs), they were deluged with calls from lawyers and prosecutors nationwide, all describing defendants who had committed violent crimes while on steroids.

By the time Barry got to Grover Cleveland High School in Reseda, he was almost muscle-bound, and his fellow students there have equally strong memories of him. They recall him as overwhelmingly strange, someone struggling to be liked and forever trying to buy friendship and admiration. Barry once paid a girl $100 to go out with him. He was very pushy and something of a bully who enjoyed picking fights in front of girls. He was smart in school but not excessively intellectual, and he struck people as lacking in authenticity, a showoff who often seemed to be playing a role. If the word "phony" means anything in describing an adolescent, Barry was one. He inspired a combination of derision and awe.

"He came to school in a brown polyester suit, a striped tie and tennis shoes, and he carried an attaché case," says Nancy Wilson, who knew him at Cleveland. Brian McGregor, a friend and student body president in Barry's senior year, recalls: "When I first met Barry, he wrote one-dollar or two-dollar checks. He'd pull out his briefcase and write a check for a dollar so he could buy a burrito."

Sometimes these checks would bounce, but that didn't stop Barry, and when he finally got his business going, he started to throw his money around grandly. He'd take a dozen friends to dinner and pick up the check. He'd take his male buddies down to a Chinese massage parlor in Hollywood. At Christmas, "He'd buy them ski boots, bindings, poles—the whole outfit," says Wilson. Mary Lauffer, another Minkow friend in high school, recalls that he actually brought a gold bar to school one day—"it was about a foot long."

The guys would always send Barry on beer runs, even though he hardly ever drank, because they knew he'd always come back with lots of food to impress them. Money was his solution to every problem.

"One time we were playing football and we needed an extra player; he paid somebody five dollars to play," recalls one former friend. Wilson adds: "He thought all the girls would like him because he had a business and a fancy car."

Anthony Scamardo, a close friend since eleventh grade, tried to warn Barry that people were taking advantage of him, that they knew he was a soft touch for money, but Barry didn't seem to care.

One former schoolmate recalls that when the gang would get together to watch videos, Barry would bring over porno tapes and insist that the guys watch with him. The girls would protest, and after a few minutes, even the guys would give up. But Barry would persist, watching alone if necessary when the others left the room.

For a while Barry was especially jealous of Bret Saberhagen, the pitching ace for the Cleveland High School baseball team who was something of a school idol. In 1982, Saberhagen's senior year, he threw a no-hitter for Cleveland in the city championship at Dodger Stadium. He later became a big-league star with the Kansas City Royals. Early on at Cleveland, Barry resolved to become more famous than Saberhagen.

"No one ever knew the real Barry," says Scott Balachio, who calls himself Barry's best friend during tenth and eleventh grades. "He had different personalities around different people."

One day, while visiting Sherri in the hospital, Barry met another pretty young girl who was also being treated for an eating disorder. Her name was Joyce Lipman, and soon she and Barry were dating. Tall, blonde, and slightly bewildered-looking, Joyce was the hazel-eyed daughter of Dr. Harold Lipman, a retired assistant superintendent of schools in the community of Simi Valley, just beyond the San Fernando Valley. She is two years younger than Barry.

Unlike Joyce, Barry seemed to his friends especially careful about nutrition, telling Brian McGregor, with whom he drank on New Year's Eve 1983, that he had never tasted alcohol before. His other friends can't remember him taking drugs either. On the contrary; they say he was always popping vitamins, slurping raw eggs and taking amino acids. He was adamantly opposed to narcotics, even though some of his friends were serious users. Almost no one knew about the steroids.

Barry was much bigger now, but he always remained the class cutup. In a stroke of unwitting genius, his graduating class voted him both Most Likely to Succeed and Class Clown, perhaps in reward for an ultimate Minkow stunt: at Cleveland, one of Barry's classes was Work Experience, which meant getting a job and having one's employer submit a grade to the school. Barry was self-employed, and therefore graded himself. He gave himself an F.

4

In the summer after Barry's twelfth birthday, his mother used to take him along to her job at Same-Day Carpet Care, where he learned the carpet-cleaning business from the pile up. Before long Barry was working the phones. He solicited customers with a prepared script, his high-pitched voice giving the impression he was a young girl. Men sometimes asked him for dates. Later, in his early teens, Barry worked for a couple of other local carpet-cleaning companies, and eventually started going out on jobs with one or another of the more experienced men. He learned a lot at Dunn-Rite Carpet Cleaning from Joel Hochberg, for example, a raspy-voiced former New York cabbie, recovering alcoholic and ex-cocaine user.

Carpet cleaning is a dirty business, but it's not a bad line for a kid who wants to work. As the economists are wont to say, there are few barriers to entry, which means that like journalists, no testing, license or registration is required, and there is little need for capital or training. Pretty much anyone can get into the business, and pretty much anyone is who you're likely to get if you open up the phone book and call your average rug-cleaning company.

"Carpet cleaning is a major complaint area," says Timothy Bissell, chief investigator for the Los Angeles County Department of Consumer Affairs. David Tuck, past president of a trade association called the Carpet Cleaners Institute, acknowledges that the business has plenty of rotten apples. "The most visible part of our industry is the most embarrassing," he says. "It's a bait-and-switch rip-off game."

Carpet cleaning has its share of reformers. In California, for example, the Carpet Cleaners Institute sponsors courses with a curriculum including "Fiber Identification," "Cleaning and Crew Procedure" and "What Is Soil?" Instructors have included Michael E. West, described in an institute brochure as "Third generation in the Cleaning Industry . . . Past Editor of *Western Carpet Cleaner* . . . Three-time recipient of Joe Laurino Carpet Cleaner of the Year Award." Mr. West was joined on the faculty by a smiling Carl F. Williams, described as "Hard driving, motivated builder with a keen sense of humor . . . people-, task-, and goal-oriented. Truly a communicator in our industry."

Aware that their vocation is not on a par with neurosurgery, carpet cleaners refer to themselves disparagingly as "rug suckers," in allusion to the wet vacuuming they do all day. You clean a carpet by pumping a cleanser in, section by section, scrubbing a little as you go. Professionals do this using an electric steamcleaner; heat helps. The cleanser loosens the dirt, and when you're finished you vacuum out the whole mess. If you're lucky, the carpet will be considerably cleaner and none the worse for the experience.

The good thing about carpet cleaning is that there is potentially lots of business. Carpet is an essential part of the Southern California landscape, like palm trees and sunshine, and sometimes in considering the vast surfaces of the region covered by the stuff, it's comforting to think about the profound historical continuity of it all. It's almost moving.

In a place without much respect for the past, it is through carpet that Californians unconsciously hark back to their most distant ancestors. Think of cave dwellers huddled in their dripping holes, surrounded by discarded bones and the dancing shadows of the fire. They laid down animal skins to take the chill off the dirt floor at night. Later, rulers from one end of the earth to the other differed in culture, language and faith, but shared a dislike for walking on a naked floor. Greek heroes got to tread on purple cloth, and everybody knows about Oriental rugs. At Graceland, Elvis Presley carpeted some of the walls and ceilings. Carpeting can make a place feel cozy, and more important, it's a lot cheaper for a builder to put in a plywood or concrete floor and a roll of broadloom than it is to install hardwood. Anyway, wood scratches easily and makes life noisy downstairs, while linoleum seems spartan. So tastes and economics came together, and in the great postwar Southern California land-rush, the place was paved with pile. Carpets like the Minkow's mustard-colored shag became fashionable, and apartments throughout the region have sliding aluminum windows, cottage-cheese ceilings and shag carpet in common. Consider the implications for Barry. Carpets cover things up. Rugs lie. And of course Barry made rug suckers of all of us.

By the time he was a teenager, Barry knew all the angles. He knew that in his business, the great majority of the work is selling; cleaning is almost a sideline. The selling begins in the office, where a roomful of people sit working the phones. They ring strangers day and night, calling and calling and calling to persuade people that their carpets are dirty. When these mad dialers are lucky enough to book a job, a cleaner is sent out. Even before setting to work, this individual often tries to sell the customer more of his dubious product. Bait-and-switch tactics, in which absurdly low prices are quoted only to vaporize when the cleaner arrives, are common; the mailboxes of Southern California overflow with postcards from companies offering to clean acres of carpet for $6.95 (direct mail is probably even more common than telephone sales). The cards typically show a nozzle-wielding "technician" in spanking overalls, determinedly scouring the filth from a section of pile. The reality is usually somewhat different: a poorly trained rug sucker and an unexpectedly high price are likelier.

Always a lightning study, Barry caught on fast. He learned, for instance, that when a customer orders a stainproof coating, you spray the stuff only on the major-traffic areas, because no one walks or spills things under the sofa.

Barry also noticed that carpet-cleaning companies offered restoration services to homeowners coping with damage from an overflowing toilet, a broken waterpipe, etc. He learned that carpet companies commonly referred to themselves as "insurance restoration experts," and highlighted such services in the Yellow Pages.

"I realized that I needed to let my imagination run," Barry says in the autobiography, which was printed at his own expense and used as a promotional tool (the book was never sold in stores). Elsewhere it says, "By the time I was fifteen, I knew I was unique. My idols weren't football players. They were people who owned their own corporations."

During the summer of 1982, Barry's body building had advanced far enough for him to become a gym instructor. On weekends he cleaned carpets. That fall, at the ripe old age of sixteen, Barry Minkow decided he had had enough of working for others. He wanted to make more than an hourly wage or a commission on sales. He wanted to have money in his pocket, and he wanted to be the boss. In October he went into business for himself.

"Because I'd been immersed in the carpet-cleaning business since I was nine," Barry's autobiography says, "I knew every side of that operation. Naturally I'd start my own version of that type of outfit, and I'd build it into a huge winner. That was the plan."

Dan Krowpman Sr., Barry's hero at the gym, apparently lent him a couple of thousand dollars to get started. On the witness stand Barry said Krowpman put up $1,600 in return for 50 percent of any profits. Barry was to do the work, keeping 50 percent for himself.

Not everybody was happy with the arrangement. Krowpman's wife got mad at him for bankrolling Barry instead of his own son. But Barry was ecstatic. Money in hand, he rushed out and bought a shampooer and a steam-cleaning machine. He also bought cleaning chemicals, which he stored in his bedroom, and then he set up shop in his family's barebones garage on Lull Street in Reseda. His father thought it was a pretty good idea. His mother disagreed.

"He came to us and said he wanted to open his own business," his mother recalled during a 1985 interview. "I said, 'You have rocks in your head.' "

Indeed, Barry knew a great deal about cleaning rugs and chiseling customers, but little about running a business, and he would have to overcome a host of obstacles that stand in the way of any teenager launching a commercial undertaking more elaborate than baby-sitting. Banks wouldn't lend him money, or even open an account for him. Customers tended not to be filled with confidence, and while the carpet-cleaning business is a good one for an uneducated person with few skills, it also had specific drawbacks for Barry. For example, it takes hours for a freshly cleaned carpet to dry, and during that time you can't walk on it. Therefore, most people want their carpets cleaned in the morning. But Barry was in school mornings. So he hired his mother to make phone calls for him, and he'd suck rugs in the afternoon and on weekends. Later he hired someone else to go out on any weekday cleaning jobs his mother could scare up.

"I worked real hard for him," Carole Minkow said later. "I was the only employee. He was doing well, he was enjoying it, and it was better than being on drugs like the other kids."

Pretty soon there were four phone lines in the garage, and Barry was getting some business. An early business card says:

YOU'VE HAD THE REST, NOW TRY

ZZZZ
BEST

CARPET AND FURNITURE CLEANING COMPANY
"NO ONE DOES IT BETTER!"

Later on, Barry told anyone who would listen that he chose the name ZZZZ Best because he wanted four children someday, but it's likelier just an intentional corruption of "the best," possibly suggested by Barry's early mentor, Joel Hochberg. "I named that company," says Hochberg, who later worked for Barry as a telephone salesman. "I said, 'You tried the rest, now come to zbest.' "

It didn't take long for Robert Minkow to sour on the idea. He didn't mind Barry being in business. But the business was making a circus of the Minkows' home. The arrangement lasted just a few months.

"There were so many people in and out of that garage, they were inundating the house," the elder Minkow recalls. "Both bathrooms were always being used, the refrigerator . . ." Robert shrugs. He says he kept after Barry to move somewhere else, someplace more spacious, but to no avail. "So I threatened to charge him one hundred and fifty dollars a month rent if he didn't find larger quarters. That's how I got him out of here."

For Barry, moving to an actual professional office was a big step that he couldn't really afford, even if it was a slummy little place not far from home. But an office was a sign of legitimacy, which was important to Barry, who absolutely loved being in business and acted the part even at school, with his polyester suits and briefcase. In class he would fret over how he was going to make payroll. Barry was long on instinct and short on skills—he claims he failed accounting in eleventh grade—and keeping ZZZZ Best alive was a huge struggle.

The truth is, Barry Minkow was a terrible businessman, and his company was already taking on the characteristics that would later become hallmarks: overexpansion, inadequate controls and a tendency to implode if Barry let up for even an instant.

Already, he was careering from crisis to crisis, rushing around to beg, borrow or steal enough to keep his money-losing enterprise afloat. Barry's cleaning equipment was supposedly stolen from his parents' house, ostensibly by a carpet cleaner but possibly by Barry, who then asked Krowpman for money to replace it. Barry probably hocked it or pocketed the replacement money and presented the old equipment as new. Intriguingly for Freudians, Carole Minkow's wedding ring was stolen in the same alleged burglary. No one in Barry's family seemed safe. He borrowed $2,000 from his grandmother and then stole her pearls to meet expenses. Barry denied taking them at first, but confessed when his father threatened him with a polygraph. Distressed at Barry's constant lying, his forging of school passes and his evident belief that rules didn't apply to him, his parents finally sent him to a therapist. Within a year he had what appeared to be a bleeding ulcer.

Barry worried about his stomach but wouldn't do anything about it. "Finally, we told him we were going to play football," Scott Balachio says, "and we took him to Tarzana Hospital instead. They admitted him."

Balachio was one of Barry's first employees.

"He set me up with a table, a phone and the White Pages," Scott says, adding that for only twenty hours of work per week after school, "he was paying really well, one hundred and fifty dollars a week in the eleventh grade." At first it was telephone solicitation—Scott was in charge of all four people in that aspect of the business—but eventually ZZZZ Best solicitors went door-to-door. Barry even wrote out a little script, so his untried employees would have some idea what to say. And in those days there was no "Mr. Minkow." Barry was so uncertain he sometimes asked Scott what to do. "I'd tell him I can't help you," Scott says now, adding that he quit after several months for one simple reason: "He started to bounce checks on everybody."

By all rights, Barry shouldn't even have had a checking account. Most banks wouldn't give him one. But in late 1982 or early 1983 he managed to establish an account at tiny West Valley Bank on Ventura Boulevard in nearby Tarzana, thanks to the good offices of bank manager Robert Turnbow, who took a shine to the kid.

When Barry came in, the woman who normally opened new accounts was on vacation, and her substitute allowed Barry to get started. Turnbow stumbled across Barry's signature card when he was reviewing the new accounts, and realized that the customer in question was only sixteen years old. He called the number on the form and told Barry he wanted to see him. He also called Barry's father, who was strangely defensive.

"I don't have anything to do with that," the elder Minkow insisted. "I take no responsibility for any of Barry's financial dealings."

When Barry came in, he said his father wasn't very bright, and that he didn't get along with him terribly well. Turnbow was sympathetic. He had had a stormy relationship with his own father, and Barry was clearly eager to succeed. Turnbow agreed to keep the account open as long as Barry met with him every day and kept the account clean. The banker and the boy would talk about Barry's business, about activity in the account, and eventually, about Barry's personal problems as well.

"I liked him very much and felt I was a bit of a father image to him," Turnbow, then forty-seven, said later. Barry reinforced those feelings by telling him, "Gee, it's too bad my own father doesn't treat me like you do."

The banking went well at first. Barry was depositing $1,000 a day in gross receipts, and the balance was growing. The daily meetings continued, and sometimes Krowpman would come along. He had the offices of his Cornwell Tool distributorship downstairs in the same building as ZZZZ Best, at 7040 Darby Ave., in Reseda, and he would stop up every morning and say hello.

Before long Barry started to become a problem for Turnbow. Checks would sometimes bounce, or his account would become overdrawn. Turnbow stayed with him; he claims it was easier and safer to work things out than to close the account and write off the losses. In 1984, for example, Barry deposited some large checks, and Turnbow allowed him to draw on the funds before they cleared. The checks bounced, and Barry was overdrawn by about $20,000. So Turnbow arranged a $20,000 loan for Barry, and in fact Barry paid it off, averting a loss to the bank and affirming Turnbow's faith in him.

"Don't worry, Bob," Barry would say reassuringly. "You've been real good to me. I would never do anything to hurt you."

Barry liked having his friends around the business, even the ones he couldn't hire. Tom Padgett came by about once a week, and in early 1983 began giving ZZZZ Best some "rain jobs."

In those days Padgett was working as a claims adjuster for Allstate Insurance, and heavy rains brought in a torrent of claims. Barry wanted business, so Padgett started using ZZZZ Best. Barry in turn kicked back a few dollars and took his friend to lunch now and then. One of Barry's first repair assignments seems to have been at the home of unlucky Arnelda Monroe in Van Nuys, who felt the damage was so bad she ought to have new carpets. Padgett sent his friend over to try and patch them up. Monroe complained that Barry hadn't done a good job, and she wouldn't sign the form he needed to get paid. Barry blithely forged her signature, and Padgett kept sending him on rain jobs. In the summer of 1983, Padgett moved over to automobile claims, but he still made a point of distributing Barry's business cards and introducing him to other adjusters who might help him.

Barry needed all the help he could get. In April 1983, he opened a new office, in the fast-growing suburb of Thousand Oaks, west of the San Fernando Valley. Like most of Barry's initiatives, this one was a disaster. Payroll and overhead were rising, one of his employees was diverting business to himself, and Barry was strapped.

Desperate for cash, in July or August he staged a phony burglary at his office to collect from his insurance company. Barry saw to it that the door was kicked in, and the next morning he called police. He claimed steam cleaners and various other tools were taken, and when he had to be more specific, he cooked up the Cornwell Triple-Vac Dual Pump Waterheated Steamcleaner, a mythical beast that might have dwelt in the land of Seuss or Mary Poppins. The Cornwell Triple-Vac was based on real machines except that "waterheated" was added. But Cornwell Quality Tool Co., a large, legitimate company for which Krowpman was an independent distributor, never made any such animal. The scam worked so well that Barry pulled this stunt again and again, until he was claiming ZZZZ Best was victimized by thieves half a dozen times. Barry was learning that it pays to have imagination.

It was also during 1983 that Barry had his first experience with credit cards. He somehow got hold of a Diners Club card and ran up $5,500 in debt taking his friends out to dinner.

In the early fall of 1983, Barry told Padgett he was having trouble making his payroll. Indeed, on October 3, 1983, Ben Aliav, owner of Rick's Liquor and Check Cashing in Reseda, sued Barry in Small Claims Court for $1,500 worth of bounced checks going back to July. The case was dismissed on October 30, presumably because Barry paid up, but the Aliav lawsuit wasn't to be the last.

Barry spent these months in a characteristic frenzy, dashing frantically from place to place in an effort to keep all his plates spinning in the air. In the two weeks beginning June 17, he was ticketed three times for speeding on the freeways, and on September 14 he was ticketed for speeding on a street and running a stop sign. Throughout his career, Barry's reckless driving and disregard for licensing and registration requirements earned him ticket after ticket. He had moving violations, parking violations and equipment violations. He made illegal u-turns, blocked crosswalks and exceeded speed limits from Palm Springs to Beverly Hills. In just five years on the road, he was cited at least eighteen times. When cited, Barry didn't pay the fine and didn't appear in court. Cited again, he would again ignore the ticket and the judge. When his license was suspended he drove anyway. Revocation didn't stop him either. Barry's offenses seemed to come in clusters. He had about one a month during the last half of 1984, for example.

To help Barry with his continuing financial crises, Padgett obligingly took out a $4,500 passbook loan secured by his savings. Around Thanksgiving 1983, Padgett learned that his friend had missed a loan payment. Still in the role of older brother, Padgett chastised him over the phone. "Barry, what is this? We're supposed to be helping my credit." That weekend, Barry went over to Padgett's apartment with a fancy car radio he said he'd gotten somewhere. He even had a screwdriver. Padgett had a houseful of people, so when Barry asked for the car keys, he just handed them over and went back to his guests.

Five or ten minutes later Barry was back.

"Tom, the radio's not going to fit."

"Fine," said Padgett, distracted by his visitors. "Thanks for the thought. And listen, you're going to keep paying the loan, right?"

Barry said sure he would.

On Monday Padgett went back to work, only to discover that a couple of Allstate bank drafts were missing from the glove box of his car. These were like checks, and were used by adjusters to settle small claims on the spot. Padgett told his boss to stop payment on the missing drafts and figured that was the end of it. But three weeks later Padgett was summoned to a meeting with the regional manager in Pasadena. Padgett was nervous, and when he arrived, claims manager Robert J. Pastorini proceeded to interrogate him. Padgett admitted lending Barry $4,500, giving him business and recommending him to other adjusters.

"Did he ever offer you any bribes or gratuities?" Pastorini demanded.

Lying, Padgett said no.

"You mean to tell me you loaned four thousand five hundred dollars from your own pocket to some teenaged kid? And he's one of our contractors? Don't you see the conflict of interest?"

Padgett finally asked what had happened to the drafts missing from his car. The answer was that they had been filled in for $4,762 and $2,672, marked with bogus claim numbers and signed by Barry, who had forged Padgett's signature. Then Barry deposited them at West Valley Bank, where his account was badly overdrawn. He even had an unidentified girlfriend call Turnbow, posing as Padgett's secretary, to let him know the drafts had been issued and would be coming in soon.

Padgett was angry and depressed. Not only had he been betrayed by someone he had tried to help, but the whole thing was stupid; did Barry really think he was going to get away with it?

When Padgett finally caught up with him, Barry was so contrite that Padgett couldn't stay mad. Barry also promised to talk Pastorini into letting Padgett keep his job, which he had held since March 1980, or nearly four years. Padgett was still depressed and missed the next two days' work. He even missed his Thursday-night workout at the gym. He liked Allstate, he felt his co-workers cared for him and he enjoyed the spirit of the place. On Fridays everyone came to work in casual clothes, and once when Padgett came in all black and blue from another unsuccessful amateur boxing match, the office manager demanded to know why Padgett hadn't told anyone he'd be boxing, so his co-workers might have been there to cheer for him.

On December 8, 1983, a Thursday, Barry drove to Pasadena and met with Pastorini and a subordinate, Jack L. Martin. For forty-five minutes, in a performance that was vintage Minkow, Barry impressed the older men with his deep sincerity. He said he was desperate because on November 17 his bank had informed him that he was $14,000 in arrears. So he took the checks from Padgett's gym bag while Padgett was in the sauna. Afterward Martin wrote a three-page memo to his boss recounting Barry's tale. "He readily admitted that he stole two drafts from Tom Padgett," the memo says, "forged the necessary information on the drafts and fraudulently presented them to West Valley Bank for payment. . . ."

Barry said he knew he'd be caught, but assumed (correctly) that he'd get off with a slap on the wrist because he was a minor. He repaid the money and urged the men to go easy on his friend.

Padgett had to quit anyway. His superiors felt he had shown terrible judgment giving insurance work to a seventeen-year-old kid, and recommending an incompetent to his fellow adjusters. Worse, Barry hadn't been making the loan payments, and the bank took the money out of Padgett's account. So, thanks to Barry Minkow, Padgett lost his job and most of his savings in the span of a few short weeks, leaving him jobless and broke for Christmas.

Barry hadn't solved his own financial problems, either. Small

Claims suits filed December 30, 1983, and January 20, 1984, accused him of bouncing checks. A Van Nuys auto repair shop sued for the same reason on February 16, 1984. An $800 Small Claims suit filed the same day accused Barry of damaging a mirrored wall and two glass tables at a residence in Calabasas; the dispute almost made "The People's Court" television show, but Barry eventually settled. Indeed, most of those who took him to Small Claims Court got their money. But they had to work for it—and they had to wait.

Thus ZZZZ Best kept growing, swelling with fraud the way Barry's body was puffed up on steroids. In February 1984, ZZZZ Best opened a third location, in Anaheim, to tap the lucrative Orange County market. It was yet another drain on his company's resources. Meanwhile Padgett remained friends with Barry, who sought to make amends for the stolen drafts. "Tom, look, you can work for me, I'll put you on the payroll," he offered.

Padgett refused. Instead he became a Herbalife salesman.

Any student in the school of Barry Minkow needs a quick primer in Herbalife International Inc. Based in Inglewood, Barry's early hometown, Herbalife makes various pills and potions that are supposed to be healthful, but over the years it has been assailed for selling products that many doctors consider useless. The company was founded by a twenty-four-year-old named Mark Hughes, whose adolescence was marred by three-and-one-half years at a home for emotionally disturbed youth. He has told interviewers he got interested in nutrition at the age of eighteen, when his mother died from an overdose of diet pills.

Hughes started the company with help from another diet-products veteran in February 1980. Just five years later, Hughes told *Forbes* that his company had annual sales of $488 million for the fiscal year ended January 31, 1985, generated by more than 700,000 distributors. Hughes had married a Swedish beauty queen and bought a mansion in swank Bel Air for $7 million. He was only twenty-nine.

Forbes also said "some physicians and nutritionists warned that Herbalife's 20-pill-a-day regimen contained potentially harmful laxatives, diuretics and caffeine, and the investigators were circling." California, for example, accused the company of making false claims in promoting its products, and of being organized as an "endless chain" marketing program—in other words, a pyramid scheme in which salesmen make money not only by selling the company's products, but also by recruiting other salesmen and collecting royalties on their sales as well. In 1986 the company settled with California by paying

$850,000 in costs and penalties. It also agreed not to make "curative or medicinal claims" for its diet products. And to satisfy the Food and Drug Administration, it agreed to remove two products from its line altogether. Herbalife has had other problems, but still managed to become a public company—to have its stock held and traded by outside investors—in 1986 by quietly merging with a Nevada "shell" company. Companies that go public in this expedited fashion can avoid some of the federal government's more onerous disclosure requirements. But Herbalife investors took it in the neck; shares fell from a high of $9.125 in July 1987 to about 50 cents eighteen months later.

As a Herbalife salesman, Padgett didn't fare too well either, even though he was able to get lots of business at the gym—from Krowpman, for example. But mostly it was a struggle. Padgett was always fighting with his landlady, who shut off his utilities at one point, and he never had any money. Selling Herbalife to strangers wasn't easy. He tried putting sales flyers on the windshields of parked cars, and a security guard chased him all over the parking lot around the Universal Pictures complex while he was at it. Barry had agreed to pay off his debt to Padgett at $50 a week, but he'd disappear when Padgett turned up looking for money on Fridays. Padgett ended up having to take a job at a pistol range, and even had to sweep out the place—a sad comedown for a Viking—when things got slow.

Finally, after missing three Fridays in a row, Barry turned up with some money. He also told Padgett he was starting to get some substantial insurance restoration jobs from a guy named Jim, who was somehow connected to big money back East.

5

As ZZZZ Best grew, Barry developed his own management style. Besides lying and cheating, he was turning into a youthful martinet who brooked no challenge. Around the office people had to call him Mr. Minkow, including his own mother, and everyone except Barry was supposed to wear a necktie. He told questioners he had learned the importance of discipline in military school. "My way or the highway," he liked to say. Barry ran the business with all the collegiality of a Central American tyrant.

He particularly relished humiliating older men—especially his dull-witted father. Once, at a ZZZZ Best function, Barry got up and spoke in praise of the elder Minkow, who was just beaming as a Harry Chapin song called "Cat's in the Cradle" was played on the sound system. A few people in the room understood what Barry was up to and shook their heads. "Cat's in the Cradle" is all about a father who doesn't have any time for his son, and whose son, when grown, has no time for the father. "He'd grown up just like me," the father laments.

Barry's father wasn't the only one who came in for this sort of thing, and it wasn't often so subtle. "Get the hell out of here," Barry would bark at executives twice his age, and for some reason, perhaps because he was the boss, perhaps because they needed the job or never before had such a fancy title or such good money or so much faith, these men took it, slunk out of sight and stayed on.

Among those who put up with abuse from Barry was the formidably named Charles Breckenridge Arrington III. Chip Arrington is nothing like his starchy full name. Arrington is handsome, warm and unpretentious, with bright eyes that make him seem open and alert, dark hair and a big smile hooded by a humorous-looking mustache. He started working as a carpet cleaner in 1980, a year after finishing high school, and met Barry in 1982 while both were working at Dunn-Rite.

Chip was struggling, and did a few jobs for Barry's fledgling company. By the following year he and his partner were top producers at Dunn-Rite, and in May of 1983 he went to work for Barry full-time, although he was still allowed to do some jobs of his own. That would stop soon; ZZZZ Best and its founder would come to dominate Arrington's life. Even though Chip was six years older than Barry, he became enamored of his boss and tried hard to please him. Arrington is intelligent but uneducated, and later told police Barry offered him $700 a week to start, at that point a lot of money for Chip. Arrington was no naïf. He knew his way around the carpet business, but he didn't really know Barry. All he saw was a chance for himself to rise above the level of rug sucker and become somebody. Barry proved by example that it could be done, and Chip worked hard to follow suit.

Before long he was chief operating officer, overseeing the company's cleaning operations and working to open new offices. The company had about seventy-five employees in 1984, but despite Arrington's best efforts, it still wasn't making any money. ZZZZ Best suffered from the same cutthroat competition that had beset others in the industry for years. It arose partly from the ease with which anyone can get into the carpet-cleaning business—even a pathologically dishonest sixteen-year-old with no capital. The competitive environment bred ferocious price-cutting, which would seem inevitable except that there's so much carpet in the area, and industry estimates are that 80 percent of it has never been professionally cleaned.

ZZZZ Best was also inept. For all Barry's rhetoric about motivation, for all his rules about attire and honorifics, his business was actually a shambles. ZZZZ Best wasn't even good at cleaning carpets. Late in 1984, for example, a woman in the Valley called upon ZZZZ Best to clean a pair of Oriental rugs. They were worth several thousand dollars, but they had a much greater sentimental value to their owner, who wanted them cleaned carefully. ZZZZ Best destroyed them, and Barry refused to make amends. Finally the woman sued.

Arrington was always after Barry to resolve such matters, but as usual, he ignored the Municipal Court subpoena, and the woman's attorney, Stuart Zimring, won by default. Barry was subpoenaed again, this time for questioning about his assets. Once again he ignored the subpoena. Now he was cited for contempt, and a bench warrant was issued. When Barry was stopped on one of his many traffic violations, the cop punched him into the computer, the warrant popped up and Barry was arrested. To Joyce's consternation, he spent the night of February 14, 1985—Valentine's Day—in custody. He never did pay the entire judgment. After much harassment from Zimring, Barry turned up one day in shorts and a tank top at the lawyer's office. "What does the bitch want?" he demanded. "This is so insignificant I can't even bother with it."

Zimring finally got most of the money out of him.

Cash remained Barry's biggest problem. He was like an addict, and the more he used, the more he needed. How could he pay attention to operations—to actually cleaning carpets—when he had to worry night and day about raising more money? He had already begun kiting checks, for example, by manipulating his accounts at Valley State Bank and Lloyd's Bank in Woodland Hills. Check-kiting is illegal. It means depositing, say, a Valley State check at Lloyd's, while depositing a Lloyd's check at Valley State. The results are bank balances inflated by nonexistent funds.

This kind of thing tended not to get much notice, but Barry's precocious industrialism did. Maybe it was the universality of carpet that gave Barry's business exploits such resonance, but they might have escaped notice if the fates hadn't intervened and, probably with a nasty snicker, introduced him to Jeri Carr.

To me Jeri Carr is a flack's flack, the PR person Plato had in mind when he conceived of an ideal world in which there was one of everything. When I met her she wore enormous hoop earrings of black plastic, her black hair swept up and pomaded and her eyes ringed with so much black makeup she looked like a spoiled raccoon. Jeri is in her early thirties and kind of pretty despite all the goop on her face. Perhaps to evoke sympathy, she brought along her easygoing husband and her beautiful new baby. Jeri is enthusiastic and a touch sexy on the phone, with that husky, breathless public relations sound that reporters everywhere know.

In October of 1983, Jeri Carr too was bitten by the entrepreneurial bug, and after working in other publicity jobs and as a fashion buyer, she decided to start her own public relations company in her one-bedroom apartment in North Hollywood, just a few miles east of ZZZZ Best.

In the world of Los Angeles "praiseries," as Hollywood public relations firms are known in *Variety*, Jeri Carr is nobody, a small, poorly pitched voice in a heavenly chorus of approbation. But for a while, at least, Carr outshined them all. She was like the ballplayer who toils for years in the minors, where his entire career seems likely to pass, when by some fluke he is called up to the parent club and tears up the league, transforming a ragtag collection of losers into champions.

It happened because Carr hired a young woman named Ana Madrinan to work in her fledgling public relations business. Ana's younger sister, Elenora, attended Cleveland High School with Barry, who offered Elenora a job. According to Carr, Barry learned that Elenora's sister worked in public relations: "Barry said to Elenora, 'Do we have what the media would want?' There was no cockiness at all." Soon after, Ana approached her boss about getting Barry as a client.

Carr went over to see Barry, who was wearing a characteristically skin-tight tank top to show off his muscles, and her first impression was that the carpets in his office were filthy. But her attitude changed when she heard him speak: "The first sentence out of Barry's mouth, I was mesmerized."

Carr listened to this charismatic seventeen-year-old talk for a while and was stunned. "There's nobody at that age who is that smart, that directed," she says. "He talked about helping youth, fighting drugs, building a business. He was great. He was a PR person's dream. He was a *mother's* dream. He really believed in himself."

Jeri was hooked; she knows a story when she sees one, and it must have seemed to her on that fateful day in the kid's office that the gods of public relations truly smiled upon her. Carr recalls: "Barry said, 'We'll try it for three months. If you can get me three different things, you've got me forever.' "

Three different things meant getting Barry mentioned in three different places in the media. Carr knew that Barry particularly loved listening to Cleve Hermann, a veteran reporter on KFWB-AM, an all-news radio station in Los Angeles. So she went after Hermann first, and persuaded him to come out and do an on-location interview with Barry. "I didn't have to do anything else," Carr says. "He hired me."

Barry had always wanted attention; now he was about to get it. Jeri Carr was glad for the new business—Barry would soon become her biggest source of billings—and threw herself into the task. It was like the fable about the woman whose kiss turns the frog into a prince, although in this case it's not clear which of the two was the frog. Anyway, "I took Barry because he was wonderful," Carr says. "I would have wanted my son to grow up and turn out like Barry."

It was 1984. Orwell's fateful year was significant for Barry Minkow. On March 22 he turned eighteen, the age of legal majority for most purposes in California. In June he graduated from Grover Cleveland High School, and his friend Tom Padgett was hired as an auto-damage appraiser by the local Travelers Insurance unit of Travelers Corp., a major insurance company based in Hartford, Connecticut. This wasn't entirely accidental; Barry had pushed him to go back into the insurance business. But Padgett was happy to get the Travelers job, which was hardly demanding. He had to assess four cars a day and spend one day a week in the office. On most days he was home at noon to catch "Twilight Zone" reruns on television.

It was the year of the Summer Olympics in Los Angeles, and contrary to the predictions of gridlock that preceded the games, things went extraordinarily smoothly thanks to staggered work hours and other special arrangements. People wondered why the city couldn't be this way all the time.

Things looked equally rosy for Barry and his company. Barry was free of high school and could at last concentrate on his business. He had his own offices and his own publicist on monthly retainer, and the company was growing fast. Barry was starting to get noticed. Around the office, at least, so was Padgett, who turned up about once a week. Barry explained to Arrington that ZZZZ Best had begun getting restoration jobs from him. This came as something of a surprise to Chip, who thought he was working in a carpet-cleaning company. But Barry said that someday Arrington himself might have a role in this lucrative end of the business.

Meanwhile, the ruddy glow of ZZZZ Best was only cheap rouge. On July 17, 1984, Barry was accused in a Small Claims suit of failing to pay for $927.37 worth of janitorial supplies. Three months before, ZZZZ Best had been sued over supplies by another vendor stuck with a bounced check, this one for $714.59. Barry wasn't even forwarding to the federal government the payroll taxes he withheld from his workers; he owed Uncle Sam money for this all through 1984, according to federal tax liens filed the next year. Despite outward appearances, Barry and his business were still thrashing around, struggling to survive.

On July 31, for example, in an ironic recapitulation of his family's embarrassing past, Barry wrote to an official of Pacific Bell, begging him not to turn off the ZZZZ Best phones again. Without them, Barry explained, the company would be virtually out of business.

That summer, Barry placed an advertisement in the *Los Angeles Times* saying, essentially, "money wanted." A man named Wallace Berrie responded. To impress him, Barry went over and cleaned his carpets, which were white wool. "Hard to clean," Barry said later in a telegraphic aside to the jury. "Had to use cold water." Barry told Berrie he needed the money for new offices and for buying drapery-cleaning equipment. Berrie lent him $30,000, which helped for a while, but of course Barry had to pay a healthy return, and since ZZZZ Best was a chronic money-loser, it would have to run that much faster to stay in place.

Even Jeri Carr had her first fleeting taste of reality on the subject of Barry Minkow. Soon after the Cleve Hermann radio interview, she got an angry call from another publicist demanding, "How dare you steal my client?" The other publicist never had a contract with Barry, but was doing public relations work for him and thought he was hers exclusively. The other publicist, whom Carr knew, never spoke to Carr again.

In the fall, Barry forged some paystubs for himself to show a weekly salary of $1,100 so he could get a car loan to buy a Datsun 300ZX. He put $6,000 down, got Krowpman to guarantee the balance and drove away. He also somehow stole and forged about $13,000 worth of money orders from a Reseda liquor store to pay company bills. In November the store sued, and the case was settled out of court. As usual, hardly anyone ever found out about it, but by that time Barry had found a more efficient way to raise money.

In September, West Valley Bank, where Barry had established a relationship with Bob Turnbow, approved a ZZZZ Best application to establish a "merchant account" so Barry's business could accept credit cards. When a customer buys something on a credit card, the merchant customarily takes the charge slip to the bank and deposits it in his merchant account. The bank credits the merchant with cash immediately, and then forwards the slip through one or another of the charge-slip-processing networks to collect payment from the bank that issued the credit card in the first place. When Barry opened his merchant account at West Valley Bank—the fee was $35—ZZZZ Best began accepting credit cards for its services. Almost immediately, Barry began using customers' charge numbers to forge charge slips, which he would deposit at West Valley like cash.

The American economy is rife with credit-card fraud, but it usually involves someone getting hold of your card number and using it to buy goods and services before disappearing. Even though most Americans don't even look at their charge-card statements every month, it's hard for a going business to submit forged credit-card slips on an ongoing basis and get away with it. Barry, who isn't stupid, knew this. But it is a measure of his chutzpah that he went ahead and did it anyway. For a while, at least, he had a license to print money.

Sure enough, in late 1984 or early 1985, a former Army intelligence officer named Gil Lopez began to hear more about Barry Minkow than he ever wanted to know.

A friendly but taciturn man, Lopez was branch investigations manager at First Data Resources in Santa Ana, California, a unit of American Express that does credit-card processing for banks. Lopez's job was to track down fraud, and he pursued it vigorously. Around the New Year, he started to get a lot of disputed MasterCard and Visa charges from ZZZZ Best. All were telephone orders, meaning a card had never been presented for imprint. Instead, someone merely used the card numbers to fill out drafts that could be deposited in the ZZZZ Best merchant account, just like cash. Through the usual clearing system—in this case, First Data Resources—the customer's credit-card account at some other bank would be debited, and in the case of false charges, the customer might complain if he or she even noticed.

Lucille Frost was one of those who fell victim to Barry's credit-card scam. On a Saturday, February 9, 1985, she had a ZZZZ Best crew come out to her home in Santa Ana to clean and Scotchguard the carpets. Some people were already starting to wonder if ZZZZ Best really used protective chemicals, or instead sprayed water on the rug and called it protected, but Frost didn't know anything about that. The bill was $75, and for some reason she paid $60 cash and $15 by check. A ZZZZ Best crew member asked for a Visa or MasterCard number as identification, and so Frost wrote her Bank of America Visa number on the face of the check. In other words, she never charged anything with ZZZZ Best.

But the next day, February 10, ZZZZ Best generated a charge of $389.50. On February 12, there was a charge of $800. On February 13, there was another $200. The total of phony charges was $1,389.50. Lucille Frost was horrified. She was even more horrified when she discovered that ZZZZ Best submitted $1,710.57 in bogus charges on her *MasterCard*, the number of which she never even gave to the workmen. Frost later surmised that one of them must have cribbed it from her purse when she wasn't looking.

Lucille Frost never had to pay any of this, because when her statements came, the phony charges were so large they jumped out at her. Federal law gives credit-card users the right not to pay most disputed charges, so the burden ultimately fell back on West Valley Bank, where Minkow had his merchant account.

It must have been obvious to Barry that most of the bogus charges would be uncovered sooner or later, but meanwhile it afforded ZZZZ Best a nice little float. Gil Lopez says that by the time a phony charge is posted, billed, complained about, tracked down, resolved and repaid, months can go by. Barry filled out all the forged credit-card drafts personally, in his own large, childish scrawl. The amount of money involved isn't clear. At one point Barry said the figure was $150,000 to $200,000, but later he insisted it was just $72,000. The scam went on for several months, straddling the 1985 New Year.

One of Barry's victims was venture capitalist Earl Needham. When he called to complain, he got Barry on the phone. In fact, he talked to Barry twice more, and was amazed at the young man's financial sophistication. Barry tried to get Needham to help turn ZZZZ Best into a public company with freely trading stock. Even then, Barry had big ideas.

For reasons unrelated to Barry Minkow, West Valley Bank was declared insolvent by federal regulators in February 1985, and was taken over by First Interstate Bank, one of the nation's larger financial institutions. Bob Turnbow quit and went to work at Valley State Bank, also in the San Fernando Valley, as a branch manager. The ZZZZ Best account went with him.

Around the time Turnbow took over his new job, Barry told him he was getting into the restoration business and had done a number of smaller jobs for insurance companies. Now Barry claimed he had a big job in Arroyo Grande, near Santa Barbara, for $3 million, and Turnbow was impressed. Actually, the notion was preposterous. Arroyo Grande is a pleasant town of 13,000 souls and five traffic lights. There isn't a building over three stories for miles around. But Barry's invention and Turnbow's reaction are significant. Barry was to make up many more insurance jobs during the next three years, and Turnbow's credulous response would prove more or less typical.

Probably the first time Barry made up one of these insurance contracts was in trying to borrow money from Wallace Berrie. With Turnbow, Barry said the Arroyo Grande job was being financed by

Union Bank and First Interstate; Valley State was just too small. But Turnbow's bank would be permitted to consider making a $15,000 loan so that ZZZZ Best could complete a $61,000 insurance job at 1102 Hope St., in downtown Los Angeles. Barry showed Turnbow what was supposedly a work order dated March 3, 1985, from State Farm. Barry also submitted a personal financial statement that showed a net worth of $228,548. Turnbow approved the loan on March 18, knowing that it was collateralized by cash on deposit at the bank; a month before, Barry had borrowed $15,000 more from Berrie.

Some of that cash might also have come from credit-card victims like Lucille Frost, but Gil Lopez was about to put an end to that.

"I contacted Barry Minkow at the time," he recalls. "His story was, he had an employee in one of his shops generating these credit-card sales."

Since Barry's bank—West Valley—wasn't a customer of First Data Resources, Lopez sent the unpaid charges back, and by April 29, they had begun to reach their destination. On that day, Bob Turnbow got a call from Peggy Ingram, a former West Valley colleague who had stayed on under First Interstate.

"Did you open another account for Barry Minkow?" she asked. "Be careful, because a lot of the charges are coming back."

Almost as soon as Turnbow put down the phone, it rang again. This time it was someone in his own operations department, reporting a problem in the ZZZZ Best merchant account. Bogus credit-card charges were being returned. The account would have to be closed.

It was not a pleasant Monday for Turnbow. He called Barry and confronted him with the credit-card problems. Barry immediately blamed them on some crooked former employees and said everything had been straightened out. But Turnbow insisted that the account be closed and that Barry pay off the $15,000 loan.

Barry seemed truly hurt by what was happening to him. He asked Turnbow for one last favor: would he approve immediate credit for a $10,000 check from Wallace Berrie? That way Barry could get a cashier's check to open an account elsewhere without having his funds—and potentially his business—frozen for several days. Turnbow agreed. Later in the week his heart sank when the Berrie check came back stamped "Payment Stopped" on the back. Fortunately, Barry made good on that one too. Sooner or later Barry always seemed to make good.

But hardly anyone knew about Barry's conniving, and Jeri Carr was still hard at work promoting the wonder boy. In March 1985 she managed to get Barry an official commendation from Los Angeles Mayor Tom Bradley, who routinely issues flocks of these, and who said the young businessman "has set a fine entrepreneurial example of obtaining the status of a millionaire at the age of 18. . . ." The commendation is a comic paean, raving on about his "reputable and reliable carpet cleaning services," his "tremendous struggle being accepted as a knowing businessman," and his "list of clientelle" (sic). The mayor's office says pointedly that they don't write the things; they just sign and issue them as submitted.

Thus did the public and private Barry Minkows diverge. But ZZZZ Best didn't stop at credit-card fraud. Minkow and Padgett were still friends, and in June or July of 1985 Barry asked for a favor. It seemed that "Jim" was giving Barry so much work it was starting to look bad. Would Padgett tell any inquiring bankers that the restoration contract they might happen to be asking about had actually come from Travelers? There would be something in it for Padgett, of course: $100 a week.

"But Barry, what if they call the boss?"

"They won't," Barry assured him. "It's just procedure."

Tom Padgett is kind of a likable guy, aside from his fascistic tendencies, and his profound gullibility would almost be endearing if it weren't so dangerous. Practically anyone else would have realized that Barry Minkow might once again cost him his job, but Padgett just didn't look at it that way. He needed more money to impress a woman he was after, and his take-home pay at Travelers was only $550 every two weeks. Therefore he went along. Soon he was telling callers that, yes, Travelers certainly was giving ZZZZ Best hundreds of thousands of dollars' worth of insurance jobs. Padgett seems to have believed these jobs existed; he was merely disguising their source. From this tiny acorn grew the mighty oak of ZZZZ Best fraud.

It wasn't just that Padgett wanted a woman. He was also good at taking orders, and badly needed to belong to something larger than himself. He joined the Army for the first time when he was seventeen and served two separate stints, including a tour of duty as a mortarman in Vietnam during 1969 and 1970. A student of Germany between the wars, Padgett must have drawn strong parallels between himself as a returning veteran of the miserable and unsuccessful war in Southeast Asia, and the valorous German fighting man returning home from his brutal struggle in the trenches. Padgett could say that both warriors saw their efforts undermined by divisiveness at home, and both found that when the war was finally over, there seemed little place for them in the society they had fought for.

Padgett's self-awareness is such that he can recommend an excellent guide to his own personality: Eric Hoffer's *The True Believer*, a spare and remarkable study of precisely such spirits. Indeed, Padgett always seemed in the throes of some unwarranted disaffection. Vietnam, he says, "made me look for causes, and causes where the rug wouldn't be pulled out." He is a strange mixture of egotism and powerlessness, and also a kind of cosmic ignorance. There is an air of grievance about Padgett, as if he were somehow thwarted by forces larger than himself, and of vague recklessness, like someone ready to do anything. Padgett is one of those people who never really grasped that the universe wasn't created to thwart him.

But he isn't unschooled. Padgett is well informed and widely read, especially in military and political history. He holds a bachelor's degree in political science from Kent State University, where he attended one meeting of Students for a Democratic Society, but mainly hung out with bikers and sometimes dressed like one. He says he once broke up a left-wing political rally with what he described to the crowd as an anticommunist boa constrictor, the sort of story Padgett loves to tell. He can be an electrifying storyteller, and when he really gets going he has an unsettling tendency to cackle like a loon. Still, he took his studies seriously enough to get a master's degree in international relations from Boston University. Tom Padgett had aspirations. He had planned to get a PhD and become a professor, or perhaps go to law school and be an attorney. But an old Army buddy had a tile business in Southern California, and somehow Padgett went west, where he ended up following Barry Minkow.

In those days, that might not have seemed such a terrible idea. In March 1985 Barry bought himself a condominium, paying $109,189 for unit No. 25 at 7211 Cozycroft Ave., a year-old building at the corner of Sherman Way in Canoga Park. It wasn't Beverly Hills, but the place had two bedrooms, two baths and 1,033 square feet of living space. Through his uncle, builder Joe Mark, Barry got a deal. Like moving ZZZZ Best from his parents' garage to a real office, moving out of his parents' house was a major step on Barry's road to independence. He closed on the place the day before his nineteenth birthday.

But like everything else about Barry, this deal was done with mirrors. He borrowed $25,000 for the down payment from Hal Berman, his hulking trainer at Gold's Gym in Reseda, where Barry went when Valley Gym closed. He also staged another phony break-in during March, claiming to State Farm that the robbers took $20,380 worth of equipment from the ZZZZ Best offices in Reseda.

Padgett, meanwhile, was still a big help. Besides telling people he was giving Minkow business, he also supplied Barry with Travelers stationery. For example, a letter on the Travelers letterhead of supervisor David L. Tengberg dated August 19, 1985, confirms that ZZZZ Best was awarded a $1.5 million repair job "in National City in San Diego, California." The letter, probably written later and backdated, purports to be signed by "Thomas Padgett, Property Appraiser." Padgett was no property appraiser, and there was no such repair job.

Around the same time, Barry asked his friend for another favor in the same line. Padgett was about to go on vacation when Barry said he'd pay him $500 to put on a necktie and business suit and take part in a meeting with an investor named Jack Catain. Minkow would tell him what to say. Padgett agreed, and when Catain arrived for a meeting at Barry's office, Barry and Padgett were busily—and noisily—going over a rehearsed list of purported damage-restoration jobs that ZZZZ Best was performing on behalf of insurance companies.

Gravelly-voiced and gruff, Catain sounded like a tough guy and looked like one who was perhaps a little over the hill, but who knew people who could make your life difficult. He had a fleshy face with a dour expression and a pug nose, a strange pallor from his circulatory problems, and he moved stiffly thanks to a pair of artificial hips. Catain was five feet eight inches tall and weighed 200 pounds. "He was the kind of guy who'd get a haircut every other day," says a former lawman who once arrested him.

Padgett and Minkow talked animatedly about making sure the electricians did a good job and so forth. None of the jobs existed, of course. Some of the addresses weren't even buildings. But Jack Catain seemed fooled.

6

Any beatification campaign launched on behalf of the late Jack M. Catain Jr. seems destined to fail. A well-known loanshark, racketeer, counterfeiter, money launderer, extortion artist, looter of public companies and eluder of law enforcement, Jack Catain was truly a renaissance man of white-collar crime.

He was born May 29, 1930, in Chicago, the son of a produce worker whose family name was originally Catania, like the seaport in eastern Sicily. Jack Jr. moved to California in the late 1950s, but there is evidence that he left his heart in the Windy City, which has always had a more powerful underworld than Los Angeles. Some people call Los Angeles' gangsters "the Mickey Mouse mob" for their petty crimes and residence in the land of Disney.

The Mafia is weaker in Southern California than in cities like Chicago or New York for several reasons. Los Angeles has a smaller proportion of Italian-Americans, and although La Cosa Nostra has dealings with every ethnic group, membership requires Italian heritage. Also, unions aren't as powerful or ubiquitous in Los Angeles, and there isn't nearly the level of official and police corruption that seems to thrive elsewhere. Lately Los Angeles is spawning its own brand of organized crime. Black and Latino street gangs meet any reasonable definition of the term, and illegal drugs today are the bootleg whiskey of Prohibition. Immigration plays an important role too. Just as Jewish, Irish and Italian criminals got organized earlier in this century, L.A.'s huge immigrant population has sprouted an Asian mob with ties to the Far Eastern financial world.

Jack Catain was a Los Angeles mobster with connections to crime families in New York, Philadelphia and Detroit as well as Chicago. In March 1976, for example, Angelo Bruno, the aging Mafia patriarch of Philadelphia, met twice with Catain in Southern California. Several weeks earlier, Bruno lieutenant Frank Sindone also visited Los Angeles to see Catain about laundering more than $3 million in illicit funds. Bruno and Sindone are both dead now, victims of a mob war apparently unrelated to Catain.

"He was a guy that did it all with a pencil, the kind of guy that gathers strength in organized crime because he makes money for people," one former federal investigator says of Catain. "He laundered the money for the Chicago mob out here."

Catain had long ago established himself as a shady business executive by taking control of Rusco Industries Inc., a publicly held building-supply concern. During the late 1960s and throughout the 1970s, he ran the company with flagrant disregard for any shareholders other than himself, and some of Catain's dealings neatly foreshadowed what would happen later with ZZZZ Best.

In 1971, for instance, Rusco and Catain settled a Securities and Exchange Commission lawsuit accusing them of defrauding investors and manipulating Rusco stock. The SEC said the company hyped its shares by announcing a contract to supply panels for a new steel-shell home system. But the ostensible buyer of the panels was a barely established company run by one of Catain's business partners, and it depended on Rusco for financing. Rusco was also involved in a bogus joint venture to make credit-card-protection systems that led to losses of nearly $1 million. Catain eventually had to pay $800,000 to cover Rusco's losses from his dealings. But neither Catain nor Rusco admitted wrongdoing or suffered criminal penalties.

In 1975 Catain sued an associate over a disputed finder's fee during Catain's unsuccessful attempt to buy a Las Vegas casino-hotel, demonstrating an unusual characteristic for a mobster: he would go to court to collect a debt. But then, Jack Catain was never Al Capone.

Sleazy dealings continued at Rusco, which was supposed to be a public company owned by its stockholders, not Catain's personal preserve. Yet he used it to buy businesses owned by his relatives, and in 1978 Catain was reported to be under Justice Department investigation for acting as a conduit in the laundering of at least $10 million in organized-crime money. The department was also said to be considering the possibility that Rusco was a front for this purpose. Catain denied the allegations.

For the uninitiated, "laundering" is a way of making ill-gotten gains look legitimate. Someone who makes millions selling drugs, for example, can't just deposit a suitcase full of cash in the local savings and loan. Financial institutions are required to report transactions of $10,000 or more to the IRS, which demands to know where the money came from. (It's taxable even if procured illegally; that was Capone's downfall.) But if the money can be deposited offshore and then repatriated through a foreign bank, or if it can be invested somehow, it can be moved into the banking system and used for the benefit of its owner. Billions of dollars in drug profits are laundered annually. One way is to buy a business, paying the owner partly with legitimate funds and partly with dirty money. The seller reports only the price paid by check, and keeps the rest tax-free. The buyer has laundered his dough.

In 1980 the SEC finally forced Catain out of Rusco, after he got the company to advance $507,000 to a couple of friends without ever trying to collect repayment. Catain himself owed the company $2.7 million for insider transactions. Just before quitting, he got a contract from Rusco giving him $157,500 a year for five years as a "senior employee." The payments didn't last even though Catain (again, characteristically) sued to try to make the contract stick.

Catain also had connections to some of Los Angeles' beautiful people. His divorce was handled by the law firm of Henry Bushkin, who was for years Johnny Carson's lawyer and confidant, and for a while Catain was a major customer at the Commercial Bank of California. Carson and Bushkin together owned about a quarter of that bank and were co-chairmen for a time. Catain generously brought in friends and associates as new borrowers and secured their loans with his $1 million home. Unfortunately for the bank, the house burned down in 1981, and at least some of the loans it secured went sour. Bad debts prompted regulators to close the bank in May 1983, leaving behind some hard feelings. The ensuing litigation included a civil suit by the Federal Deposit Insurance Corporation that accused Bushkin, Carson and other directors of allowing loans to individuals "directly or indirectly associated with organized crime." It was settled on undisclosed terms.

During all this time Catain eluded the law, but he had other troubles. He got divorced, had serious health problems and wasn't going to skirt prosecution forever. On top of everything else, he was soon to meet Barry Minkow.

The summer of 1985 was brutally hot in the San Fernando Valley.

In its further reaches, a few miles northwest of Barry's headquarters, desertlike winds blew so warm that if you drove with the windows down the air would bake your face. The hills surrounding the Valley's great plain disappeared in the smog, and life took on the groggy quality of a day in the sun following a night of strong drink.

Barry's life in those days seemed rich with promise. He was the owner and president of an apparently booming business that was claiming net income of $322,000 on revenue of $1,240,000 for the twelve months ended April 30. He was starting to get noticed in the media. He had just moved into his very own "luxury" condominium. And he was still only nineteen. On the other hand, he owed money all over the place, and ZZZZ Best was hardly a cash cow. Barry had to find some money. As usual, he succeeded.

Barry claims he met Catain one morning in May of 1985, when he was dispatched by an uncle in the construction business to repair a torn carpet in Catain's new town house. Barry knew about Catain's sordid reputation almost from the outset because someone in his own family, perhaps the same uncle, had warned him. But Barry didn't care. Maybe he knew how useful Jack Catain could be. Perhaps he somehow foresaw that he would gain access to his first real money through the aging mobster, who introduced him to banks and investors that would eventually plow millions into ZZZZ Best and enable Barry's business to take off.

Catain was a heavy drinker as well as a hood, but he always had a soft spot for kids. When his criminal lawyer, a former federal organized-crime prosecutor named James A. Twitty, had children, Catain opened what Twitty calls "a substantial" savings account for them as a present. A gregarious Texan with a Lone Star voice, Twitty recalls that when he couldn't always find enough time for Catain during the week, he would visit the ailing mobster at home on weekends, infants in tow. "We'd go to places like McDonald's, me and Jack eating Big Macs and my babies having a great old time. Jack was one of my favorite clients. He never, ever cried about what he was being charged with."

Catain's encounter with Barry was another example of the latter's amazing eye for corruptibility. Perhaps the two men saw only raw opportunity when they met, but I suspect that each appealed to something deeper in the other. Barry was always conscripting fathers from among the men he encountered, and Catain must have been favorably predisposed. In 1976 his teenage son Alan died of leukemia. Barry was an eager substitute, ready to learn whatever Catain could teach him about financial manipulations. "He wouldn't tie his shoes unless Jack said to do it—at least in the beginning," says one Catain associate. Barry appears to have learned much, but he would someday teach his mentor a lesson as well.

Neither man wasted much time. Barry claims Catain was home when he got there, and asked a lot of questions about ZZZZ Best. Barry told him what he really needed was money. Catain said, "You've come to the right place."

That very night, he and Barry met with John Miller, who had a company called Direct Professional Funding, to discuss arranging enough bank financing to give Barry a little breathing room. Direct Professional Funding was a mortgage company just up the street from Barry's offices in Reseda, and Catain had lent Miller money to help him through a rough spot with the business. Miller had also arranged a mortgage for Catain to buy a condominium from Barry's uncle's company in the Valley. Barry says he brought along his bogus financial statements and a fee of $2,500 in cash.

Miller wasn't too keen on Barry. Catain wanted him to arrange some bank loans for the kid, but Barry was only nineteen, and he smelled phony. Miller didn't for one minute believe all that baloney about insurance restoration jobs, and Barry's financials, which he admitted were bogus, were so amateurish they wouldn't do any good. But Catain was insistent; in one of their many arguments over Barry, Catain accused Miller of being jealous and pounded his cane on the desk. "You just won't listen to me, will you?" Catain demanded. "You just won't believe what I'm telling you."

Miller knew Barry was a fraud and hated to risk any of his banking contacts, but he got some friends at Rancho National Bank in Agoura, California, to give Barry a checking account.

"Keep the account current and I'll get you a line of credit in thirty to sixty days," said a bank officer.

"Great," said Barry.

That very same day the account was overdrawn. Barry, it seemed, began kiting his new checks as soon as he got his hands on them. Incredulous bank officers closed the account.

Catain and Miller would bawl Barry out for this sort of thing, but Catain wouldn't give up. He said Barry was closer to him than his own son, and Barry was always respectful, calling Jack "sir." Bridgette Bridges, then Miller's wife and receptionist, says Barry and Catain came around virtually every day for months. Barry would wait outside with her while the two men had closed-door meetings, occasionally shouting at one another and summoning their young "client" for just a few minutes at a time. It must have galled Barry. Sometimes they'd send him out for pizza and Cokes.

Catain's attachment to his young friend grew quickly. One day during that hot summer in 1985, Barry called Chip Arrington into his office and introduced him to Catain. "Mr. Catain is going to be a consultant," Barry explained; he would help get the business organized, smooth the paper flow and so forth. Apparently Catain even made some recommendations. He urged that a computer system be installed, and discussed with Barry the possibility of franchising ZZZZ Best. Catain was also going to help finance the growing restoration business, and took an office in the Darby Ave. building, right next to the offices occupied by ZZZZ Best.

Maybe he really could help. ZZZZ Best had a bad reputation among community bankers in the San Fernando Valley—who were reluctant to deal with Barry all along because of his age—and the company still wasn't making any money on operations. Barry's determination and ingenuity were the only things keeping it afloat. At one point Catain arranged a $25,000 loan from a gentleman who was described by Miller in court as "a bad guy . . . right out of 'The Untouchables.' " The guy brought the cash around in a brown paper bag and gave it to Catain as Barry stood by. He wanted Catain to be responsible for the dough. "Don't worry about a thing," Catain said, and Barry in fact repaid the loan.

By now fund-raising had surpassed carpet cleaning as Barry's main occupation, and the strain was tremendous. Barry's stomach troubles flared up, and, vomiting blood, he landed in the hospital for three days starting July 22. Veteran internist Dr. Harold Lovitz thought it was an ulcer, even though upper gastrointestinal tests—a GI series—proved negative. He prescribed daily doses of Zantac (a standard ulcer medication), and more elaborate tests, which were never done. Barry told him nothing of the steroids.

"Since I was in desperate need of money at that time," Barry said subsequently in a legal declaration, "I agreed that, if Mr. Catain could assist me in obtaining financing for particular insurance jobs, then I would pay him a percentage of the profits. . . ." Barry went on to say that, ". . . from June through the middle of August 1985, Mr. Catain did assist me in obtaining loans which I desperately needed for my business."

Catain did this mainly by introducing Barry to Ellen C. Rozario, an Australian émigrée known to her friends as Kay.

A large woman with platinum-blonde hair, Kay was in her early fifties and knew Jack through his wife, Phyllis, with whom Kay had been friends for years. Kay lived in Agoura, on the western fringe of the San Fernando Valley, but she had also lived in Las Vegas (her husband Bobby was a bandleader), and she had affluent friends in both places. Among them was a group of older, divorced women that included Ann Randall, Elaine Orlando, Ada Cohen and Suzette Whitmore. All aging beauties, they had varying levels of business sophistication ranging from slight to none, and most were in some way needy.

They met Barry at various times in late 1985 and early 1986 either at Kay's house or at Barry's, and in the ensuing months his manipulation of these women bordered on the diabolical. He would stand beside Kay Rozario, encircle her shoulders with his powerful arm, and say, "This is my mom," making her flush with happiness and bringing out the strong maternal feelings deep within all the others.

"I wish my mom was like you, Kay," Barry would say, while the others clucked and admonished. "My mother embarrasses me. She's got no class."

Like Max Bialystok in Mel Brooks' film *The Producers*, Barry overwhelmed all of these women with energy and affection, showering each with individual attention. He included them in various ZZZZ Best social events and invited them to his house again and again, where they got tours of the place and chatted with Joyce. Everyone had a good look at the fancy cars in the driveway, and when the women ate, there was usually a butler. They took special pleasure in a series of investor luncheons to which Barry invited them and a few other pigeons who shared their naïve search for epic returns through ZZZZ Best. Since all of these investors were concerned about the safety of their money, Barry guaranteed each of their investments personally, in addition to the company's promise to pay. Both Barry and his company were obviously doing very, very well. To these foolish and faintly greedy older women, it seemed perfectly safe. They and one or two others of their ilk invested a total of roughly $1 million with Barry, to whom they were the fattest pigeons he had yet encountered. He seems to have assessed each of these aging glamour girls and zeroed in on their deepest needs—for love and admiration in most cases, but also for the security they hoped to obtain from a quick buck. Returns varied, but 1 percent a week wasn't uncommon.

In Rozario's case, for example, there wasn't much call for bandleaders anymore, so Kay was delighted to have a rich new source of income in Barry. Catain and his protégé had already told her all about his great success with the damage-restoration business. They said Barry was starting to get large contracts from insurance companies and only needed financing to carry out these profitable jobs. Barry even showed her letters from Travelers Insurance, certifying that ZZZZ Best had been assigned certain projects. Kay was impressed, and on June 24, shortly after her first meeting with him, she lent ZZZZ Best $25,000 guaranteed by Catain. The interest was 5 percent per week, Barry said in court. On July 11, she lent ZZZZ Best another $25,000 guaranteed by Barry, at 3 percent a week. And on August 12, she lent ZZZZ Best $40,000 more at 2 percent a week, guaranteed both by Catain and by Barry. The terms supposedly improved because Barry was making his cash payments to Catain on time.

Some of this money appears to have come from Kay's friends, who at that point had never met Barry but trusted Kay to keep track of their money and disburse the payments. They would meet Barry soon enough, however, and they would put more and more of their cash in his hands.

In Ann Randall and Elaine Orlando, Barry saw women eager to establish themselves independently of their willful, soon-to-be-ex-husbands.

Ann Randall is a former singer and child television star who was about forty-five when she began investing with Barry. Her second husband, from whom she was being divorced at the time, was a former stuntman. Her first husband, whom she married while she was a nightclub performer, was twenty-seven years her senior. Randall is a gentle soul, originally from Missouri, a Baha'i by faith, and although she has some experience in business—she has been in antiques and cosmetics—she is not a person of great financial expertise. The dissolution of her second marriage devastated her, and she found the court proceedings a nightmare. When Kay told her about Barry, he seemed just the thing to help her rebuild her life. She was eager to make a fresh start; she was considering buying a new home, or perhaps moving to Australia, a place she had always loved. Ultimately she invested her life savings with Barry, pouring $150,000 into ZZZZ Best. He told her ZZZZ Best was planning to expand into Australia, and she could run its operations there. Randall was delighted.

Elaine Orlando was in somewhat similar circumstances. She was going through a divorce from entertainer Tony Orlando at the time. She had known Kay Rozario since 1973 because Bobby Rozario had worked for her husband. In July of 1985, Kay told Elaine that she had met an extraordinary young man who had a terrific, growing business and who needed help with financing. Elaine Orlando wasn't poor and decided to give it a try. She began investing with Barry even before she met him, providing $25,000 through Rozario in three cashier's checks of $9,000, $9,000 and $7,000. Kay said Barry preferred it that way, and had specified the amounts himself. While Orlando's money was outstanding, she got 1 percent a week in cash via Kay, and eventually she also got her principal back, so she invested similar amounts twice more in the ensuing months, with equally gratifying results.

Orlando was deeply impressed with Barry when she met him in December of 1985. He was cheerful, gregarious and extremely ambitious. She was also pleased that he was Jewish. He told of starting ZZZZ Best when he was fifteen in his parents' garage, of the booming restoration business, and of his difficulties in borrowing from banks. His company had a future, he said; all he needed was money to buy the materials for his restoration work.

A few months later, in May of 1986, Barry told his investors at one of their luncheon gatherings about a big new insurance job in Sacramento, and he asked for more money.

This Sacramento contract, supposedly for $7 million, was to become central to the ZZZZ Best fraud. He probably chose Sacramento because it was far enough to be inconvenient yet close enough to reasonably fall within the company's California purview. But the job was not reasonable in any other way. In the small world of water- and fire-damage restoration business, such a contract would be the biggest news since the Chicago fire. A $7 million contract is virtually inconceivable; the company that cleaned up the Las Vegas Hilton after the catastrophic fire there several years ago says that contract was worth just $2.1 million.

When Barry told his lunch guests of the big new job, Orlando and Ada Cohen, another investor, asked to visit the site. Barry said that wouldn't be possible, the insurance company would object, hard hats were required and so forth.

"I wouldn't mind wearing a hard hat," Cohen said.

Barry said he would see what he could do.

Over the next twelve months, Orlando's investments escalated, and before long she was pouring hundreds of thousands of dollars into Barry's company and reaping succulent returns for her trouble. By January 14, 1987, she had sunk $450,000 into ZZZZ Best and was hoping for a huge payoff nine months later.

Ada Cohen knew Kay Rozario from the University of Nevada–Las Vegas, where both had studied a dozen years before they had ever heard of Barry Minkow. An immigrant from Yugoslavia, Cohen was divorced but still owned half of a Las Vegas motel with her ex-husband. She was worried. Business was bad, and she was beginning to think the motel was no longer worthwhile; it was only later, she said on the witness stand, that she discovered an employee had been stealing $10,000 a month, or one-seventh of monthly revenues. Through Kay, Ada began pouring money into ZZZZ Best. Like some of her fellow investors, she wasn't even sure whether she was lending or investing, but it didn't seem to matter. She had a new boyfriend, she trusted Kay and she had been told ZZZZ Best had a top accounting firm looking things over.

"I was absolutely sure that I was in good hands," she said later.

Cohen was promised a return of half a percent per week while her money was outstanding, plus some vague share of the profits from the restoration jobs she was financing. In 1986 she invested $200,000 with Barry and got envelopes full of cash every few weeks while the money was outstanding. Then she got back the entire principal—and a $20,000 bonus! She was eager to continue giving Barry money.

"I wanted my son to meet Barry," Cohen said later. "I thought so highly of Barry, I wanted my son to have some of the qualities that Barry had."

Cohen sold off some gold and land to invest with Barry. She got so carried away that she borrowed thousands of dollars from a bank, from several friends, and from her adopted daughter. When she said she was considering relocating to Los Angeles, Barry said he'd give her a seat on the ZZZZ Best board of directors, and she was ecstatic. Barry told her she would make so much money she could buy the beach house she had been dreaming about.

"He was so loving and understanding and eager to help you fulfill your dreams," Cohen said later. "I just adored him."

At one of the luncheons she attended at his house, Barry described a restoration job in great detail, including an exquisite Oriental rug that he got down and painstakingly cleaned personally. Imagining Barry down on his knees, poring over the fiber, Cohen was moved almost to tears.

Although she never got to visit a job site, she did get to see financial projections and architectural plans for the Sacramento building that ZZZZ Best was supposedly restoring.

"Kay," she whispered to her friend. "Did you notice that the word 'architectural' is misspelled?"

Cohen says they figured Barry was a whiz at business but lacked formal schooling, and maybe he should pursue that next. She didn't say anything to Barry for fear of embarrassing him—or provoking him to exclude her from what she called "this wonderful dream." She wasn't excluded. During 1987 she got to reinvest her $200,000 with Barry.

Suzette Whitmore is a little harder-headed than most of the others in the luncheon group, but in the end she wasn't much less susceptible. Originally a *pied-noir*—a Frenchwoman from colonial Algiers—Whitmore met an American soldier from Las Vegas during World War II, married him, and came to this country in 1946. He later became Las Vegas city attorney, and they had three children before their eventual divorce. Whitmore, who is about sixty-two now, worked for ten years as a cocktail waitress at the Flamingo Hilton, and eventually gained the cigarette concession at Bally's Grand in Reno. Later she got another such concession, in Las Vegas, and so she too was a businesswoman.

Whitmore and Cohen had both been married to lawyers and renewed their old acquaintance after their marriages ended. Thus Whitmore met Rozario, who had lived nearby in Las Vegas. Early in 1986, Ada and Kay told her about ZZZZ Best. "They said Barry was very friendly, very ambitious, very cute," Whitmore said later in her heavy French accent. She first met Barry around April, beside Rozario's swimming pool in Agoura, where he said casually, "Come on, I'll make you some money."

A week or two later, she cautiously lent ZZZZ Best $5,000, for which she was promised a return of 1 percent per week. Once a month, while visiting her doctor in Los Angeles, she would pick up $200 in cash from Rozario. Then she got her $5,000 back.

In June of 1986, she lent Barry $40,000, and in August followed up with $55,000 more. She made $19,400 in profit on this money, and on December 16 got her principal back and—that Minkow touch—a $10,000 bonus.

Delighted, she called Barry to say she had done something special with the $10,000. She had made three Christmas trees of $100 bills, one for each of her three children, and set them on the dinner table. Not long after, Barry got a photo of the scene in the mail, and in January of 1987, Whitmore invested another $100,000 with him.

Besides loving the profits, Suzette loved Barry. She felt motherly toward him—her heart ached when she saw him later in handcuffs—but he was always at pains to flirt with her, and always greeted her with a hug.

"I love French girls," Barry would exclaim with a big kiss.

"Well, Barry, I don't want to be Mrs. Robinson," Whitmore would exclaim with a laugh.

None of these women had any clear idea what they were getting into. Rozario and Whitmore are probably the only ones who even understood what they were *supposedly* getting into. Certainly greed played a role: Barry paid a lot better return than any bank. Ignorance helped too. Most relied so completely on Rozario that they can't describe the terms of their deals, or accurately calculate what they invested and how much they got back. At one point, for example, Cohen "invested" $50,000 with Barry ostensibly for ZZZZ Best to acquire a company called Flexpipe. A month later Cohen heard from Rozario that the acquisition never happened, but Barry said he'd just keep her $50,000 with the rest of her cash in ZZZZ Best. Cohen said that was just fine.

Through her tears on the witness stand, Orlando described the terms of her investments this way: "We were to receive, umm, stock and a bonus down the line; participation in a company that was going places, and we were also told that if Barry liked you and you were in and supporting him and in on the bottom rung, that you would participate in any profits later on because he intended to be the General Motors of carpet cleaning."

Catain was going to help. Working to secure conventional financing, he told John Miller to get Barry some decent-looking financial statements and tax returns. Miller, who was a little afraid of Catain, turned to Mark Morze, who ran a bookkeeping service and often visited some of Miller's officemates at Direct Professional Funding.

It's an open question how far Barry would have gone without Catain, or at least without the money he managed to get through Catain. Mark Morze, the bookkeeping wizard he met as a result of Catain, was just as important.

Like almost everyone involved with ZZZZ Best, Mark L. Morze would be an early pick if the United States ever needed to field a sumo wrestling team in a real hurry. Morze is a big blond man with a suntanned face and a pale beard who immediately conveys intelligence and some sensitivity, which isn't easy when you're his size. Morze has completed most of the course work for a doctorate in the history of science at the University of California–Los Angeles. He was also a benchwarming fullback and linebacker for the powerhouse UCLA football team from 1971 to 1973, lead by coach Pepper Rodgers and quarterbacked by Mark Harmon. He played rugby for eight or nine years too, and belonged to a fraternity, though he wasn't the animal-house type. Morze claims he fully intended to be a professor, but was discouraged by the experience of other graduate students in his department, who would do well at UCLA and then "go to Left Elbow State" to teach. There just weren't any jobs.

If Morze is scholarly, he is nevertheless no scholar, and his face shows that too. There is something just a little sly about him, almost slick. Mark is clever, a man of the world more than a cloistered schoolman discoursing on the choreography of angels. He is a ladies' man, too, and by instinct an entrepreneur. He always managed to make money, but he hated wearing a coat and tie and working on someone else's schedule. Instead he would sell annuities by day and tend bar at night and make $30,000 to $50,000 a year. In 1979 he started a company called Marbil Marketing with a partner named Bill Little (thus, Marbil) who left almost immediately. Morze had been selling accounting services for others and decided instead to try selling his own service to mom-and-pop businesses.

"I figured I could buy an Apple computer and crank out P and Ls," he says, referring to profit and loss statements. He took a five- or six-week tax class, and he was in business: "My average client was about one hundred dollars a month, and I had over one hundred of them. I was thirty, thirty-one years old, making one hundred thousand dollars a year."

Disastrously, Morze decided to branch out. He'd always done a lot of weight training, so in December of 1983 he teamed up with a former UCLA fraternity brother to open a health club in Woodland Hills. The place broke even, the lease expired in September 1984 and the partners decided to open a fitness center in the Sherman Oaks Galleria, a mall known as Mecca for Valley girls. Morze's partner had experience in the health-club business, but the Galleria venture was a flop and started consuming the partners' time. Morze's bookkeeping business sagged; the health club collapsed as well.

"I had to file Chapter 11 for the business, and then, because it was a partnership, I had to file personally," Morze says. "I've always had a strong work ethic. To me bankruptcy was one notch above child molestation."

It was a difficult time for Morze. He was struggling to save a doomed business stuck in a ten-year lease at a high-priced shopping mall, and his failure at it left him deeply embarrassed and financially ruined. He must have found it discouraging. Yet Barry was never discouraged. With Barry everything seemed possible.

"Is life completely a matter of how you see it, or is it a rock-bottom reality for all of us with very few differences?" Barry asked philosophically in his autobiography. The answer was clear: ". . . Life certainly is an issue of how you see it."

This flight from circumstance was just what Morze needed, and Barry didn't merely preach it. He lived it. He simply would not let anything get in his way. Morze met Barry around September of 1985, shortly after Morze filed for personal bankruptcy. He says he thought, "This kid's going somewhere."

Through Miller's good offices, Morze prepared the necessary phony financial statements and tax returns, and ZZZZ Best became one of Morze's clients. Morze says his bookkeeping business had taught him how lending requirements vary from bank to bank: which banks required extensive financial statements, for example, which others would just accept an application, which had a fetish for debt-to-equity ratios, etc. (Morze doesn't mention that he was willing to concoct whatever was needed.) So he could help ZZZZ Best get loans, which to Barry made him a very valuable person. Barry had always embraced the idea that money motivates, so he promised to pay Morze 10 percent of whatever he managed to raise, and the arrangement seemed to work out. For three months Morze worked one day a week at ZZZZ Best. "Barry knew I wouldn't call him Mr. Minkow and wear a tie," says Morze. But Barry was also a pragmatist, and before long he had the older man on the payroll full time, even if he had to put up with being called "Barry."

Morze, who would eventually become vice-president in charge of the ZZZZ Best restoration division, provided Barry with some down-to-earth business savvy. He was a credible grown-up who would also engage in forgery, check-kiting and fraud in order to help ZZZZ Best. In his way, Morze is a hustler too, even if he does have a conscience, and like Barry, he lives in a whirl of activity, so that he always seemed harried and rushed. He is yet another of those hyper personalities that Barry seemed to attract.

Morze and Barry may have spotted larceny in one another immediately, but Morze didn't much like Barry, and the feeling was probably mutual. Barry wanted his chief lieutenant to hang out with him, but to Morze the idea of socializing with a semiliterate teenager who had no appreciation of food or wine was ridiculous. Morze hated Barry's attitude toward women, and, fearing AIDS, was repelled by his use of prostitutes. Morze generally kept apart from the other ZZZZ Best characters as well, and Barry did his best to assist in this segregation. He worked hard to keep Morze from talking to Padgett, for example.

"He told me Padgett is an idiot," Morze says. "He probably told Padgett that about me."

Morze says people always ask, "Who gave Barry the idea?" Morze shakes his head. "That implies an idea." Morze insists that ZZZZ Best was no grand conspiracy, but rather the result of a terrifying congruence of greed, stupidity, charisma and chance. He says neither he nor Barry, together probably the heart of the blossoming ZZZZ Best fraud, had any notion at the beginning of what they would do next or how things would end up. They just put one foot in front of the other and kept moving.

Morze's first task for Barry was preparing financial statements that would impress lenders. As a forger, Morze would soon become both prolific and proficient, a virtuoso whose handiwork held up Barry's house of cards. His early work was amateurish, and no one was too impressed with the financial statements he created. But at least the numbers were impressive.

Anyway, Barry was filled with scorn for bankers and often complained that they were boring, jealous little men who couldn't stand his success and certainly weren't going to help him outdistance them even further by lending him money. But he could still make many of them eat out of his hand, and armed with Morze's handiwork, Barry began pursuing bank financing in earnest.

"He told everybody they were like a father," says Maurice Rind, another potential father who would later play a key role in Barry's success. "The kid was good."

The bankers were cautious, but Barry would give them Padgett's name, and Padgett didn't have any trouble satisfying them on the phone that Travelers was assigning restoration jobs to ZZZZ Best. They would call and ask general sorts of questions, and anyway, Padgett could always claim his own clients' confidentiality rules prevented his disclosing more information. ZZZZ Best was also using letters written on Travelers stationery to show its bankers it was legitimate.

Padgett was increasingly impressed. There were repair jobs for $100,000, for $200,000, eventually for $1 million or $2 million!

Padgett knew enough about the insurance business to know that these are very big jobs, and that it takes quite a lot for a building to sustain $1 million in damages of the sort that can be restored by a company like ZZZZ Best. Where on earth was Barry getting these jobs?

From "Jim," of course. In October of 1985, Barry finally took Padgett to Bakers Square to meet his mysterious benefactor—if there was such a person, and if that's whom Padgett actually met. He found Jim to be a cold, aloof, blond-haired guy of average build in a three-piece pinstripe suit. As usual, Padgett and Minkow ate heartily. Jim ate nothing.

"You got it?" he asked Barry.

"Here," Barry responded, handing across an envelope. He told Padgett it contained $25,000.

Padgett never learned Jim's full name, never saw him again and eventually decided that "Jim" was just like Padgett himself—a guy Barry paid to act a part. By this time Catain was much more important.

In December of 1985, for example, a friend of Catain's in the garment business referred him and Barry to Susan Russell, a vice-president in the commercial loan department at the 9100 S. Main St. office of Union Bank downtown. Brisk and businesslike, Susan McNamara Russell had been with Union Bank for six years and is nobody's fool. When Barry and Catain came to visit, she listened patiently as they described the carpet-cleaning business, Barry's need for more working capital and his company's building-restoration jobs. The two men provided shabby-looking financial statements for ZZZZ Best, and for Barry personally as well. Catain called himself a father figure to the young businessman. The meeting lasted thirty or forty minutes, and Barry applied for a $200,000 loan.

Russell rejected the request. It wasn't a hard decision. She considered Barry, at nineteen, too young, his business too tenuous, and his home equity too low. She didn't even know at the time how much tearing of hair and beating of breasts Barry had caused other bankers, usually at smaller institutions out in the Valley. For instance, on July 3, 1985, ostensibly with Catain's help, Barry had borrowed $38,000 from Charter Pacific Bank. But somewhere along the line, Barry accidentally sent in two different—and fraudulent—financial statements, an easy mistake for him to make considering that he often used a variety of phony documents and tax returns, the latter with a phony Social Security number to get around his terrible credit record. Charter Pacific called the loan early.

Jack Catain didn't like this kind of snafu, but it only made him think Barry was a screw-up, not a fraud. Catain never considered Barry honest, in the sense most of us understand the word. Catain just thought he understood the way Barry was dishonest. Believing Barry an honorable thief, he always thought the insurance jobs were real. All this was affirmed for Catain during November of 1985, when he had lunch with Barry and his friend Tom Padgett. Padgett was passed off as a Travelers Insurance official who had grown wealthy thanks to Barry's kickbacks.

"Really, Jack," Padgett said jovially, "on the salary that Travelers pays me, what I make and what I show are two different things."

Catain laughed sympathetically. As usual, Barry and Tom feasted on cheeseburgers, Coke and pie, while the aging mobster dined with more restraint. They ate at Bakers Square, where Padgett had explained to Barry the costs of the kosher symbol on the ketchup bottle. This time Padgett explained that he was starting his own appraisal company to get even bigger jobs for ZZZZ Best. Padgett was dressed up, and Catain was apparently fooled again. Throughout lunch, he tried to interest Padgett in various tax-shelter schemes.

Catain apparently thought everything was fine, and presumably saw Barry as a source of continued profit. By the end of 1985, though, Barry had won the confidence of Rozario and her friends, and was well on his way toward slaying his newest father. Jack Catain may have thought he was exploiting Barry, but in fact Barry was exploiting Catain, and when Barry found that he could get by without the aging racketeer, who was becoming an expensive pain in the neck, he moved firmly and daringly to get rid of the older man.

7

arry always yearned for admiration, and therefore loved
publicity. It also helped him raise money. Publicity was a
cheap way to buy legitimacy. He was like products that say
on the label: "As Advertised on TV!" as if that were somehow in their favor. But he also liked the images of himself that he
saw in the media, which portrayed him as strong, successful and
charitable—in short, the son any parents would want for their own.
Jeri Carr worked hard at this, but Barry's big break had very little to
do with her. The truth is that I was to blame.

It was October of 1985. I was a reporter for the *Los Angeles Times*,
and on a slow news day I read that a teenager who started a multi-
million-dollar business was to address a bunch of aspiring entrepreneurs at California State University–Northridge.

Covering business and in need of a story, I drove over to hear
Barry. It was hot, and I arrived sweaty and late, hating the whole
thing in advance and therefore forcing myself to bend over backward
to be fair. The room was packed with serious-looking collegians, and
to my surprise I was impressed with Barry's talk. I congratulated
myself on my open-mindedness—how well I had suppressed my
sneering instincts—and afterward scribbled notes as the young
phenom and I chatted over Cokes in the cafeteria. I wasn't planning
to write about the speech. Instead I saw a feature. Barry had the
cocksure energy of a kid, but he was also intelligent and articulate.
He made the college students all around us seem somnolent and puerile
by comparison. Here is how I began my article: "Nineteen-year-old
Barry Minkow's life seems a kind of parody at first, an elaborate spoof
of society's obsession with success."

The piece was moderately skeptical, all things considered. I correctly focused on Barry's obsessive need to succeed and his resentment toward his father, but I got snookered too. My nominal checking failed to unearth anything untoward; the Better Business Bureau and Los Angeles County Department of Consumer Affairs, for example, had had no complaints about ZZZZ Best. At one point in the story I described Barry as "charismatic, funny and unpretentious," sides of him I certainly wasn't to see again. Running on October 29, 1985, in Southern California's dominant newspaper, the piece was duplicated by various other television and print media. It helped make Barry famous.

With her cupid's-bow lipstick and eager phone calls, Carr also did her part. Soon after the *Times* story, she found that her young client's popularity with other reporters had soared, and afterward she never missed a chance to disseminate the piece further. Meanwhile I got one or two calls of the barely credible but nevertheless unsettling variety that reporters always hate, the kind that suggest maybe you missed something. One caller told of a lurid sex-discrimination complaint that turned out not to exist. Another suggested banking problems, always hard to pin down.

Barry had only had about an hour to address the budding entrepreneurs at Cal State–Northridge, so he left a lot out that I was too dumb to learn on my own. He didn't mention Jack Catain, for example. He didn't give any tips on using credit-card fraud to finance a struggling business. And he said nothing about bouncing checks, paying kickbacks or staging burglaries to rob your insurance company.

Nevertheless, Richard B. Sadler III read the October 29 *Times* article with interest. Special Agent Sadler was an organized-crime investigator in the Los Angeles office of the FBI, and he had only recently received a nebulous tip that someone named Barry, who had a carpet-cleaning business in the San Fernando Valley, had borrowed $150,000 at loanshark rates from the notorious Jack Catain. The tipster didn't even have Barry's last name, and until October 29, neither did Sadler.

Now all of a sudden here was an article about a carpet-cleaning wunderkind named Barry Minkow. Bucky Sadler—his middle name is Buchanan—and fellow agent Jerry G. West visited ZZZZ Best in Reseda on November 7 to see if Barry Minkow was borrowing money from a loanshark (that wouldn't be illegal; the crime is using strong-arm tactics to collect). Barry fervently denied any such borrowing.

When the agents asked him about Catain, he told them what a wonderful guy Jack was.

The agents didn't know that the very same day, Barry got a $75,000 loan from Charter Pacific Bank guaranteed by Phyllis Sherwood, Catain's wife and financial alter-ego. A week later Barry got another $50,000 from Charter Pacific, again thanks to his crooked mentor. All told, Catain had brought Barry more than $400,000, ensuring the survival of ZZZZ Best and inadvertently helping to support Barry's lavish life-style.

It was around this time that Barry bought a 3,600-square-foot Spanish-style house for $700,000 in a gated community called Westchester County, in the Valley's posh Woodland Hills section. It wasn't far from the site of the former military school where Barry had been bullied as a kid. Actress Heather Locklear lived next door. Barry put $221,000 down and would eventually spend $55,000 on furniture. He could keep his new $60,000 Ferrari in the driveway.

Barry must have thought good and hard about the FBI's visit. He had already begun subtly betraying Catain by cementing his relationship with Kay Rozario. He learned from Rozario herself that he could borrow from her directly at a lower interest rate, and she was also mad at Catain over a deed of trust, or second mortgage, that she had bought from him. As early as July of 1985, Rozario told her friend Elaine Orlando that Barry needed financing partly because he was dealing with an older man who wasn't being fair to him.

"Catain was a mediocre middleman who collected money from little old ladies," Morze says bluntly. "When Barry learned this, he circumvented Catain."

In truth, Barry's teacher, protector and sometime intimidator was a toothless tiger in fragile health who was already beginning to get suspicious. He usually called Arrington into his office at ZZZZ Best once a day, just to chat. Catain was a consultant, after all. One day in September, he asked about the insurance jobs.

"Is Barry really investing all the money I give him in these jobs?" Catain asked.

"I really don't know anything about that," Arrington replied nervously.

"I mean, do you think Barry has a safe deposit box somewhere with all kinds of money in it?"

"I don't know," Arrington said, wishing he could leave.

Chip Arrington bowled on Tuesday nights. On his next bowling night, Barry came down to the alley and exploded.

"Why would you talk behind my back to Catain?" he demanded. "Why don't you believe in me anymore? Why don't you trust me?"

Barry was ranting and raving this way, but Chip finally managed to placate him by explaining that he'd been in a spot, that he'd tried politely to get out of Catain's office without saying anything.

"What we're going to do," Barry said more calmly, "is get Jack Catain on the telephone right now."

Barry dialed and began screaming again. "Why are you talking to my people behind my back?" he yelled. Then he put Arrington on the phone, and Chip dutifully said he wouldn't talk to Catain anymore because he didn't want to be in the middle of anything.

He already was. As Barry's gofer, Arrington was willing to follow his boss's increasingly suspicious instructions. Layer by layer, he shed his honesty like a stripper shedding her clothes, nervously at first, but before long routinely. One of Arrington's main roles was to be Barry's bagman, delivering cash to a host of ZZZZ Best lenders and investors who, unlike the banks, didn't want to have a check arrive by mail. At various times Arrington carried money to Jack Catain, Kay Rozario, Hal Berman, Wallace Berrie or Barry himself. Often Arrington cashed checks for this purpose. He also signed what he was told, however potentially significant, and wrote up invoices to bury supposed restoration revenue in the cleaning operations. Barry told him big companies did that sort of thing all the time.

Arrington believed the restoration jobs were real, but the business always seemed oddly shadowy to ZZZZ Best insiders who weren't in the know. There was little evidence of any refurbishing business around the office, yet it seemed to monopolize more and more of Barry's time. Barry usually got to work before seven-thirty A.M., for example, but for a couple of months he came in late, saying he had trouble at a restoration job in Westminster, over an hour away. At one point Barry said his crews were working too slowly, so he got up on a stack of lumber and gave them a pep talk. The men were sup- posedly so fired up that as a result the job went much more smoothly from then on. Arrington was sure this actually happened; he had seen Barry give such talks before, and the workers who received them always came away inspired. Yet there was nary a trace of these work- ers, or anything else to do with restoration, around headquarters. Even Rozario secretly worried. Around October or November of 1985, she went to see Catain's skeptical friend John Miller, whom she knew.

"Barry's into me for three hundred forty thousand dollars and I'm worried," Rozario said. "I don't really know if these jobs are for real."

"Kay, I've always said these things weren't for real," Miller said. "I don't believe in them."

Rozario showed him a letter from Travelers Insurance that Barry had given her. It was signed by Tom Padgett. Miller dialed Travelers and learned that Padgett was an adjuster.

"If you want my opinion," Miller told Rozario, "an adjuster can't sign these things."

Barry must have assuaged Rozario's fears somehow, because she and her friends kept investing. Perhaps all that cash they were getting back had a tonic effect. Perhaps it was Barry's personal warmth—he dated Rozario's daughter and joked about marrying her. But the closer Barry got to Rozario, the less he needed Catain.

Barry also moved to rationalize his insurance racket. Why not set up a legitimate-sounding company to provide ZZZZ Best with the same supposed insurance restoration jobs Barry was claiming came through Jim? And why not institutionalize the function Padgett was performing? Instead of having him give bogus assurances that Travelers was granting ZZZZ Best major contracts, why not set Padgett up in business to grant ZZZZ Best phony contracts. Who would ever know?

That autumn, Barry urged Padgett to get into the insurance-adjusting business on his own to save Barry from Jim, who was supposedly gouging him for excessive kickbacks. Ostensibly, the idea was for Padgett to secure legitimate refurbishing jobs of the sort ZZZZ Best was growing to depend upon, and let the contracts to his friend. Until Padgett could secure real jobs, his company would merely confirm to outsiders jobs that continued to come from others. Of course there were no jobs of any kind, from Jim or anyone else, but Padgett says he didn't know this yet.

He and Barry had talked about setting up an adjusting business before. Now Barry said he would pay the expenses needed for Padgett to get started, and apparently neither man was overly concerned about the outrageous conflict of interest—if not outright fraud—this would entail for Padgett even if the jobs were real.

Padgett was supposed to be starting an *independent* appraisal service. Such things do exist legitimately. Insurance companies have people on staff to handle the normal flow of claims, in the usual places where the company does business. But in the event of a sudden and overwhelming surge of claims—from a hurricane, for instance—an insurer might turn to an independent appraiser to handle the overflow. Similarly, an insurer confronted with a small, far-flung claim might find it easier to use an independent appraiser based in the area instead of sending one of its own people. Independent appraisers are also used in complex reinsurance situations, in which several insurers might share the same liability. An outside appraiser can serve impartially to resolve the claim.

But the whole premise is that the independent appraisal firm operates in the interest of the insurance company or companies that hired it. If it is beholden to one of its contractors, as Padgett was to Barry, it couldn't very well decide objectively who should get a repair contract, or even how much repairs were warranted or what they should realistically cost. Of course, Padgett was already lying regularly for his friend and taking bribes for doing it. He was also helping Barry commit fraud by giving him Travelers stationery, which baby-sitter-turned-secretary Sherrie Maloney used to type phony documents. Now Padgett intended to go further and start his own appraisal firm—which would presumably seek business from Travelers' competition—while still working for Travelers.

Padgett was beginning to recognize that a subtle shift had occurred. He used to be a big brother to Barry. Now, clearly, Barry was dominant. He had his own business, he had more money, and he had the superior intellect. Padgett was increasingly—and admiringly—doing the younger man's bidding.

In November 1985, Padgett and partner Michael Vecksler, who owned an auto body shop, set up Interstate Appraisal Services. Soon after, Minkow asked Padgett for some Interstate Appraisal stationery. He and Padgett were to meet at the body shop. When Padgett got there Vecksler and Minkow were screaming at each other. Minkow, it turns out, had also demanded some stationery from Vecksler's business, and Vecksler refused. He told Barry that getting loans under false pretenses is a crime.

"Fuck you!" Barry shouted back. "I can buy and sell you ten times over!"

So Vecksler dropped out of Interstate and Padgett was left to run it alone, which he did fine as long as Barry was paying the bills and telling him what to do. There was no business anyway. His first employees were two cousins named Sandra and Debbie, the latter an aspiring model with whom Padgett would soon fall madly in love. Neither woman was overworked; on the contrary, there was hardly anything for them to do.

It was around this time that Catain started to make life unpleasant for both Barry and Padgett. In late 1985, Catain called Padgett to complain that Barry was talking to the FBI. "This kid's going to get us both in trouble," he warned. Worried, Padgett called Barry, who explained that Catain was extorting him, and that he was talking to the authorities.

Fed up with paying Catain anyway, Barry must have thought the FBI's appearance was yet another sign of grace. On November 26, 1985, he stopped payment on three checks to Catain totaling $350,000. Six days later the FBI men were back with a subpoena for any checks or records that might show payments to Catain. This time Barry admitted that Catain was pressuring him for money, but he didn't mention the stop-payment orders, and he didn't produce the stopped checks. When Sadler asked if, instead of a "shylock loan," he was being extorted, Barry nodded.

Federal authorities were very interested. They had been after Catain for years, without success. Suddenly they had accusations of extortion and a witness who would testify. Barry began cooperating with a federal grand jury investigation of Catain's loansharking activities.

Catain somehow got wind of this, but perhaps Barry told him something resembling the truth: that the FBI had come to him because of a tip from someone else. Perhaps Barry even said he was doing his best to keep the agency at bay. But Catain was also worried about the insurance jobs—what if John Miller was right?—and around this time he called Interstate and left a threatening message for Padgett with Sandra. Then he called Padgett himself at Travelers.

"Those jobs better be real or you're going to regret it," he said.

Now Padgett was really upset, and he demanded a meeting with Barry. When he arrived in Reseda, Barry was with a big guy named Robert Victor, an older man with a New York accent who said, "If you have any more problems with Jack Catain, you give me a call." Padgett never heard from Catain again.

Like Mark Morze, Bobby Victor didn't call Barry "Mr. Minkow," and there wasn't a hell of a lot Barry could do about it. Victor's name was originally Robert Viggiano, but he legally changed it. He is five feet eight inches tall, weighs 240 pounds, and has a panther tattoed on one of his hamlike forearms. Viggiano was born in 1936 in Brooklyn, and according to the Los Angeles Police is a reputed member of the Mafia's Colombo crime family. Even if he isn't, he is enough of a hood to have a curriculum vitae in the form of a three-page FBI rap sheet. The charges include extortion, loansharking, robbery, forgery, conspiracy and weapons possession, among others.

Victor's main businesses are restaurants and automobiles, but among his many run-ins with the law, he was indicted in December 1968 by a federal grand jury in Brooklyn on a charge of extortionate credit transactions in an alleged loansharking scheme. The charges were dismissed in January 1972. The very next year, Victor got five years' probation after pleading guilty to attempted grand larceny in connection with the 1968 theft of $750,000 in jewels from the Long Island Diamond and Jewelry Exchange in Garden City, New York. Also arrested in that robbery was the late Joseph Colombo Sr., then the head of one of New York's Mafia families, but charges against him were later dismissed. If the robbery sounds uncharacteristic for a bunch of reputed mobsters, that's because it wasn't what it seems. Police believe instead that it was an inside job, carried out with the cooperation of someone working at the exchange.

Barry says he first came across the Victor family in June of 1983, when he went to their Sepulveda service station, Reliable Auto Repair, to get his 1963 Chevy fixed. He might have heard of Reliable through his carpet-cleaning connections; Reliable used to work on cars for the owner of Dunn-Rite, where Barry and Chip used to work, and the Victors had helped Arrington when he had car trouble in 1982. Barry ended up trading in the Chevy for a 1972 Buick, after which he began making weekly payments and playing on the Reliable softball team. Barry became friendly with Steve, Victor's grown son.

With Victor on Barry's team and the FBI still interested, it was getting easier and easier to squeeze Catain out. Just as Barry had found a way of getting into the insurance business without Catain, he also found ways of raising money without him.

As ZZZZ Best later told the SEC, "The company terminated its relationship with Mr. Catain in November 1985, after repaying all amounts advanced by or through Mr. Catain, with interest at the rate charged by Mr. Catain, which exceeded the maximum rate permitted by law." But if the company had terminated its relationship with Catain, Barry had not, and Catain was to haunt him for quite a while longer during Barry's meteoric rise to the top.

8

ichie Schulman visited Los Angeles for the first time in perhaps twenty years during the final days of August 1985. He did not make the trip lightly. Like many aging hoods, Schulman wasn't in the best of health. Grossly overweight, he suffered from high blood pressure, diabetes and gout, and perhaps the years in and out of jail and the stress of so much duplicity had also taken their toll.

"They don't live healthy lives," a former federal agent says with a laugh. "They don't jog."

Schulman didn't even like taking an airplane. But Bobby Victor had his eye on a few money-making opportunities in Los Angeles, and eagerly urged his old pal to come. He told Schulman about the success of his son's friend Barry Minkow; he was so excited he offered to pay for Schulman's trip. Both New Yorkers, Victor and Schulman got to know each other during a stint in the federal penetentiary at Lewisburg, Pennsylvania, during the early 1970s. Viggiano, as he was known at the time, was in for theft and Schulman was in for extortion. The two men became fast friends. When Victor got out he went to work in Schulman's garbage-disposal business in New Paltz, New York. Schulman fit the profile of someone who could be involved with ZZZZ Best: he was five feet eight inches tall, roughly 300 pounds, and had an extensive criminal background, including charges of book-making, assault, loansharking and receiving stolen goods. Born in 1934, Schulman grew up in Queens, New York, where his boyhood friends included Maurice Rind, a financial maven who was also living in the San Fernando Valley, and Joseph Mangiapane, who did a little boxing and later became Rind's driver. None of these men was des-

tined to give the Swedish Academy pause in its Nobel Prize deliberations. Schulman hadn't been in trouble in perhaps fifteen years,
but Los Angeles Police have identified him publicly as an associate
of the Genovese Mafia family. Rind says it isn't so.

Barry met Schulman and Rind sometime around Labor Day of
1985, and he told them about a major restoration project ZZZZ Best
was undertaking in San Diego. Barry said they could make a 100
percent return in a short time if they would finance the job.

As the police put it, Victor "was always looking for various ways
to make money," so he and Barry formed something called B&M
Insurance Services Inc. B&M was to provide financing for the restoration work at ZZZZ Best, collect payments from insurance companies (presumably through Tom Padgett's Interstate Appraisal) and
pass the money along to ZZZZ Best. Apparently B&M was to deduct
half the profit for itself in return for its cash up front.

According to Rind, Victor put up $250,000 and Schulman, who
spent most of his time in New York and Florida, provided another
$90,000. Rind put up nothing—he was in debt to Schulman already—
but was enlisted to keep an eye on Schulman's investment.

"This is either the greatest deal in the world, or it's a Ponzi," Rind
claims to have said of ZZZZ Best. But Schulman was convinced Barry
was legit. He had Victor's assurances, after all, and none of the three
had ever come across a guy quite like Barry, who sat at Rind's kitchen
table one night and said, "I'd sell my mother to the devil to make it."

B&M made some money for its backers, but the funny thing about
Barry was that he was constantly short of cash. "Barry always was
in money trouble," Victor wrote later in a semiliterate narrative seized
by police. Like Jack Catain and John Miller, Barry's backers tried
to arrange bank loans for him, without success. Finally, Rind says,
"Richie asked me to help ZZZZ Best go public."

Rind was certainly qualified. A shrewd former stockbroker, he knew
the securities business, the laws governing it and the people who could
help. Chances are he also knew that huge profits might be possible
by converting ZZZZ Best from a private concern owned solely by
Barry into a public company with stock that could be traded by
anyone.

Maurice Rind is the guy a director has in mind when he wants to
cast the role of Meyer Wolfsheim, the fictional World Series fixer, in
a television remake of *The Great Gatsby*. His style is agitated and nasal,
and when he gets on the subject of his law-enforcement troubles, his
speech turns to harangue. Maurice is a likable fanatic. Sit with him

in the eerie fluorescence of his kitchen and he will charge back and forth, pouring out amazing tales of persecution and coincidence that resulted, tragically and unbelievably, in his own incarceration. Maurice will stalk while you sit, and he will punctuate what he says with loud flicks of his fingers, as if flicking away the petty and ludicrous transgressions of which he has been accused. Every now and then, instead of flicking, he will give you a little push with his hand— on the shoulder, on the leg—as if to make sure he has your undivided attention, as if what he's about to say now is even more amazing than all the words that have tumbled out before. Maurice writes long, detailed reports of the wrongs he has suffered. He assembles thick, neatly photocopied collections of newspaper clippings on subjects of interest. All he cares about is the truth. He is an honest investor and friend pursued by the unforeseen shadow of his own good deeds.

Not everybody sees it this way, of course. Los Angeles police say Rind associates with mobsters—which he denies—and to the SEC, he is a three-time loser.

On July 22, 1976, Rind was sentenced to eighteen months in prison and fined $10,000 by a federal judge in New York for securities fraud and other charges stemming from the collapse of Packer, Wilbur & Co., a securities firm of which Rind had been president. He and others were charged with misappropriating clients' securities, selling them using forged stock-transfer documents and then using the $200,000 in proceeds for their own benefit. Rind's sentence was later reduced to a year and a day, but the SEC stripped him of his broker's license and barred him from any future association with a securities broker or dealer.

Less than four months later, Rind was indicted for securities fraud by a federal grand jury yet again, this time in connection with a company called Industries International Inc. that looks suspiciously like ZZZZ Best in an earlier life.

At first little more than a suburban Denver machine shop, Industries International supposedly held the license to manufacture some kind of miracle pneumatic pump that was to earn the company millions. In a bold and elaborate scheme, a group of swindlers took the company public—by fraudulently merging it with a public "shell" company— and then pumped up the stock price from 50 cents a share to $6.50 in just one month of illegal manipulations in early 1973. They put out phony financial statements and sold lots of stock to Des Moines-area investors in private transactions while secretly dumping their own shares. Investors reportedly lost more than $1.5 million; the government says the swindlers pocketed most of it. Rind says his role was minor, and that he was only prosecuted because, as a former International Brotherhood of Teamsters consultant, the government wanted information from him about Jimmy Hoffa. Nevertheless, Maurice pleaded guilty to fraud and conspiracy and was sentenced to a term concurrent with his earlier conviction in the Packer, Wilbur scam.

In 1983 Rind was in more trouble. The SEC contended that beginning in January of that year Rind and others bought more than $10 million worth of stock in a Los Angeles real estate concern called First City Properties, Inc. without ever intending to pay for it. Such "free riding," as the practice is known, is illegal.

The First City case was one of the whackiest in a long time. The key to it was a friend of Rind's named Thomas W. Reid, an extraordinary figure who moved to tiny Cleburne, Texas, threw around his money like there was no tomorrow, and got the whole place to load up on First City shares. Overnight, the town was in an uproar. Of the 30 percent of First City in public hands, almost half was held by the 19,000 men, women and children of Cleburne, who were more familiar with cattle stock than any other kind before Reid hit town. He was sort of like Robert Preston in *The Music Man*. On some days, the folks in Cleburne accounted for almost all the open trading in First City.

According to the SEC, Reid and his associates had First City's stock on a roller coaster. Their huge buying would run First City shares up so Cleburne investors could make money. Then they would fail to pay for the shares, forcing brokers to dump them. That would depress the price briefly, enabling Cleburners to buy more shares cheaply. Ultimately, the price of First City shares roughly doubled as a result of all this, presumably allowing Reid and his confederates to profit mightily.

When everything came out, Reid, Rind and the others got off with a slap on the wrist. In 1985, without admitting any guilt, Reid and Rind consented to permanent injunctions barring them from violating the antifraud and margin provisions of federal securities law. Such violations are illegal anyway, and there were no criminal charges. Reid also agreed to pay two brokerage firms nearly $160,000 secured by liens on his $2.5 million yacht and Texas ranch. Both men were required to show a copy of their consent decrees to any brokerage firm they might try to do business with or any bank from which they might seek a loan collateralized by securities.

First City was controlled by the wealthy Belzbergs of Canada, who weren't implicated. But their control gave First City something in common with ZZZZ Best: during Rind's alleged machinations, the Belzbergs held 70 percent of its shares, leaving only 30 percent in public hands. Similarly, ZZZZ Best had less than half of its eleven million shares in circulation even at its peak. A small float means a small supply and a limited market. Like anything scarce, a sudden increase in demand makes for sharp increases in price.

Rind and Barry met just a few months after Rind settled his First City legal troubles. Rind lives in an Encino condominium almost literally underneath the Ventura Freeway, the world's busiest, where his living room is dominated by an enormous pool table. The kitchen has plaid wallpaper, and the whole place has those awful cottage-cheese ceilings that are everywhere in Southern California.

Maurice Rind is not a big guy, but he looks quick and solid, the kind of fellow with good hand-eye coordination despite his fleshy face and growing gut. He claims he was an all-Queens basketball player at Forest Hills High School, and then went on to play at Hofstra University on Long Island. He was born on December 16, 1938, and fifty years later carried just 160 pounds on his five-foot ten-inch frame. He says he still plays ball, and his sons are athletes too.

Rind's background shows that his agility extends beyond a basketball court, and in the fall of 1985 he applied himself to making some money on ZZZZ Best.

"ZZZZ Best Carpet and Furniture Cleaning Company, Inc. is a privately held California corporation that desires to become a public corporation," says an oafish letter "to whom it may concern" dated October 4, 1985, on ZZZZ Best letterhead. "I hereby authorize one Maurice Rind the authority to perform in a business-like and professional manner whatever duties are necessary in order to achieve this goal."

The letter is signed by Barry Minkow, and it goes on to say that "Rind has power of attorney to sign any and all documents" necessary to accomplish the task. The letter doesn't sound like much, but it was a fateful, even a visionary agreement. It was the first big step in elevating ZZZZ Best from a two-bit neighborhood scam onto a level of fraud so great that it would rank with the very biggest, the sort of scandals that bring warm smiles to the faces of a certain class of lawyer, investigator and journalist who get nostalgic for such things years after the fact.

The idea was to merge ZZZZ Best into a public shell company—

just as Herbalife and Industries International had done—that ZZZZ Best would ultimately control. Barry's company could thus become a public concern quickly and cheaply, without all the expensive, embarrassing and time-consuming disclosures that would be required if it tried to go public by itself. What Rind wanted for ZZZZ Best is often called a reverse merger, and is analogous to *Invasion of the Body Snatchers* in that a very slimy creature takes over a human body and then thinks it can mingle with the rest of us.

Taking ZZZZ Best public in this way could mean millions in profits. The shell can usually be acquired for a nominal cost from people who make it their business to have such entities ready when needed, and the stock, originally worth pennies, can easily be controlled by a few shareholders who "box" the shares, holding them off the market while hyping the company and trading amongst themselves to propel the price skyward. Insiders lucky enough to have bought shares for pennies can get rich.

Rind got moving. On November 6, 1985, he sent a handwritten note to a New York attorney named Harold Fischman by overnight mail, along with copies of Barry's tax returns and other personal financial information, my October 29 *Los Angeles Times* article and a previous overnight mailer which he'd sent to the wrong address; Rind says he wanted to prove he had tried to send the material earlier.

"I would like to move yesterday on this deal," he wrote.

Rind was seeking Fischman's help in finding a shell company, and in order to oblige, Fischman looked to Utah.

Colorado is Mecca for the notoriously corrupt penny-stock industry. Nevada is big on securities fraud, particularly in mining and precious metals. But Salt Lake City is the undisputed center of the shell corporation, otherwise known as a blind pool.

In a blind pool, a couple of people get together and form a company with little or no capital and a business plan to match. They sell stock to the public, often for a penny a share, and avoid registering the stock with the SEC by raising less than $1 million. (In the interest of promoting capital formation, the federal agency doesn't make the smallest issuers of stock go through the registration process.) In some cases the founders either hype the stock before unloading their own shares at a profit, or let the business lie dormant until a larger private company like ZZZZ Best comes along wanting to go public. The shell or blind pool is usually formed at the behest of a local securities firm, which keeps it on hand for whenever it might be needed.

Blind pools are legal in only a few states, and even Utah cracked down in 1986, curtailing the number of new ones sharply after 450 were formed from 1983 to 1985. Still, many people consider Utah the nation's capital of stock fraud. By sheer volume, more skulduggery occurs on Wall Street, of course, but Utah is distinguished by a securities industry known primarily not for capitalizing companies, but for dirty dealings. Some have called it the "sewer of the securities industry."

Why Utah? First, states have a surprising degree of power over securities sold from or within their borders. A stock offering conducted in New York or California, for example, occurs under far more stringent standards than it would in many other states. The various state rules are called "blue-sky laws" because one of the earliest, in Kansas in 1911, was supposed to shield investors from scams with "no more basis than so many feet of blue sky." States with lax regulation can become havens for securities con-artists, and Utah was among the most lax. It not only allowed blind pools, it seemed comfortable with them. A state panel in 1984 explained, "Utahns have been interested in speculative ventures almost since the State was first settled by Mormon pioneers. Encouraged by their leaders to fund many public works as quasi-private business ventures by subscription, the Mormon people bought shares of canal companies, grain elevators, flour mills, spinning and weaving corporations, stage and freight companies, as well as other enterprises needed in their frontier communities." In the 1860s mining operations became another outlet for speculation in Utah, and a Salt Lake City Stock Exchange was established in 1883, later renamed the Intermountain Stock Exchange. A hundred years later, the stock exchange is closed, but the industry still thrives.

The lyrically named Morningstar Investments Inc. was incorporated under Utah law on August 29, 1983, and issued 900,000 shares of stock to its founders for a fraction of a penny each. It issued two million additional shares at a penny each, or $20,000 in all. The company's prospectus, which makes Morningstar sound about as attractive as a transatlantic zeppelin line, solemnly denies it was formed to create a public shell. Morningstar was instead supposed to be in the mineral, oil and gas business, but the prospectus itself says none of the founders knew the slightest thing about minerals or energy, and the company had no assets or even ideas that it could use to get into this business. Its thirty-three-year-old president and chairman, Jay D. Hall, was already the president of another shell corporation, and had mostly held unimpressive jobs in sales and personnel. His home was Morningstar's headquarters. The vice-president was in the insurance business. The secretary and treasurer was a housewife who happened to be married to Hall's brother. There was virtually no capital.

Morningstar was born during the heyday of such companies in Utah. In the twelve months ended June 30, 1984, 211 of the 282 stock offerings registered in the state were blind pools. For the same period, Colorado ranked second in blind pools. It had seventeen.

"Turning out little companies like Morningstar used to be a local cottage industry," says Ron Poulton, a well-known Salt Lake City securities lawyer.

Morningstar was the shell under which Rind was going to hide ZZZZ Best. He found it through a Utah concern called Alpine Securities. To help with the accounting, Fischman enlisted S. George Greenspan, a certified public accountant and attorney from Englewood Cliffs, New Jersey, who was associated with Fischman's law firm. Greenspan was brought in to handle the merger accounting, a tricky business important to the health of a company's financial statements.

In December of 1985, ZZZZ Best became a subsidiary of Morningstar when Barry's company was reincorporated in Nevada, which was free of state income taxes and had liberal incorporation and corporate-structure laws. "Some promoters will do everything as a matter of course through Nevada," says Poulton. "It might come in handy."

The process was just sailing along when it ran into the iceberg of Jack Catain. In December Catain sued Barry in Los Angeles Superior Court, accusing the hardworking young entrepreneur of breach of contract and fraud. Catain contended that from roughly June 24 to November 15, he arranged hundreds of thousands of dollars in financing for Barry, and that as a result, ZZZZ Best got contracts with various insurance companies worth more than $5 million. (Catain still believed there were insurance restoration jobs at ZZZZ Best.) His contention was that he never got his fair share of profits.

Barry denied the allegations, but perjured himself by insisting in a sworn declaration that there were indeed restoration jobs at ZZZZ Best. He merely claimed that his company had suffered because Catain never produced the promised financing for a big job in San Diego.

None of these fabrications really mattered. What mattered was that the judge in the Catain suit issued a temporary protective order to prevent Barry from transferring any ZZZZ Best funds until things were ironed out. That would have blocked the Morningstar deal. Catain had the reverse merger by the throat and apparently planned to squeeze until some money came out.

9

Life around Barry was rough. Paychecks didn't bounce as often, but he was under tremendous stress, and his power over those who worked for him seemed to be going to his head. ZZZZ Best had begun holding monthly managers' meetings, and Barry presided like an experienced autocrat. "My way or the highway," he would say again and again, demanding utter devotion from underlings. "If you're not behind me 110 percent, then you're not behind me."

Barry's own parents had to call him Mr. Minkow, and Arrington says they got no preferential treatment. Barry even liked to use them as an example. At one meeting he told one of the managers that he wasn't running his shop up to par. "You know, you're just like my parents," Barry said. "Anyone can be fired here."

He enjoyed reminding his father of their role reversal, exploiting his power over the older man as an expression of contempt for Robert's failings, and of fear that they might become his own. One visitor recalls getting a tour of the ZZZZ Best phone-sales operation and encountering Barry's father in the hall. "What are you doing?" Barry demanded impatiently, giving his father a series of orders. "Barry's parents were kind of frightened of him, in the same way as everyone else," recalls Ana Madrinan. "You didn't want to get Barry angry."

During the fall of 1985, the world was throwing lots of fuel into the raging furnace of Barry's ego. Moe Rind was going to take his company public, the *Los Angeles Times* had done a profile, and television shows were clamoring for interviews. Barry grew cockier every day, and anyone reckless enough to challenge or question him provoked a tirade of ear-splitting abuse. Says Madrinan: "You felt like you were a little girl and Dad was scolding you. It was weird, the power he had over people."

This sort of thing was particularly difficult for Arrington because his wife, LuLu, also worked for the company, and she hated Barry. Chip, who was by now also delivering sealed envelopes to Victor and Rind, felt it would be better all around to find something else for LuLu, and one day in the fall of 1985 Barry said he saw a flower shop for sale in the paper. The sellers were a married couple named Chai and Thomas Lee, and the store was in Canoga Park, near Reseda.

Barry said he was getting so much publicity lately he didn't want to let anyone get the idea he was diverting his attention from the carpet-cleaning business, but that the flower shop might be a good spot for LuLu, who could be the manager. Would Chip be willing to let Barry buy it in Arrington's name? Chip agreed, and in October Barry bought Floral Fantasies from the Lees for $20,000. The business was registered in Arrington's name, but there was a secret agreement in which Barry was named as the true owner and pledged to indemnify Arrington in the event of trouble.

In December, when the Arringtons left for a three-week Christmas visit with family in Michigan, Chip left Barry a batch of signed, blank deposit slips so the Floral Fantasies receipts could continue to be deposited in his absence. The store's bank account, like the store itself, was in Arrington's name.

Soon after their return, a Floral Fantasies customer complained to LuLu about excessive charges on his credit card. LuLu didn't recall putting through such large purchases, and she told Chip, who remembered that such complaints used to occur at ZZZZ Best. When they started, Barry had said any such inquiries should always be referred directly to him. To Chip, that seemed like a good idea this time around as well.

"Don't worry," Barry soothed. "It's not your problem. I'll straighten it out."

But the Arringtons were worried, and with reason. As it turned out, Barry forged over $100,000 in phony credit-card charges at Floral Fantasies, in many cases allegedly using charge-card numbers obtained from Bob Victor's service station. Barry even forged Arrington's name sometimes in order to deposit them. LuLu soon quit, and in January or February of 1986, Arrington told Barry that since his wife wasn't working there anymore, there wasn't much point in Arrington lending his name to the shop. Chip had to nag Barry about this repeatedly until, in May of 1986, Barry sold the place. The buyer was Bob Victor.

Just as Chip Arrington had hoped Floral Fantasies would work out for his wife, Tom Padgett was hoping Interstate Appraisal would work out for him. He knew it wasn't altogether on the up and up, but he actually did try to drum up some legitimate business, and he hoped ultimately that Interstate could be aboveboard. After much effort, Interstate actually did land a real insurance claim, but not until September of 1986. It was for a garage fire in South-Central Los Angeles that left about $35,000 in damage. Padgett was elated until it suddenly hit him: who was he going to get to do the work? ZZZZ Best certainly couldn't manage it. It didn't even have a contractor's license.

Meanwhile, Interstate wasn't generating any revenue, so in December of 1985 Padgett was still relying on his Travelers wages when he got a call at Travelers from a loan company called Thomas Funding Corp. Barry was trying to borrow $300,000 from Thomas Funding to finance a supposed $622,000 restoration job, and had told Thomas he would have Travelers repay the money directly from funds due ZZZZ Best. Travelers owed ZZZZ Best nothing, of course; Travelers had never even heard of ZZZZ Best.

Padgett's job was to convince the man from Thomas otherwise. But the guy from the loan company wasn't happy with telephone assurances. He wanted to see some documentation on the ZZZZ Best work. Padgett tried to put him off, but the man was insistent.

"Look," the caller said. "I'm only ten minutes away, I'll come by right now." Then he hung up.

In terror, Padgett called Barry, who told him to stay put.

"Tom, you've got to convince him."

"I can't," said Padgett, who wasn't even wearing a necktie.

"You've just got to convince him. And if it goes good, I'll give you ten thousand dollars for it."

Padgett needed the money, and he couldn't flee because the guy might ask someone else about ZZZZ Best, or Padgett's job, or whether it was even the fire- and water-damage department he was standing in. So when the man from the loan company arrived, Padgett coolly told him he had sent the file to Hartford for review. "They know all about the payment," he explained. "It's got to come from them."

The visitor left, apparently satisfied, but he later called Padgett's boss, Leland McDonald, who found the whole thing alarming. The man from Thomas Funding showed McDonald all sorts of bogus paperwork given to him by ZZZZ Best, paperwork intended to prove that Travelers had given a big insurance-restoration contract to Barry's company. Among the documents was a promise by Travelers to pay a sum of money directly to Thomas. It was on Travelers letterhead, and was signed by Padgett as claims manager. McDonald reported all this to *his* boss, David Tengberg.

For the second time, Barry had cost Padgett his job. Despondent, Padgett turned in the keys to his company car and quit. Then he set out for home, crying as he walked along Western Avenue.

Padgett wouldn't starve. Barry put him on the payroll full time, at $500 a week. It made sense. Interstate had already been formed, and although it didn't have any business, it did have ZZZZ Best. "Tom, this is going to be the best thing that ever happened to you," Barry promised.

ZZZZ Best also had Padgett. At the company's Christmas party that year, Barry used cocaine and gave out gag gifts. Padgett got a magnifying glass, for the intense scrutiny under which he supposedly placed ZZZZ Best's work. Arrington got a bottle of milk of magnesia.

Once Padgett was on the payroll as the head of "independent" Interstate Appraisal, he found that life wasn't too bad. He would go to the gym and lift weights in the morning, take his two secretaries out to lunch, then study his business books in the afternoon. Always the scholar, Padgett was reading up on insurance and finance. He had Debbie around, he had a regular paycheck and he was working on his dream of getting his own business going.

Life was a lot more demanding for Barry. On January 16, 1986, and again a week later, while Barry was wrangling with Catain and trying to do the Morningstar deal, he went to see his internist, elderly Dr. Lovitz, not for any physical ailment, but just to talk about his troubles. He told the doctor he was under tremendous pressure, that everything was on his shoulders. The responsibility was crushing. Dr. Lovitz urged him to delegate more.

At this point Barry remained deeply alone with his own moral turpitude. It's likely he was still the only one who knew everything that was going on in his scam. He hadn't fully confided in Morze yet, or Padgett or Rind or anyone else.

Yet Barry couldn't stand actually being alone, and since his house was enormous and several of his friends were between jobs, marriages or homes, he had them move in with him. During December of 1985, Barry's Woodland Hills home was occupied by Sherrie Maloney and three of her four children; Dan Krowpman Sr.; high school friend

Tony Scamardo and his sister, who served as Barry's maid; and occasionally Joyce, Barry's girlfriend, whose parents sometimes allowed her to stay over. There was no furniture yet, so they mostly slept and ate on the floors. Barry seemed to enjoy being the breadwinner for this surrogate family. He would come home and roughhouse with Eddie, Maloney's youngest, until January 18, when Maloney and her kids moved into a condominium in the same building as Barry's. He gave her $8,000 for the down payment.

So Barry had the cars, the house, the great wealth, the svelte blonde girlfriend and the world's admiration. But he also had the stomach troubles, and he had a secret. Barry's secret was that, already, he had more in common with Charles Ponzi than Horatio Alger.

Charles Ponzi was one of those people who did something so extraordinary that his name entered the language. A thirty-seven-year-old Italian immigrant to Boston, in 1919 he hit upon a clever way to fulfill the American dream using something called international reply coupons. These are things people enclose in an envelope in order to prepay the postage for a return letter. At the time, World War I had ended and European currencies were low in relation to the dollar. But European countries didn't seem to figure currency fluctuations into the price of their international reply coupons. For example, a coupon that cost 10 francs when the French currency was strong still cost 10 francs now that the currency was weak. But in dollars, the price of that same coupon was much lower, which was crucial, because the coupons could be exchanged for a fixed amount of American postage in the United States. So suddenly there was a way to get U.S. stamps at far less than face value. The man who performed this international monetary prestidigitation would be left with a huge profit. Charles Ponzi figured he was that man. He planned to send dollars overseas to some European associates, who would exchange them for the local currency, buy international reply coupons and send those back to Ponzi, who could convert them to stamps and then to a larger amount of American cash than he'd started with. Ponzi planned a form of arbitrage.

He raised money for his venture from the public, promising a 50 percent return in just forty-five days. People soon lined up around the block. And Ponzi soon realized that, rather than messing with transatlantic currency arbitrage, he'd be better off paying earlier investors with funds raised from those who came later.

Like all subsequent Ponzi schemes, Ponzi's was predicated on the idea of infinity, on raising more and more money from new investors to pay off the old, presumably in a world without end. Ponzi himself took in $10 million, an enormous sum in 1920, but failed to heed one of the essential implications of his own scheme: the need to run away. Even the best Ponzi scheme will someday run up against the limits of all the money in the world. So Ponzi's Ponzi failed; he was imprisoned and then deported to Italy.

In 1949 Ponzi died penniless in Brazil, but his scheme lived on, and variations abound to this day. The notorious Home-Stake Production tax-shelter swindle of the 1960s and 1970s, ably chronicled by David McClintick, is a prime example. Investors included former Citibank chairman Walter Wriston, financial journalist George J. W. Goodman (his pseudonym is Adam Smith), the late Senator Jacob Javits, Barbara Walters, Barbra Streisand and dozens of other luminaries in business, entertainment and law. Home-Stake went on for eighteen years. Losses exceeded $112 million (and would be far higher in today's dollars), with more than two-thirds of that suffered by the U.S. Treasury in the form of bogus tax deductions. The statute of limitations made it impossible for the government to recoup.

More recently, there was the case of J. David & Co. Apparently motivated by his love for an attractive socialite, shy, frumpy Jerry David Dominelli ran a San Diego investment firm that echoed Ponzi's almost perfectly. In 1984 investors lost more than $80 million in his bogus foreign-currency trading scheme. Dominelli was sentenced to twenty years.

Most people didn't know it yet, but ZZZZ Best was a similar operation. Like any really good Ponzi operator, Minkow found it dizzyingly easy to raise money at first, but quickly realized he was on a fund-raising treadmill that made him run faster and faster to stay in place. He raised money by promising enormous returns. The enormous returns meant he needed more and more money. A Ponzi scheme is insatiable that way, and as a result, Barry and his co-conspirators were forever scrambling to cook up new documents, con someone else, raise more money and then repeat the process for the next crisis to come down the pike. There was always a crisis, and it was usually something Barry and his friends had done in response to the last crisis.

A good example occurred January 21, 1986, when Barry resolved his legal differences with Catain by means of a one-sided settlement. Barry had no choice. He needed for his company to go public, and Catain's suit stood in the way. In an agreement drafted by Lawrence Brown, an Encino attorney who represented Catain (and at one time or another, Victor), Barry granted the sun, the moon and the stars.

He even waived his right to counsel. Barry agreed to pay Catain $50,000 up front, $2,500 every Friday through December 19, plus huge block payments every couple of months, along with interest and attorneys fees. The total exceeded $650,000 *before* interest and fees. Barry would be in default if he was more than three days late with one of the weekly installments or five days late with any of the larger payments, and the penalty was Draconian: $950,000 plus interest. And of course the agreement was to be kept confidential, perhaps at the request of both signatories.

It was expensive, but it worked. Catain dropped his lawsuit, and the protective order was lifted. A few days later, Barry and the other major ZZZZ Best players gathered in one of the big Las Vegas casino-hotels, where they consummated the ZZZZ Best merger with Morningstar. Barry, Rind, Fischman, Chip and LuLu Arrington, Bobby Victor and Krowpman were present, and the company was in gay spirits on this happy occasion. By a circuitous means, nearly 2.2 million of the 2.9 million freely tradeable Morningstar shares ended up in the hands of Rind, Victor, Schulman and Barry, who purchased them for 2 to 5 cents a share, or less than $100,000 in all. (They had a sense of irony. Perhaps half these shares were held by a company called Brooklyn Enterprises, and someone had a bank account in the name of Wise Guys, Inc.) Within a year ZZZZ Best shares were trading at $4 each, which meant that Barry and the three ex-cons had seen the value of their joint stake rise to $8.8 million. Brooklyn Enterprises offers insight into at least some of the profits. Brooklyn Enterprises bought a million shares for $50,000; eventually they were sold by Brooklyn or by Richman Financial, another Rind-Schulman company, for $6,138,250.

Barry, meanwhile, traded his ownership of ZZZZ Best for 12 million shiny new shares of Morningstar, which he got all to himself. Federal law bars shares acquired under these circumstances from being sold right away in the open market, in order to keep the market from being swamped and keep promoters from taking the money and running. So Barry's shares were restricted, but investigators later came to suspect that the 700,000 or so remaining Morningstar shares were in the hands of others who might be holding them for him.

The merged entity took the ZZZZ Best name, and Morningstar shares became ZZZZ Best shares. Barry, who wasn't old enough to gamble in the casino downstairs, was now the chairman and chief executive of a publicly traded corporation, and owned about three-quarters of its roughly 15 million common shares.

10

The settlement agreement with Catain cleared the way for the merger, but it only exacerbated Barry's never-ending need for cash. Barry was barely keeping his business alive, so often robbing Peter to pay Paul that he could hardly tell one from the other. His tendency to bounce checks and commit credit-card fraud hadn't endeared him to bankers, so borrowing from traditional sources wouldn't work, and anyway, lenders tend to ask what the money is for, and Barry was running a Ponzi scheme. He needed ever-larger loans just to pay back old borrowings. Barry had already raised large sums by claiming to perform refurbishing jobs, even though those didn't exist. Why limit the idea to restoration work? Lots of things don't exist. The possibilities are endless.

Equipment, for example. Ken Pavia and David McHugh have a company called Fiduciary Funding Corp. FFC is a finance company based in Hilton Head, South Carolina, where McHugh works, but Pavia lives in Newport Beach, California, and heard about Barry through a friendly banker at Security Pacific Bank. Pretty soon, McHugh and Minkow got to talking about equipment leasing. Barry seemed interested in doing business, so McHugh asked to see some financial statements.

"No problem, we'll get them right out to you," Barry said.

When they arrived, McHugh was struck by their amateurish presentation. When he asked if he could speak to Richard Evans, the Valley accountant who supposedly prepared them, he wasn't surprised when Barry told him that wouldn't be possible.

"We're changing accountants," Barry said, not mentioning that

Richard Evans was actually Mark Morze. "We weren't happy with Evans. But I can answer any questions for you myself."

Indeed, Barry's grasp of his company's finances was thorough and impressive, and he told McHugh all about his dynamic young company. "Think big, be big," he said.

Barry also said he was looking to finance nineteen or twenty Cornwell Triple-Vac Dual Pump Waterheated Steamcleaners—mythical beasts of the very same genus that had supposedly been stolen in Barry's first phony burglary. Barry was asking FFC to put up $100,000 to buy the nonexistent machines and be their legal owner, leasing them to ZZZZ Best until they were paid for.

FFC does such deals every day, and never looks at the equipment. It had examined ZZZZ Best's financials. It got Cornwell (or at least Dan Krowpman's end of it) to promise it would buy back the machines if ZZZZ Best defaulted. It got a life insurance policy on Barry. And as collateral, FFC got the machines, Barry's 1985 Ferrari 308, his Datsun 300ZX, and three ZZZZ Best vans. In January of 1986 it was a done deal. Dan Krowpman's Cornwell Tool distributorship billed FFC for roughly $94,000, FFC paid the money, the equipment was theoretically delivered to Barry's company, and ZZZZ Best began making lease payments. Everything was just fine.

Pavia and McHugh were so satisfied that they also invested, as joint-venture partners, in some ZZZZ Best restoration work, and got some of their own investors involved as well. First was the big job ZZZZ Best was claiming in Sacramento. Barry gave McHugh his standard spiel about paying cash to get the best deal on supplies. McHugh wanted to know more about the job. Who were the insurers involved, for example? Could McHugh call them? Barry was adamant about not being able to disclose any more information. His explanation? As a small company competing against much larger concerns, he didn't want his insurance company clients to know he was using joint-venture partners, and he didn't want to bother them about confirming jobs; only a small-fry would do such a thing, and they couldn't be plagued by callers checking every little contract.

"Look," Barry said, "if ZZZZ Best wasn't so new, any bank in the country would finance these receivables. I wouldn't need you."

All this sounded reasonable to McHugh. FFC plowed $250,000 into the first job, and as promised, got back a 100 percent return plus principal within ninety days. Or so Barry said. McHugh never actually saw this money, because FFC just rolled it over and let it ride with ZZZZ Best.

Like many people who did business with Barry, FFC went out of its way to be nice to him. After he'd been making lease payments on the cleaning equipment for a few months, Barry called and said he wanted to buy himself a new Ferrari, a top-of-the-line Testarossa this time. It would make life a lot easier if FFC would let go of the title to the old one. McHugh obliged. Pavia had a special relationship with Barry. A literature student in college, he later became a private investment banker who took special pleasure in doing business with people he liked and trusted, and he counted Barry firmly in that category. Pavia was delighted that Barry went out with his daughter once or twice, and told her he was just the sort of person she should be dating. But the romance never caught fire; she didn't like Barry.

Leasing worked so well for ZZZZ Best that in February of 1986, Barry did a similar deal with Perry Morris Corp. of Newport Beach, another leasing concern. Perry Morris prides itself on quick decision-making, and it decided to do the deal the same day Barry met with three of its representatives. A week or two later Morris paid Krowpman's company $100,000. Soon Barry was back; he needed still more equipment, so before the month was out he had gotten another $64,000 out of Morris for a nonexistent Cornwell Consolidated 2120 Dry Cleaning Machine supposedly intended for draperies.

Barry was finding leasing a very rewarding technique, and he went from leasing company to leasing company, harvesting more cash at each. He was like Chichikov, Gogol's fictional con man who traveled the Russian countryside buying up male serfs dead since the last government census. These "dead souls" were officially still alive, and Chichikov hoped to use the transfers as collateral for fraudulent borrowing.

Similarly, Barry's victims would have been very surprised to learn that the equipment that secured his borrowings didn't exist. Just as surprising, their checks to Cornwell were paid over to Barry's company. And although the leasing deals burdened ZZZZ Best with hefty monthly payments, nobody knew better than Barry the meaning of the phrase "Time is money." What counted was not small monthly payments for years and years, but large sums of cash, *now*.

In keeping with this idea, around March of 1986 Barry and Mark Morze approached California Factors, a Burbank finance company, about buying some ZZZZ Best receivables. If you have receivables and need money, a factor can come in handy. He'll give you immediate cash in return for the debts that others owe you for goods or services.

Usually you get something less than face value, which is what the factor charges instead of interest. The factor recoups his investment by collecting the full IOU when it's due. Factoring is common in agriculture and textiles. It can be expensive compared to borrowing from a bank, but compared to loansharks it's cheap, and Barry couldn't afford to be picky.

Dale Buteyn (pronounced "butane") is one of the people at California Factors who handled the ZZZZ Best account. He talks like Joe Friday, the Jack Webb character in "Dragnet," and he had some questions for Padgett, who was supposedly giving ZZZZ Best the insurance jobs.

"Who are your insurance companies?" he demanded.

"We can't tell you," Padgett replied. "If everybody called every company, they'd do nothing but take calls confirming contracts and so forth. Some of the companies aren't from around here; some aren't even from this country. But I'm not even supposed to say that."

"Well, can we see the jobs?"

"No, I'm afraid you can't. They've gotten real strict about that. We had a guy who fell and had a broken kneecap, so we can't do it. But I'm working on getting the restrictions lifted."

Cal Factors started buying ZZZZ Best receivables anyway, but Buteyn still wasn't happy. Interstate Appraisal, which was responsible for the supposed receivables, had been paying Cal Factors with cashier's checks. Now Buteyn wanted to see a draft from an insurance company. This seemed like a stumper. For a while Minkow, Morze and Padgett considered wiring a couple of hundred thousand dollars into a Travelers' bank account. The mistake would be discovered fairly quickly, and Travelers would issue a check in repayment. That check might satisfy Cal Factors.

But it didn't come to that, and somehow ZZZZ Best put Cal Factors off. At one point Barry even sent Morze up to Arroyo Grande, where ZZZZ Best supposedly was doing a job that Cal Factors was helping finance. Morze claims this was the first time Barry revealed that he'd made up a restoration job. Whether this is so or not, Morze was certainly ready to help.

"Go up there and find a building—any building—and take some pictures," Barry commanded.

Morze arrived and found nothing that fit the bill. Arroyo Grande is a sleepy place without a building that could hold millions in fire or water damage and still stand. Ever resourceful, Morze lay down on the sidewalk and shot some pictures of a smaller building at a steep angle.

Cal Factors still wanted to find those insurance jobs, though, and Buteyn was leaving messages for Padgett, who by now had established a policy of never taking phone calls and never answering messages from anyone but one of his cohorts. "What if Barry had told somebody about the Boston job—the whole city of Boston burned down?" Padgett might not know about it, and their stories wouldn't jibe. Finally Buteyn called him at home.

"Listen, I'm going up to Arroyo Grande with the wife and kids. You mind giving me the address up there?"

Padgett refused, of course.

Maurice Rind, meanwhile, was working on bringing in new capital too. He did this through a man he faintly knew named Jay Botchman, whose company, JLB Equities of Montvale, New Jersey, makes, according to police, short-term loans at high interest rates to people who can't borrow elsewhere. Botchman had known Schulman for perhaps twenty-five years and had also met Rind. Botchman told police that Schulman called one day and said he and Rind were "onto something really great" that was making both of them a lot of money.

Botchman flew out and met with Barry, Rind and Padgett in California. Botchman is a big man and puffed on a cigar. He seemed jovial, but everybody treated him with great deference, and after a discussion of ZZZZ Best's financing needs, he said to Barry, "Now do you mind if we investigate you a little?"

Barry didn't mind. In fact, he helped. Two days later, he called Botchman in New Jersey, claimed he was Padgett, and answered some questions. Calling people as Padgett was one of Barry's favorite things, and he would do so repeatedly during the next eighteen months.

Barry got money from Kay Rozario's friends in bits and pieces. Now, thanks to Botchman, Schulman and Rind, Barry started to see some real money, all at once. In January of 1986, JLB had loaned B&M Insurance $1 million at 24 percent annual interest plus attorneys' fees to finance the supposed San Diego restoration job. The money was plowed into ZZZZ Best, and Padgett assigned to JLB the supposed contract proceeds from the supposed insurance companies that were paying for these renovation jobs in the first place. Barry and his friends repaid the money on time and everybody was happy.

Now it was time for Barry and Moe to swing for the fences: in the spring, they asked Botchman for $2.1 million to finance the purchase

of supplies for another nonexistent contract, the giant $7 million res-
toration job in Sacramento. In May of 1986, he granted them a $2.1
million line of credit, once again at 24 percent annual interest. Barry
immediately drew down $1.1 million, hoping to take the rest soon
after. But he would never get more than another $100,000 from
Botchman, who because of some repayment snag decided he didn't
like the risk.

Dale Buteyn, meanwhile, still wasn't satisfied. He found ZZZZ
Best suspicious and thought Barry was a jerk. He couldn't stand the
way Barry came into the office and acted like he owned the place,
flashing V signs around as if for victory, or peace. Finally Buteyn
demanded a meeting with Minkow, Morze and Padgett. It was a
Friday morning in April. Padgett and Morze were scared, but Barry
seemed perfectly calm. When everyone was assembled, Buteyn told
the group that Cal Factors was canceling ZZZZ Best's line of credit
and wouldn't buy any more receivables.

"These jobs don't exist," Buteyn said simply.

Padgett was terrified and said nothing, but Barry went on and on
trying to talk his way out of it. It was all a misunderstanding, he said.
Hadn't ZZZZ Best always been good for the money? Hadn't Cal
Factors *made* money?

Buteyn just shook his head. Cal Factors had checked with Travelers
Insurance and learned that Travelers had no contracts with Interstate
Appraisal. Perhaps Buteyn also learned the circumstances of Padgett's
termination there.

"I don't want any excuses," he said. "I just want a cashier's check,
now."

"Look," Barry pleaded, "what can we do to make this right?"

"Pay me," said Buteyn.

Barry, Morze and Padgett left in Barry's Ferrari, headed straight
for their next big crisis: they owed Jay Botchman $400,000 that they
didn't have. The money was due that very same day, and no matter
how many debts Barry had due, Botchman always got priority.

With no more credit from Cal Factors—the boys somehow came
up with $212,000 to settle that problem—and Jack Catain out of the
picture, there wasn't a prayer of making the payment to Botchman
on time. Not only that, but Padgett and Morze had never met before;
Barry had always done a careful job of keeping them apart. Later that
day, though, Padgett needed a ride and Morze gave him one. The
two men got to talking, and Padgett explained how Barry had cost

him his job at Travelers. Morze and Padgett also discussed "the library job"; the main branch of the Los Angeles Public Library had recently suffered a devastating fire.

"Jim's business must be going really great," Padgett said to Morze. "Barry says he's got the library fire."

Morze looked over for an instant before responding.

"Tom, Barry said *you've* got the library fire."

Padgett had had his suspicions about things before, but had always wanted to believe. Like many who followed Barry, he thought the boss was only bending the rules, or was about as crooked as everybody else. Padgett claims he thought the jobs were real but were coming to Barry from Jim instead of from Interstate, and that he was merely disguising their source, not their absence. Thus, Buteyn could plausibly be a problem even if the jobs were real. Now, all of a sudden, Padgett felt a little chill and accepted that something was very wrong.

But that didn't make him stop. An elaborate conference call was arranged with Barry, Padgett, Rind, Schulman and Botchman. Jay Botchman was concerned. Since the money was ostensibly coming from Interstate Appraisal, he questioned Padgett closely, but every time he asked something, Barry jumped in to answer. Finally Rind burst in: "Barry, shut the fuck up! Tommy, you answer."

Barry promised to have the money by Monday, and told Padgett he'd scraped up $300,000 over the weekend, supposedly from the mysterious "Jim." Botchman apparently was paid the rest within a few days. Where Barry got all that money so fast is one of those ZZZZ Best imponderables, but chances are he didn't get it from Jack Catain, who was still a huge headache.

According to federal law enforcement authorities, Barry paid Catain more than $500,000 from December of 1985 to July of 1986 as the result of their settlement agreement. One of Victor's jobs was supposedly protecting Barry from Catain. He never quite succeeded, angering Schulman and Rind, who were furious that so much money was being paid out to Catain. But Barry continued talking to the FBI. On February 21, 1986, he explained his onerous settlement with Catain, again insisting that no one physically threatened him. It was more a case of economic blackmail. Soon after, Barry once again benefited from divine intervention. On April 17, 1986, Catain was indicted by a federal grand jury—not for loansharking or extortion, but on counterfeiting charges! He was arrested that day by a Secret Service agent and two Los Angeles Police detectives, one of whom was named Mike Brambles.

Barry soon stopped paying, although he kept saying he would continue. In late April and again in mid-June, he and Catain, who was out on bail, worked out new payment schedules. Each time Barry failed to meet them. On July 4, his final deadline, Barry called Catain in the hospital and combatively refused to pay. Five days later Catain sued him again.

Catain was no longer acting much like a fearsome mobster. When he called Arrington to ask if he could retrieve his personal effects from ZZZZ Best, Barry at first refused, relenting only after Catain called a second time.

"Let him get his personal belongings, but that's it," said Barry. Looking sickly and walking with a cane, Catain finally came over to pick up his things. This time he was accompanied by his real son.

To help Barry extricate himself from the Catain quagmire and work out his cooperation with the government, he retained Arthur Barens. Barens is a well-known criminal lawyer who has represented some of Los Angeles' most notorious defendants, including Joe Hunt, a Dostoyevskian figure convicted of murder in connection with the Billionaire Boys Club, a group of rich young Southern Californians dedicated to getting richer by any means. Hunt was their charismatic leader, and Barry would later follow the BBC trial with great interest, reading about it in the papers and watching the subsequent television movie.

On July 31, 1986, the Justice Department's Organized Crime Strike Force formally granted Barry immunity from prosecution—in connection with Catain—in order to learn from him whatever more it could about the man the government was finally going to nail. Barry says he told the grand jury that Catain was extorting him and had threatened to blow up the ZZZZ Best headquarters. The prosecutors couldn't have known that the big fish they thought they had landed would turn out to be a minnow next to the one they had just thrown back.

11

With Padgett and Morze aboard, the ingenious form of the ZZZZ Best Ponzi scheme had by now assumed its final shape. Although Barry told the world his main business was cleaning carpets and restoring damaged buildings, ZZZZ Best was actually a relatively simple contraption whose purpose was financial alchemy.

It worked this way: ZZZZ Best would raise money from investors, banks or anyone else. It would pay this money out to Marbil Marketing, Morze's old company, which was supposedly an employment contractor that hired workers to perform the ZZZZ Best restoration jobs awarded by Padgett's Interstate Appraisal. Marbil would recycle the money back to ZZZZ Best either directly or through Barry's personal account. Marbil and Interstate were beyond scrutiny, since both were private companies, and the true nature of the banking activity at ZZZZ Best was masked by a series of checks to Barry's company from Interstate Appraisal representing money paid by Padgett's concern for work performed by ZZZZ Best. These Interstate Appraisal checks were never deposited. They were just forgeries created by Morze to match ZZZZ Best deposit slips and thereby fool the accountants. Those deposits actually came to ZZZZ Best from Marbil, from Barry's own account or from lenders or investors, some of whom provided money secretly. In 1986 about $10 million moved between Marbil and ZZZZ Best. In the first half of 1987 the figure was $44 million. Of course it wasn't a closed system: there was substantial leakage as Barry's closest colleagues in crime benefited from a kind of Minkow "Share the Wealth" program that paid for houses, cars and women. But that was the course the money took, and that was how Barry and his friends made it look like ZZZZ Best actually generated revenue, received payments and so forth. Moving this money around necessitated a frenzy of bank activity, and Barry and his friends often took advantage of what might be called the centrifugal powers of their machine to increase the amount of money in the system without adding any. It was just a matter of moving the money around so fast that there was more of it, the way a person in a group photo taken with a slow shutter can run around back and be at both ends of the picture simultaneously. When it comes to money, ZZZZ Best proved that velocity and mass are related.

In a sense Barry and his company were a fine metaphor for so much that was going on around them. They aptly reflected the larger regression of our securities markets into casinos, for example, and the substitution of debt for equity across the board. Consumers were encouraged to trade savings for debt years ago. Corporations and the federal government have recently followed suit. Soaring stock prices, asset liquidations, junk bonds and the budget and trade deficits all hinted at a giant Ponzi scheme while Barry was at his peak, and the shift of our economy to services, which his firm exemplified, enhanced the general impression. How many people do you know who actually *make* anything for a living? How many can even say what they do in a single sentence, without using words like "coordinate"? ZZZZ Best may be the perfect expression of our fast-talking, debt-laden, paper-shuffling society, where consuming has replaced conserving and being has supplanted doing. ZZZZ Best might have been a David Mamet nightmare if it wasn't so real.

Of course there was also an element of parody about Barry, the strong suggestion of spoof. In his heyday he brought to mind *Edwin Mullhouse*, Steven Millhauser's fictional tour de force about a literary genius who dies at the age of eleven. The kid's Boswell is an elementary-school classmate. Barry was similarly situated in the myth of business manhood that seemed so predominant in the 1980s, a decade given over to the frantic pursuit of gain. Investment banking was the occupation of choice, MBA the preferred degree, the "fast track" the path to success. Barry's brief but incandescent business career was spent in the middle of a raging bull stock market that heightened the sense of easy money for those in the know. There was an explosion in business journalism; much was written about power in the executive suite, about the proper necktie or desk height to intimidate a colleague or competitor, two categories that began to seem indistinguishable. Profit was wanted *now*. Never before, it seemed, had so many carried to its logical conclusion Keynes's comment that "in the long run, we are all dead."

In a Ponzi scheme, there is no long run. The demands of investors and lenders, Barry's life-style, and his company's own money-losing operations were such that there was still never enough money. He already had millions of dollars racing around in an ever-escalating spiral of fraud, but the system required ever-larger infusions to keep it running. Barry spent the summer of 1986 in a frenzy. Although he had much to be thankful for—he had finally got Catain off his back, he was living well and he was getting the admiration he had always craved—he had to work harder and harder to make the fraud work. Like many businesses, it needed to grow to survive.

Now that ZZZZ Best was a public company, Barry and his friends wanted to make its shares more readily tradeable in order to unlock the great value they might hold. To do that, they needed to get ZZZZ Best traded on the National Association of Securities Dealers Automated Quotation system, or Nasdaq.

Shares of companies like General Motors and IBM are traded every day on the New York Stock Exchange, where there are almost always buyers and sellers, and where there are all kinds of rules to ensure at least a rudimentary level of propriety. Shares in other legitimate companies trade on the American Stock Exchange, one of the regional markets such as the Pacific Stock Exchange or "over the counter" via Nasdaq.

Virtually throughout 1986, though, the price of ZZZZ Best stock was listed only in the "pink sheets," an atavistic over-the-counter system whereby stock quotes for thousands of little companies are reported daily on paper. Each company has one or more "market makers" for its stock. These securities firms have agreed to buy and sell the shares, and they provide the quotes to the pink-sheet publishers. But the figure is often outdated, since the printed sheets are distributed the following morning. To buy a pink-sheet security, a broker has to call market makers for a bid. By the time a second or third quote is received, the market may shift, rendering the first quote stale.

Nasdaq, by contrast, brings to smaller companies many of the advantages offered by the major stock exchanges, without a trading floor. Run by the National Association of Securities Dealers under the aegis of the SEC, since 1971 Nasdaq has used computers to provide up-to-the minute, automated quotations for what has lately grown to more than 5,000 issues. It is much easier to buy shares of a Nasdaq-listed company than a pink-sheet company, and Rind knew that if ZZZZ Best could get on Nasdaq, it would open up the whole investment world, inevitably helping to raise the price of ZZZZ Best shares.

Although the New York Stock Exchange is still the Big Board, Nasdaq also bestows a certain legitimacy. Before it will list a company's shares, Nasdaq requires it to have at least two market makers, at least 100,000 freely tradeable shares and at least 300 different shareholders. Total assets must be $2 million or more, and net worth must be at least $1 million. The company must also be registered with the SEC, meaning that it files quarterly and annual reports, has an independent outside auditor, follows generally accepted accounting principles, etc.

ZZZZ Best couldn't meet all these requirements, at least not yet. It certainly wasn't ready to begin reporting to the SEC—its record keeping was a joke—and it was small enough and had few enough shareholders to be exempt. But around May of 1986, ZZZZ Best moved to meet Nasdaq's financial requirements. ZZZZ Best had virtually no assets, and since net worth is just the difference between assets and liabilities, no net worth. To solve this problem, the company acquired twenty-two secondhand electric generators for just under $2 million.

The ostensible purpose of these generators was for ZZZZ Best to have electricity at damage-restoration sites. Barry had complained to Rind that he was spending a fortune renting portable generators; now ZZZZ Best would have some of its own. But mainly they sat in a warehouse, where Barry could use them to impress visitors. Rind pleaded for permission to rent them out, and once he managed to do so, providing some of the power used outside the 1987 Super Bowl.

The generators were more important as paper assets than as producers of electricity. Rind bought them through a Miami broker for just $580,000. Then a ZZZZ Best subsidiary was established called 4Z Equipment Co., which supposedly bought the generators for $1.1 million in cash and 217,500 shares of ZZZZ Best stock (Rind says he sold the stock to Barry for $1 a share a year later). Barry says documents in the transaction were then backdated to February.

Accounting rules say that assets must be recorded at the lower of market value or purchase price, but ZZZZ Best didn't traffic with any such prissiness. It booked those generators at $2 million, which is what it claimed to have paid, and never mind that four of the generators were never delivered, or that Rind was able to get the whole pack for just $580,000, or that the machines were sold later in bankruptcy for $109,000. Suddenly the company met some of Nasdaq's requirements to be listed. The others would be met later.

But this approach wasn't bringing in money now, and immediate cash is what ZZZZ Best always needed. How much money was going out, and to whom, is difficult to sort out, since ZZZZ Best generated thousands of checks and banking transactions, and Arrington, Maloney, Barry himself and God knows who else delivered currency for the company. Rind, Victor, Schulman and a host of others received payments of one kind or another, either directly or through their companies.

New expenses were always springing up. Around May of 1986, Barry got an ominous call from Irv Rubin, chairman of the Jewish Defense League. Rubin runs the entire national organization (founded by Rabbi Meir Kahane) from the San Fernando Valley, and he had done his homework on ZZZZ Best. For one thing, he had known Rind for years. Rind had first approached the JDL about Dirk Summers, a man with whom Rind had a long-standing feud. Rind was convinced Summers was actually an ex-Nazi, which Summers denies. Over the years Rind gave money to the JDL, and Art Auctions Inc., another company Rind was involved with, hired Los Angeles chapter chairman Earl Krugel. Rind and Schulman even raised $35,000 for a float in the 1987 Israel Independence Day parade in Los Angeles.

Rubin knew who Padgett was. The JDL confronts anti-Semitism with violence, and the organization had brawled with some of Metzger's followers that same month—May of 1986—at Union Station downtown. Padgett, who doesn't shy away from a fight, took part. But the JDL doesn't shy away from a fight either. Krugel, for example, is built like one of those Inuit sculptures, without much in the way of a neck. He looks like a center or a small tackle on a mediocre semipro football team.

When Rubin first visited ZZZZ Best, he told Barry that his main source of contracts, Tom Padgett, was a Nazi. Barry listened calmly and replied masterfully. He said he was sorry but he had a fiduciary obligation to his shareholders and therefore couldn't stop doing business with Padgett, whose company was just too important to ZZZZ Best. Ultimately, according to Morze, Barry managed to keep Rubin quiet by making a donation. Barry offered $1,000. Rubin, driving a hard bargain, demanded $2,000.

"Jeez, I only do business with the guy," Barry complained, paying the money with feigned reluctance.

When Rubin left, Barry and Morze marveled at his foolishness. Rubin had it within his power to destroy ZZZZ Best, and could have extorted $50,000 or even $100,000. Barry would have little choice but to pay.

But $2,000 wasn't the end of it. Months later, Barry ended up having to give Rubin $400 a week, which Rubin used to pay radio station KIEV for his talk show. Of course Barry didn't just pay the money. Rubin had to show up every Friday morning to collect, and Barry always kept him waiting. Sometimes Rubin had to come back later in the day. Overall, Rubin says, Barry gave a total of $13,000 or $14,000 to the JDL from December 1986 to April 1987.

"How can we take any support from a guy who is associating with and helping neo-Nazis?" Rubin asks rhetorically. "We decided that if Minkow's partner is going to help Nazis, Minkow should help us."

A thousand-fingered contortionist couldn't plug as many holes in the dike as Barry seemed to manage at ZZZZ Best. Yet Barry showed the world—and close associates such as Padgett and Morze—a vision of complete calm and absolute confidence, even in the face of hysteria in others. For instance, despite all his difficulties in the middle of 1986, Barry still managed to throw a big party in June at the Beverly Hilton Hotel to celebrate the opening of a couple of new ZZZZ Best offices. Padgett drank coffee, even though he was allergic to it, and discussed his no-beer diet with big Bobby Victor, who said he was on a watermelon diet. Always a performer, Barry led cheers from the various ZZZZ Best offices represented in the audience.

Barry had a lot in common with Sammy Glick, Budd Schulberg's infamous antihero who claws his way to the top in *What Makes Sammy Run?* Glick is manic, ruthless, greedy, dishonest and obsessed. Finally narrator Al Mannheim figures out how Glick does it.

"First, no qualms. . . . In the second place, he was as uninhibited as a performing seal. . . . And then there was his colossal lack of perspective. This was one of his most valuable gifts. . . ."

Of course Barry's new friends helped. Schulman was in town most of the summer, staying in the same Encino condo complex as his friend Rind. Richie and Moe had a portable phone, and would do business out by the pool. Schulman was a friendly neighbor. He left his door wide open, played with the kids and was always up for a barbeque.

Some people say Barry seemed a little scared of Richie, but the two mostly had fun together. Schulman was so fat that clothes weren't comfortable; he would sit around the house smoking stogies in his underwear. Barry would come over, strip down to his shorts and light up with him. He seemed to be having a grand old time, and Schulman took a liking to him, even feeding Barry Devil Dogs. Devil Dogs are long sandwiches of soft chocolate cake filled with some kind of creamy white stuff, and you can get them only in and around New York. They're sold in supermarkets next to every kind of harmful and disgusting junk food, and they are probably death in quantity, but with a glass of cold milk or a cup of Irish Breakfast tea with cream they're heaven. It was the height of generosity for a tub like Schulman to share these exotic treasures with Barry, who became a regular at Rind's and Schulman's condo complex. At Schulman's birthday party, he and Barry cavorted nude as a couple of prostitutes danced undressed. Even Rind started to like the kid. (Later, Schulman would come to share in the sense of betrayal Barry left in his wake, complaining bitterly that he hadn't even been invited to Barry's big twenty-first birthday bash.) Schulman impressed Scamardo as a very jolly fellow who looked "like a whale with a cigar." Barry later told a worried Dan Krowpman Sr. that Schulman's "a big nothing, that's what he is. He's a big nothing. A bag of wind."

Bob Victor helped Barry get through his first audit, another step on the road to a wider market for ZZZZ Best securities. Conducted by George Greenspan, who flew out from New Jersey, it helped reinforce the notion in Barry that auditors are easy to fool. Although Greenspan is a former accounting teacher, has four decades of experience and even knows the construction industry, his audit for the twelve months ended April 30, 1986, came off without event.

At the time ZZZZ Best was claiming to Greenspan that it had completed two restoration projects: one in Arroyo Grande and the other in San Diego. To check on the existence of these projects, Greenspan contacted Padgett, who confirmed everything. Greenspan also examined contracts for the jobs. Then, since the ZZZZ Best restoration work was financed by B&M Insurance, Greenspan contacted Bob Victor, whose comments suggest he knew about the whole scheme.

"I asked him if he had visited the contract," Greenspan later told a Congressional subcommittee. "He said he had just come back from the contract and had been banking the payroll, taking care of labor problems and watching the contract."

(It was never made clear which job Greenspan and Victor were discussing, but it doesn't matter, since neither job existed. Rind says that when Victor first assured his partners that the jobs were real, he took Barry's word. Barry apparently told him he couldn't visit the jobs because his criminal record precluded bonding. According to Rind, Victor later learned the jobs were fake, but by that time he had already gotten Schulman involved. Victor won't comment, but if Rind is right, Victor was one of many who learned the truth when they were in too deep to do anything about it.)

Greenspan still wasn't satisfied. He went on to audit the profits generated by the jobs. The two contracts together approached $3 million and threw off $186,679 in pre-tax profits, or 6 percent of the gross. Showing how easily we can be seduced by our own assumptions, Greenspan thought this very much in line with what he knew about the construction business. He had done everything short of visiting the jobs personally. ZZZZ Best got a clean bill of health, and Greenspan, who would one day describe himself as "aghast" at what happened, returned to New Jersey.

Money was still a bigger problem for Barry than nosy auditors, but time and again, by hook or by crook, his magic turned up needed cash. One of the ways he did this, witness Bruce Blair told police, was by selling cocaine.

This might surprise those who didn't know what went on at ZZZZ Best, because Barry actively crusaded against drug abuse. He was known for it. He claimed to require drug tests of his workers, and to be free of such substances himself. In a television commercial, for example, Barry told viewers he was just twenty-one years old and headed a company with 3,000 employees (an enormous exaggeration).

"That's pressure, and it's drugfree. If I can handle pressure, so can you. If you can't, don't be afraid to ask for help—please," Barry implored.

Leaving aside his years of steroid-stacking, Barry used cocaine at least a dozen times. He snorted with Joel Hochberg, who was working for him and even selling the stuff from the ZZZZ Best offices, according to a Los Angeles Police affidavit in support of a search warrant. (Hochberg himself says the police exaggerated, and instead of dealing drugs, he merely procured cocaine for his friends.) Barry also sold cocaine, dispensing it from a large stash he kept in his desk drawer, according to Blair, a ZZZZ Best carpet cleaner and later a supervisor. Many times, Blair says, he saw teenagers come in, pick up some cocaine and come back later with cash, which they handed over to

Barry. Blair, whose allegations are contained in the same police affidavit as Hochberg's, says this went on for most of 1986, although other sources say it was likelier 1985.

It's difficult to say how much cocaine moved through ZZZZ Best, but the amounts weren't substantial compared to how much money the company was consuming to service debt and support operations, and Barry appears to have insulated some of his closest supporters from that side of the business. Padgett, for example, had no idea ZZZZ Best had anything to do with drugs. Anyway, during 1986 Barry started moving ZZZZ Best toward steadier supplies of money to feed the Ponzi's raging appetite.

For example, just because Catain was out of the picture didn't mean Barry was finished with Union Bank. In June of 1986, Susan Russell, the Union Bank executive who had earlier rejected Barry's loan request, got a financial statement and slick publicity package from ZZZZ Best in the mail. The financial statement, prepared by CPA George Greenspan, was much more professional than the last one Russell had seen, and showed that the company was growing fast based on a dramatic increase in its restoration business. It was now getting large insurance contracts. Soon after, Barry called and asked for an appointment. When he got one, he went downtown and performed.

For forty-five minutes he told Russell how well ZZZZ Best was doing. He explained in detail what the insurance restoration business was all about. He told her his company got its insurance contracts through Interstate Appraisal, headed by Tom Padgett. He noted that ZZZZ Best was now a public company. He offered to assign revenue from the contracts directly to Union Bank as some kind of collateral for a loan of between $200,000 and $300,000. He even offered a lien on his house.

Barry had also given Russell a large red book containing glowing press clippings, letters of recommendation from customers, Mayor Bradley's resolution honoring him, Barry's financial statements and his income tax returns. Barry was so insistent that Russell called Padgett, who said he had indeed been giving Barry insurance-restoration jobs. But Susan Russell is more thorough than that. She ran a credit check on Interstate Appraisal and found no credit history. Worse, she couldn't determine the source of Interstate's jobs or money, and ZZZZ Best was clearly entirely dependent on Padgett's company. What if it should go into the tank? And wasn't there a potential conflict of interest between Interstate and Travelers, the two masters Padgett

was supposedly serving? Nor did Russell much like the financial statements being prepared by an accountant in New Jersey, on the other
end of the continent. Weren't there any accountants in Southern
California?

Perhaps most troubling, Russell checked ZZZZ Best's credit and
found several Small Claims judgments and tax liens. She demanded
an explanation from Barry for each one. Then she rejected his loan
request anyway.

Knocking his head against the vault of Union Bank in this way
must have been extremely frustrating, but to say that Barry is tena-
cious is like suggesting that Kareem Abdul-Jabbar might have a facility
for basketball. Barry just didn't know how to give up.

He also pestered the Valley office of Bank Hapoalim for a loan.
Howard Nissenoff, then a vice-president of the Israel-based bank,
recalls that his boss, Lazare Tannenbaum, first brought Barry in as
a potential customer. Nissenoff met with Barry at ZZZZ Best headquarters in May or June of 1986, and found him "loud, brash and
interesting." Barry gave Nissenoff a copy of the red book and tried
to borrow $100,000 or $200,000. Nissenoff ultimately said no.

But a month later, Tannenbaum asked him to reconsider. Nissenoff
met with Barry again, along with Mark Morze; ZZZZ Best's new
chief financial officer, Bruce T. Andersen; and the company's financial
consultant, Richard Charbit. This time Tannenbaum was present,
and the men from ZZZZ Best reviewed their restoration business for
the bankers. Barry said the restoration jobs ranged up to $3 million
each, and had profit margins as high as 50 percent. But the work was
capital-intensive: ZZZZ Best needed loans in order to purchase supplies cheaply in advance. Barry and his lieutenants offered two forms
of collateral: the company's receivables and the generators. The loan
request was for $1 million. Nissenoff, who examined copies of the
restoration contracts and also extracted a personal guarantee from
Barry, approved—despite his personal opposition to the deal. He later
said in court he was swayed by his boss. Barry testified that he and
Charbit paid Tannenbaum a $25,000 bribe to make the loan, which
ZZZZ Best needed badly.

"We were nothing," Barry explained. "We were losing money in
everything we did."

Tannenbaum denies taking a bribe and insists he can't remember
overruling his subordinate on the loan. He says he met Barry through
his acquaintance, Charbit. Barry seems to have met Charbit through
an Englishman named Edwin Hale, who responded to Barry's "money

wanted" ad, put together the red book for ZZZZ Best and introduced Barry to some bankers, all for $1,000, Morze says. According to Morze, Charbit drove a Rolls-Royce and had a house on Rodeo Drive in Beverly Hills, and Barry saw right away that Charbit could do things for him. So he dumped Hale and, unfortunately for the custodians of America's wealth, took on Charbit as a consultant. Morze says Charbit got ZZZZ Best in the door at Bank Hapoalim. Charbit also helped Barry met Peter Strauss.

If function subsumes personality, Peter Strauss's persona has been swallowed whole by his occupation as a low-budget movie producer. Then again, maybe personality determines function. Maybe there are qualities about Strauss that predisposed him to the movie business, some of which may have predisposed him to Barry Minkow as well. Strauss was precocious himself. He attended Oberlin College and then made money in business while attending Columbia University Law School. He lived in Paris for a while and eventually gravitated to Hollywood. For a time he worked for Ray Stark, the famous behind-the-scenes power at Columbia Pictures, and then became an independent producer. His pictures include *Dance of the Dwarfs*, *Thunder Run*, *Silent Assassins* and *Touched by Love*, that last supposedly not a bad flick about a cerebral-palsy victim who gains hope through a correspondence with Elvis Presley.

Dark and stylish, Strauss is nevertheless known on occasion to wear his collar outside his jacket. He has a beautiful wife and son, a beautiful house in Beverly Hills and a beautiful Rolls-Royce next to a beautiful Volvo in the garage. He is a man of great intelligence and business acumen whom it would seem difficult to fool. Yet he became another of those Robert Minkow stand-ins who, for love of money and love of Barry both, went out and helped harvest cash for someone who later turned out to be a crook.

In the summer of 1986, Strauss heard about Richard Charbit from his friend Lazare Tannenbaum, whom Strauss had known for five or six years. Tannenbaum apparently told Charbit that Strauss sometimes accommodated borrowers whom Bank Hapoalim couldn't. Charbit was short, plump, French and in his forties, and he and Strauss spoke to one another in French, even though Charbit speaks good but heavily accented English.

Charbit explained that Barry Minkow was a dynamic young entrepreneur who needed help financing ZZZZ Best. He provided some information about Barry and his company, including the contention that it was working with a 30 percent gross profit margin on sales.

ZZZZ Best was prepared to pay interest on any loan against receivables or contracts, and would also split the profits on a particular job 50-50 with whoever did the financing.

"Can you do it?" he asked.

Peter Strauss pondered. His experience in the movie business had taught him much about creative financing, and ZZZZ Best was promising very healthy returns. Undaunted by risk, he decided to take a closer look. He even refused to meet Barry at first, explaining that he didn't want to be confused by salesmanship. Instead he would look at the numbers. Numbers, Strauss felt, don't lie, and the numbers seemed to look good. It never crossed his mind that somebody might simply *make up* the numbers. We are all conditioned to take the word for the thing, the image for the actuality. Like everyone else, Strauss assumed the numbers meant something.

He didn't know that the company found it hard to borrow from banks not only because of Barry's age and inexperience, but also because of his wretched history of bank fraud. Whenever ZZZZ Best ran out of money, Barry and Morze would start kiting checks again. (They did it so often that Barry's cronies gave him a giant kite, with a blow-up of a Charter Pacific check on it, for his twenty-first birthday.) In the summer of 1986, Morze says, around the time Barry and Strauss connected, ZZZZ Best was booted out of the Bank of Granada Hills for kiting checks between it, Charter Pacific, Security Pacific and Wells Fargo. Checks drawn on one bank would be deposited in the next and so on down the line, with a check from the last deposited in the first to cover outgoing funds. For short periods, ZZZZ Best was able to create money for itself this way.

It was the misfortune of the Beverly Hills branch of First Interstate Bank to have Peter Strauss as an old and cherished customer. Besides his own banking, Strauss had brought in other profitable business. Now he was calling loan officer Stephen Monchamp to introduce him to ZZZZ Best, a fast-growing concern that Strauss was excited about. Strauss was willing to guarantee a First Interstate loan to ZZZZ Best, and he freely disclosed that he would be compensated by ZZZZ Best for doing so. Monchamp met with Barry and Charbit, who gave him the usual song and dance. Before long, First Interstate agreed to lend $750,000 secured by ZZZZ Best receivables and guaranteed by Strauss. Monchamp testified later that Strauss didn't lend the money himself because he wanted to help Barry's fledgling company establish credit.

On July 22, First Interstate disbursed the money in three cashier's checks: for $210,990 to Mandy's California Woodworks, for $250,000 to Cornwell Quality Tools and for $289,010 to ZZZZ Best. Unbeknownst to Monchamp and Strauss, all these checks were ultimately deposited into a ZZZZ Best account.

As was often the case the first time someone made a loan to Barry, he repaid it promptly and everyone made money. First Interstate got two points above the prime rate, and Strauss made a substantial profit without laying out a dime. Barry was able to repay the loan because in August ZZZZ Best borrowed another $750,000 from First Interstate, also guaranteed by Strauss. In other words, he repaid the bank with its own money.

With such a good record, ZZZZ Best's Strauss-backed line of credit at First Interstate was raised to $1.5 million in September, and the company immediately took advantage of it. On September 19, ZZZZ Best borrowed $741,000. On September 24, it borrowed $759,000. Thus, the August loan probably was repaid with the bank's own money as well.

First Interstate wasn't completely careless. Monchamp asked to see some restoration jobs, and Barry said that might be possible eventually, but that it was difficult because of liability considerations, and because the insurance companies insisted on confidentiality. They didn't want to get involved in this sort of thing, Barry said; that's what Interstate Appraisal was for. Barry added that in the event of a site visit, elaborate clearances, badges and secrecy agreements would be required.

With First Interstate, Barry had carried his Ponzi scheme to new heights, even if he was still on the roller coaster with no way to get off. But at last, it seemed, salvation might be at hand. Now that Barry's company had slipped into the public securities markets by merging with Morningstar, it would be possible to reach for some real money by selling stock to the public.

Rind was dead set against it. He didn't see the need, and he felt it would focus more scrutiny on ZZZZ Best than it could stand. He, Schulman and Victor (or entities they controlled) were already making money from ZZZZ Best directly as well as by trading its stock, which they had bought for pennies. Charbit, however, backed the idea, and in the subtle struggle for preeminence between these two worldly men, the one who could deliver the most money would win. The winner was chosen by a nineteen-year-old kid. The process had already been set in motion.

12

ob Grossmann says he first heard the name ZZZZ Best in January 1986, when someone who knew Greenspan, the accountant, told him, "There's this company that's putting numbers up spectacularly in Los Angeles." Grossmann was a successful Los Angeles stockbroker at the time with the faintly disreputable New York-based securities firm of Rooney, Pace Group Inc., which is now mercifully defunct. Grossmann tended to rack up healthy commissions, but he wasn't just a salesman. He was also a pretty good stock-picker, and his overall performance made him a treasured member of his firm.

Grossmann is a quiet, intense man of average height who is modestly handsome if not particularly memorable-looking. He seems younger than his forty-five years, and he has the air of a New Yorker who has come to his senses. Grossmann liked living at the beach, enjoyed the roller coaster of the over-the-counter market and drove a little red Triumph with California plates that said HOTSTOX He has a combination of attributes that would have made him a successful newspaperman: he is at once friendly and hardheaded, skeptical and open to new ideas. Also, he loves finding things out.

Grossmann especially liked finding obscure little companies that would soon become highfliers, so he decided to take a look at ZZZZ Best. He noted that it was traded in the pink sheets at around $2 a share. But he couldn't seem to get financial statements or any of the other most basic public disclosures out of the company, so he forgot about it.

In April, ZZZZ Best cropped up again. This time Grossmann's secretary took a message from a man wanting to know if unregistered

ZZZZ Best stock could be used as collateral for a $5 million loan.
ZZZZ Best shares were at $4. And the unregistered stock was worth
some $50 million.

Grossmann was stunned. His mind reeled with questions: How
could a pink-sheet company have a valuation of $50 million? How
could an insider have $50 million in unregistered shares? If the stock
was worth $50 million, why couldn't the stockholder borrow the
money some other way? And why was Grossmann hearing about
ZZZZ Best again?

Grossmann called around to his network of "bathrobe" money managers, men who run their own money from their own homes and so
can be counted on to behave differently from professional money
managers, who are scornfully dismissed by cowboys like Grossmann
as addicted to "opium," spelled OPM for Other People's Money. In
the eyes of Bob Grossmann, institutional managers hooked on OPM
are anxious to do what will *look* like the right thing, rather than what
might really make money. The bathrobe managers tended to hear
about strange little comets like ZZZZ Best, but when Grossmann
called them, they didn't know a thing about it.

Grossmann then dialed the number the ZZZZ Best caller had left
with his secretary and got Richard Charbit, who explained that the
president of the company was only nineteen years old (Barry had
actually just turned twenty), and that because of his age no one would
lend him money.

"What can you send me?" Grossmann asked. He was looking for
all the usual stuff—financial statements, annual reports, etc.

Soon a messenger arrived bearing a volume the likes of which
Grossmann had never before encountered. He holds his fingers about
four inches apart and says, "It was a big red book, about that thick,
and what it contained was the strangest compilation of business information I've ever seen. It was a paean to Barry Minkow. It went
on and on about this self-made millionaire. It had copies of his tax
returns, press clippings on his honors, including one from the mayor,
but there was very little in the way of financial information."

Grossmann also noticed that Barry held something like 12 million
out of 15 million ZZZZ Best shares, meaning that only about 3 million
shares actually traded. "The valuation was so out of whack," he recalls.
"It was eighty or one hundred times sales." Companies more typically
sell for about the equivalent of a year's sales.

Once Grossmann met Barry, he was even more intrigued. "You
look at him and talk to him and you have to keep rubbing your eyes,"

Grossmann remembers. "This kid is twenty? No way."

Grossmann found Barry dynamic and, from the perspective of generating interest in a stock, exciting. Bob Grossmann is a sentient man. He knew he was living in the age of the yuppie entrepreneur, of vast riches amassed by single-minded young people before they reached the age of thirty. He was convinced that Barry, an evident workaholic and charismatic salesman, possessed that singleness of purpose. It was clear from Barry's hulk-like physical transformation. And Grossmann also understood that greed was in. Barry's message would go over.

But Grossmann is not the sort of man swayed merely by personality. While he appreciated the power of will, the things Barry said made huge sense to him. Particularly, it was the stuff about building the General Motors of the carpet-cleaning industry.

Grossmann knew, for example, that the service sector was the fastest-growing part of the U.S. economy, and that what he called "McDonaldsization" in many service industries was inevitable. Corner burger joints had long ago become multinational fast-food chains, and in outfits like Supercuts and Century 21, he had seen what big-time management, marketing and economies of scale had done in services as diverse as hair styling and home sales.

"There'd been a recent offering of a dry-cleaning company," he recalled, and America was just absolutely full of carpets. "Here a kid had picked an industry rife with mom-and-pop operations. It was compelling. The only thing was that the numbers were whacky."

Whacky numbers or a minor as chief executive were not the sort of things to stand in the way of Rooney, Pace. Grossmann's firm specialized in selling speculative securities for hot young companies like ZZZZ Best, and wasn't overwhelmingly scrupulous about which ones it brought to market. Sometimes these hot young companies took off, but other times they turned out to be full of hot air; eventually they shriveled and their shares crashed.

Front-line investment banking houses like Morgan Stanley & Co. or Goldman, Sachs & Co. would never consider selling a piddling amount of securities for a ridiculous company like Barry's. Rooney, Pace reveled in such deals. There's nothing wrong with selling stock for small companies. Lesser securities firms serve an important function in the marketplace. By making capital available to riskier ventures, they foster innovation, competition and new jobs. Unfortunately, Rooney, Pace wasn't nearly so noble. At the same time it was handling the ZZZZ Best underwriting, the firm was under siege by the SEC for sleazy dealings on other stocks it had brought to market.

In the case of Inteleplex Corp., for example, the prospectus conveniently failed to mention that 92 percent of the $5 million in revenue the company anticipated for the following year was contingent, meaning it might never materialize. In fact, according to the SEC the revenue never did materialize. But the Inteleplex case is also an example of the snail's pace at which the SEC usually works; the Inteleplex offering occurred in 1981, yet Rooney, Pace was wrangling with the SEC about it during 1986.

Rooney, Pace was battling with the SEC over two 1983 stock offerings at the same time, and separately, the firm was censured and then-president Randolph K. Pace was suspended for three months after the SEC accused the firm of fraudulently closing another 1981 stock deal. The punishment was stayed for a while pending an appeal that was later dismissed. Rooney, Pace had been censured before, in 1983, for failing to supervise an employee whom the SEC found to have manipulated stock and misled investors.

Worst of all, business was bad at Rooney, Pace in 1986. The firm was showing disappointing financial results and was beginning to suffer an exodus of key salesmen.

If Barry and Charbit were hoping to raise money in the stock market by selling additional ZZZZ Best shares, they had come to the right place. When savvy, perceptive Bob Grossmann told his superiors about ZZZZ Best and its young founder, Randy Pace stopped in Los Angeles and met with Barry personally en route to Hawaii for a vacation. He was favorably impressed. Two or three weeks later, during the summer of 1986, Barry and Charbit flew to a sweltering New York and met with Randy Pace; Howard Sterling, a lawyer who headed the Rooney, Pace corporate finance department; and Faith Griffin, a vice-president in the same department who arrived just after the meeting started.

Barry dominated this gathering the way he dominated every other meeting he ever attended. He was confident, dynamic and articulate, convincing about his ambitions for his company and himself. He talked for an hour about the ZZZZ Best carpet-cleaning business, and about how ZZZZ Best was also able to do a little very lucrative damage-restoration business thanks to Padgett and Interstate Appraisal. Carpet cleaning wasn't as profitable as restoration, he said, but the potential for expansion was vastly greater. Barry planned to open two new carpet-cleaning outlets every month.

Griffin thought Barry's age a little ridiculous at first, but as he talked she couldn't help being impressed. Griffin herself had started out in the securities business when she was twenty, and she had also had to struggle, not only because of her youth but because of her gender: except for secretaries, the industry in those days was almost exclusively male. Just as Barry had trouble borrowing because of his youth, Griffin had had trouble with lenders more interested in her husband's income than her own. She saw that Barry was cocky—he compared himself to Apple Computer founder Steve Jobs—but he clearly had the drive Griffin had come to see as indispensable to any really successful entrepreneur. Everybody present recognized Barry as an extraordinary personality. Griffin particularly respected his knowledge of his own business. Barry wasn't removed from it, the way executives at larger companies often can be. On the contrary, it was obvious from the way he talked that he knew everything there was to know about carpet.

After he told the little group about himself and his business, the discussion turned to money. Barry said he needed about $8 million to make his company grow. He projected that in the near term it would get half its revenue from carpet cleaning and half from restoration jobs. Randy Pace was excited about doing an underwriting—selling ZZZZ Best stock to the public, thereby earning a healthy fee—and felt his firm could market ZZZZ Best shares effectively. First, the nation was in the midst of a raging bull market in which everyone was stock crazy, and almost anything would sell. Beyond that, Barry seemed especially suited to Rooney, Pace (leaving aside the propensity of both for sleazy dealings). Rooney had a lot of young stockbrokers, for example. They could identify with Barry, and their enthusiasm would give the shares a boost. America's securities markets are a wondrous thing. Rooney, Pace decided to proceed. Griffin would handle the mechanics.

Faith Griffin is an intelligent, likably straightforward woman in her late thirties who prides herself on her independence and always seems to speak her mind. She does so in a voice made raspy by two packs of cigarettes a day—smoking is rare in boardrooms and executive suites these days—and she talks with a slight New England accent that adds a patrician element to the overall impression of toughness. She is busty, handsome and blunt, and she enjoys business. Despite the occasionally deceptive practices of Rooney, Pace, Faith has a strong moral compass. Falseness of any kind makes her apoplectic.

Theoretically, that should suit her to handling a public offering, which entails, among other things, figuring out all the relevant truths about a company, disclosing them in a prospectus that meets federal requirements and then taking people's money on the premise that the information is fair, accurate and holds promise for the future. Like Grossmann, Griffin is not someone who accepts things at face value. She is a skeptic. She needs to see proof. Of all people, Faith Griffin was assigned to lead ZZZZ Best through the arduous process of selling new stock to the public.

In the ensuing months, Barry never ceased to amaze his allegorically named investment banker. One of Griffin's functions, for example, was to shepherd him around to other investment firms to generate interest in his company. When he arrived at one, Barry would usually dazzle all concerned with his knowledge of carpets. Sometimes he would peer down a long corridor and announce the square footage. Once inside an office, Barry would get down on his hands and knees, size up the quantity and grade of floor-covering and tell his astonished listeners what it would cost to put in a better grade. About to deliver a presentation at the esteemed securities firm of Bear, Stearns & Co., Barry offered to fix the torn carpet in the corridor and shampoo every rug in the place, or better yet he would pick up the old stuff and replace it all. He could give them a price on the spot. Everyone was amazed by this kind of thing—Barry's ability to assess square footage at a glance made him seem almost an idiot savant—but since no one had a tape measure or an uncle in the carpet business, who knew if what he said made any sense?

Figuring things in his head was supposed to be Barry's great strength. He claimed a 30 percent gross profit margin on the restoration work because he supposedly could bid effectively and then buy cheaply by paying cash to carpet dealers. He seemed to know all the angles. He boasted of exploiting vague contracts that gave him room to maneuver—contracts calling for "earth-tone" carpeting, for example. "What's earth tone? Brown? Rust?" Barry would say. "Earth tone" meant he had the flexibility to seek out discontinued or out-of-favor shades that would still meet the contract specifications, thereby gaining a lower price on materials—and more profit for his company. It was all so plausible, so thoroughly well-imagined.

That was Barry's genius. Consider this book: you might guess that the author embellished a few things (he didn't). You might think that perhaps someone's real name was changed (it wasn't) or that the author himself is using a pseudonym (he's not) or that he even had a ghost-writer (nope). But would you ever guess in a million years that this volume, which says nonfiction on it somewhere and purports to be the truthful account of a widely reported series of events, that this *entire* volume is a complete fabrication? That Barry Minkow never existed, that no carpet-cleaning fraud occurred, that the publisher named on the binding never heard of this book, that the whole thing is a lie from the very first word?

You wouldn't think that, and you shouldn't. People trust reality, and they trust one another. Don't be fooled by all the crime and anomie you read about. The British empiricists lost out; doubting Thomases, they would sit around denying any basis for induction, insisting that because the sun rose today we can't assume it will rise tomorrow. Then they'd file out the door and down the stairs like everybody else, instead of jumping out the window, because something told them they'd go splat. So when we encounter someone, we assume a certain verisimilitude, a certain propriety. "This person isn't going to attack me with a meat cleaver," we think. Usually we're right. And while we might not go throwing money at them right away, we might if we thought we knew them, and if they could make us rich.

People felt Barry could do that for them. His imagination was so powerful that he created a version of reality as he went along, and people believed him and lived in it. The American dream, after all, is for most people a personal financial dream. Barry's vision was so strong he got caught up in it himself, so that ultimately it was his downfall. Barry is a great example of the ties between imagination and will—*Imagination plus determination equals success*, he would write on the blackboard at many of his motivational talks—and certainly Barry's will was extraordinary. No one could be more single-minded or more heedlessly dedicated to ends, however reprehensible the means. Barry had a deep inner discipline that contrasted vividly with his disheveled clothes and carelessness about details, and he was living evidence of his own message—that you can be whatever you want with hard work and imagination. Barry worked furiously, and his imagination was unsurpassed.

One of Barry's favorite claims was that ZZZZ Best was so successful because he was such an inspired motivator. He described a work stoppage once on the big Sacramento job, and how he flew up there, stood up on a beam or something, and gave such a stirring pep-talk that the workmen let out a whoop and threw themselves right back into their jobs. Barry could be this way, everyone saw it, and his tales were so seamless and persuasively delivered that people believed. Faith herself was convinced.

He amazed her even when he infuriated her, which happened often too. One of her earliest surprises came in the financial results for the quarter ended July 31, 1986. Contrary to Barry's earlier portrayal of the restoration jobs as secondary to the residential carpet-cleaning business, the July 31 numbers showed restoration work accounting for about 80 percent of the company's roughly $5 million in revenue.

That made ZZZZ Best an altogether different company. But by then things were moving briskly ahead. In August Griffin flew to Los Angeles to discuss the proposed offering further. She was going to talk turkey: terms, conditions, fees, etc. She also wanted to meet the rest of the company's management. When she got to Reseda, Barry hurriedly introduced her to Mark Morze, whom she regarded as one of the more presentable people associated with ZZZZ Best, and then told her he had another meeting coming up, and that he would see her later. Barry and Morze then did what they were known best for doing: they raced off to the bank. Griffin was left with Charbit, whom she disliked intensely, and a few other ZZZZ Best executives. The other managers weren't particularly impressive, but they were grossly underpaid even for high-level flunkies. Barry had sung the praises of his management team, yet he was the only person in the company making more than $60,000 a year. His own salary, as reported to the SEC, was $300,000.

Griffin complained that he wasn't giving his people good incentives to perform, and that if they were really so good someone else would hire them for more money. But Barry was reluctant to grant any raises. He liked keeping Arrington relatively poor, and knew that the executives who worked for him could never get such powerful-sounding positions anywhere else. Barry told Griffin he gave Chip a few bucks out of his own pocket now and then, and "took care of him" by treating Arrington and his wife to a first-class trip to Minneapolis to see relatives, for example. But Griffin recoiled from this as cheap, paternalistic and haphazard, and finally Barry acceded to her demands that he install a fairer and more formal compensation plan.

This was the sort of thing that was starting to produce friction between Barry and Griffin. Becoming a public company means you can't do things on the kitchen table anymore, or have your brother-in-law do your taxes, and Rooney, Pace's efforts to move ZZZZ Best in the direction of corporate maturity went beyond rationalizing executive compensation. From the outset, the investment bankers demanded that Barry hire a Big Eight accounting firm and a recognized firm of securities lawyers. The imprimatur of a nationally known auditor was vital to assure investors that the company's financial statements had passed some serious scrutiny. And the nation's securities laws are a thicket requiring specialized expertise. A single screw-up could cause the SEC to reject a proposed public offering, leaving everyone involved millions of dollars poorer. Rooney, Pace recommended the bicoastal law firm of Hughes Hubbard & Reed, which accepted the assignment to its everlasting rue.

Hughes Hubbard was a logical choice. Besides its reputation, experience and West Coast office, the 260-lawyer Wall Street firm had a strong connection at Rooney, Pace through Howard Sterling, who had been a senior partner in the firm of Rifkind, Sterling & Levine. Several former Rifkind attorneys had joined Hughes Hubbard, and one of the most respected, Mark R. Moskowitz, took on ZZZZ Best. A Brooklyn native, Moskowitz was based in Los Angeles and lived in the San Fernando Valley, not far from ZZZZ Best's headquarters. He was assisted by a bright young associate, Sharon Brodwin, whose honey-blonde hair and fresh-faced charm were irresistible to Barry.

As for the auditors, Barry put up a fight at first. He said he was very attached to George Greenspan, who was "like a father" to him. But Rooney, Pace insisted, explaining that there were still lots of things Greenspan could do for ZZZZ Best as long as the big boys— one of the major firms—were brought in to do the independent audit work. ZZZZ Best settled on Ernst & Whinney.

Ernst was glad to get the job. Almost all the Big Eight firms had opened offices in the San Fernando Valley, clustering in the Woodland Hills area, and competition for new audit business was stiff. Theoretically, at least, public companies don't "hire" an independent auditor, but rather "engage" one. The key word here is "independent." The auditor gets paid by the company, and certainly wants the company's business, but he supposedly performs a watchdog function that requires a certain arm's length relationship with the client. The audit firm decides on its own how it will go about checking the client's records and operations to prepare financial statements in accord with generally accepted accounting principles, or GAAP. If things don't add up or key questions can't be answered, the auditors issue a "qualified opinion," a very bad thing which means there is some area of uncertainty about the business at hand.

Since Barry was as desperate for cash as ever, around August of 1986 he asked Rooney, Pace to put together a private placement to finance some major contracts he supposedly wanted to bid on. Barry's grasp of all this impressed everyone as nothing short of remarkable; his capacity for learning by osmosis was spongelike. In a private placement, funds are raised privately, with the result that such a deal can be done quickly and easily, with far fewer disclosure requirements than a public stock offering. Speed was of the essence. Barry said he needed the money in a hurry.

To tide him over, Rooney, Pace raised $1.5 million privately in September, placing a debt-warrant package with some of the firm's more substantial customers. The debt consisted of notes bearing interest at 10 percent, payable in a year or when the stock offering was complete, whichever came first. The notes carried the added incentive of warrants, which gave their holders the right to buy ZZZZ Best stock at a given price. If the stock should go up, the warrantholders would make money.

Carrying out the public offering now became the focus of Rooney, Pace's attention. Like any underwriter, its main job was to get a solid new security to market, deliver the cash to ZZZZ Best and keep a cut for itself. It was the lawyers' job to write the prospectus, the bible of the offering.

Modern securities regulation in this country was born of the Great Depression and delivered by Franklin Delano Roosevelt during his first term as president. The system is based entirely on disclosure. When a company wants to sell shares to the public, it must write up a booklet for potential investors revealing all sorts of financial and other information—anything "material" to the company. Hitler, Stalin and Pol Pot can serve in senior management as long as genocide is duly disclosed in the section giving biographical data on the top executives. The idea is that by making a company disclose all the relevant information about itself (other than trade secrets), investors can make an informed judgment without the government cramping up the marketplace. You can't issue a prospectus without first getting approval from the SEC, but that agency only reviews the document to make sure all the basic questions are answered. It doesn't pass judgment on whether or not the securities are a good deal.

Prospectus-writing has risen over the years to a high plane of artful pettifoggery. The prospectus always describes the company and says how much money the company wants and why. Risks are usually emphasized. Everything in that prospectus is supposed to be true, or the people responsible can at least theoretically get into serious trouble. The result is that expensive lawyers in classy suits insert sentences like, "These securities entail a high degree of risk. There can be no assurance that the sun will rise tomorrow, or that the force of gravity, on which the company and all other earthly life depend, will not cease to exist."

The ZZZZ Best prospectus was carefully prepared by a team of capable and experienced professionals who produced what is probably among the most fraudulent public-offering documents since the basic U.S. securities laws were adopted. The financial statements were cooked, the assets overstated, the main source of revenue nonexistent and the sleazy backgrounds of Barry's partners and advisers mostly omitted.

Actually, some of Barry's partners were starting to realize that a person who would sell his mother to the devil to succeed might just as easily do the same to them. Barry was always eager to pal around with Rind, Schulman and Victor, and in July Rind and Schulman lent him $250,000 interest-free. But they were starting to sour on their young friend. Richie was disgusted to attend a ZZZZ Best function and watch Barry conduct a kind of loyalty catechism with one of his managers.

"If I asked you to lick the highway from San Diego to Los Angeles, your tongue on the road the whole way, would you do it?" Barry demanded.

"Yes!" the manager responded enthusiastically.

Rind and Schulman were also unhappy about the public offering. Rind considered Rooney, Pace "a sleazy fucking company," and Harold Fischman, the attorney, said he could line up a major underwriter after another year of solid earnings.

"You're too slow for me," Barry told Fischman and Rind point-blank in his office. "I've come to another level. You guys aren't in my league anymore. I'm twice as smart as both of you put together."

Barry, Moe and Richie patched things up a couple of weeks later; they needed one another too much to do otherwise. But Schulman and Rind were in no position to interfere with the public offering, which moved ahead despite their opposition.

How this happened is a testament to Barry's brazenness, on the one hand, and the motivating powers of money, on the other. Barry is one of those rare, remorseless souls who is able to match his enormous imaginative will with the true neurotic's piercing insight into human nature, and this insight helped him enormously not just in manipulating the collection of hyperactive flakes he drew to himself, but also in handling the heavyweights he was starting to encounter in the world of high finance. Barry always seemed to know instantly what a person needed, and to be able to provide it on the spot. Often it was money, or an impressive car, or a fancy house to live in. But even more often, given the kind of people who were drawn to him, it was something else: a pretty girl, a feeling of importance, a sense of community, maybe just a little hope. Paramount was a feeling of belonging, of being part of something impressive.

"When you see him play people, you think you're watching Heifetz playing a violin," says Morze. Ron Spencer, a technician at KHJ-TV in Los Angeles, says Barry was so charismatic that when camera crews were dispatched to do stories on him, some came back and bought stock. "Even after the thing was breaking, he was so sure and strong, they bought *more* stock. The guys said, "You can't lose, this guy's going places.' He was that impressive."

The mediocre, the disaffected and life's all-around losers were Barry's perfect prey, but so were the greedy, the good and the gullible. Almost everybody would come around sooner or later.

Mark Moskowitz, for example, is a brilliant lawyer experienced at leading clients on a steady path through the jungle of the financial markets. "A tiger," one investment banker calls him, and quite honest. Short, round-faced and balding, he is a Harvard Law School graduate with a fetish for precision whose specialty is the lucrative field of securities law. He was a brilliant student, edited the *Harvard Law Review*, and later taught securities law. Born in 1946, he is in his prime, and he performs his job with manic dedication. Moskowitz must have been wary of Barry at first, but he soon developed an almost brotherly attachment to his dynamic new client. Barry confided that his great early success had made him long for the childhood he had never had, and before long he was baby-sitting the Moskowitz children, becoming especially close to his lawyer's eldest son. He impressed all the Moskowitzes with his warmth and sincerity, and there was talk of Barry and Mark buying adjoining ranches in Chatsworth, at the furthest fringes of the Valley. Moskowitz staked his good name on his young friend; he even bought 25,000 shares of ZZZZ Best for a $50,000 IOU. When Barry handed him a trophy at a ZZZZ Best awards banquet, the two men hugged and Moskowitz looked like he was going to cry.

13

Sharon Brodwin's job was tough for all the wrong reasons. She was supposed to talk to the various people at ZZZZ Best to get the information needed for the prospectus and SEC filings. Companies like ZZZZ Best agree in writing that everything they tell the Sharon Brodwins of the world is true and complete, but just to be on the safe side, a big-league accounting firm does an audit, and the lawyers take some steps to satisfy themselves as well. The checking is called "due diligence," and since ZZZZ Best was a complete fraud, gathering the information or carrying out due diligence should have been the hard part.

Instead, the hard part for Brodwin was that Barry slobbered all over her. During meetings he would take off his shoes and throw them at her under the table with his feet, or he would drape himself over her when she was taking notes. Brodwin was becoming increasingly unnerved and finally appealed to Griffin, who had seen this side of Barry before. She urged Brodwin to take her complaints to Moskowitz, and if necessary refuse to work with Barry until things changed. Early on Griffin herself had slammed the door on Barry's attempts to sweet-talk her, and she had also noticed Barry's leering fascination with Charbit's pretty French wife. Barry was even sending roses to a junior associate of Griffin's. Once at a meeting Barry sat with his fly open and his legs spread, until finally Griffin demanded, "Shove it in your pants, shove it in your briefcase, but don't put it on the table!"

Barry didn't always strike out. On the contrary, he slept with many young women, and his appetite for them was legendary, perhaps enhanced by the steroids he took. Sherrie Maloney, his adoring secretary, eagerly arranged dates, sent flowers and signed cards, partly because she thought this is what a good secretary should do, and partly because she disliked Barry's girlfriend, Joyce, and considered her unworthy. Maloney regarded Barry as a son and was jealous of Joyce and of Barry's real mother, both of whom she regarded as having certain unfortunate qualities in common. Joyce knew about Barry's infidelities, but seemed to object only when her nose was rubbed in them. She even benefited by them. One Sunday Barry's wealthy neighbor across the way, Robert D. Byers, was startled to see him appear frantically at the front door.

"Rob, I need your wife's Mercedes," Barry pleaded.

"Sure, go ahead and take it."

"You don't understand. I don't want to borrow it. I need to buy the car for Joyce. She just came home and found me in bed with a couple of other women."

Byers promptly sold him the $42,000 car. "The next day, Joyce was driving it and she seemed very satisfied," neighbor Janet Polevoi later testified. A couple of months later Barry bought her Byers' Porsche. He also gave Joyce plenty of pocket money and expensive jewelry, bought her a closetful of clothes and lent her father $25,000. To make sure of her fidelity, Barry hired a private investigator at one point to follow her around.

Once Barry sent Joyce off on a Hawaiian vacation and then had another woman over almost as soon as she left. When his date arrived she was dazzled to be served an elaborate meal by Jack and Jerry Polevoi, near-identical twins dressed up in tuxedos. Jack worked for Barry and lived two doors down in the Westchester County complex.

When Barry had guests, Joyce sometimes acted like a servant herself. Griffin dined at Barry's house once. Joyce cooked and served but didn't eat or even sit down, and other visitors report the same experience. Griffin asked Barry about it. "Oh, she's busy," he'd said. "She's got homework."

Barry's attitude toward women wasn't particularly different from his attitude toward everyone else: they were objects to be used, and they could be bought when needed. He didn't like talking to them, or dancing with them, or going out on dates. All he loved was what women could do for him. "Barry's idea of great sex was to come home at nine-thirty, have sex until nine forty-five and be asleep by ten P.M.," one friend says. "He always complained that Joyce wanted to talk. He couldn't stand it."

Barry often was loathed by the spouses of men who had already fallen under his influence, yet the women in Barry's inner circle all fell completely under his spell. Aside from his own mother, none was more devoted or protective or compliant than Maloney, who would do practically anything for Barry. By this time she was merrily typing phony letters on Travelers Insurance stationery, to which Barry would forge Padgett's signature. She would occasionally deliver cash, too, and every day she watched as Barry crossed off dates and amounts on his precious desk calendar, which he used to keep track of who was due what when.

As much as Griffin resented Barry's treatment of women, and as skeptical as she was of his company, she nevertheless helped him grow richer. She did so unwillingly; it didn't take long before her initial warmth toward him dissipated, familiarity in this case breeding much contempt on both sides. Barry grew to hate Griffin because he couldn't handle such a hard-nosed woman, and also because she was making his life miserable. For example, when Griffin learned that all the accounting for the restoration work was being handled outside the company by Mark Morze, she demanded that it immediately be brought in-house and that Ernst & Whinney pick a big job and audit every scrap of paper and every penny of expenditures and revenue associated with it. When Morze said he had all the documents in a shoebox in his garage, she demanded that the auditors review only *original* documents, checking every payable and every receivable. Barry was outraged and threatened to fire Ernst & Whinney, but there was really nothing he could do, because he desperately needed the money that a successful stock offering would raise. And who else but Rooney, Pace would take such a ramshackle company public?

Griffin also insisted that every check carry two signatures instead of one, that an in-house controller be hired, and that the company undertake no more joint ventures without approval from its board of directors. These precautions were basically futile. In July ZZZZ Best did hire Andersen, a CPA with a strong background in computers, but he followed orders and Barry retained control of the checkbook. The board of directors was no help at all. Besides Barry, who was chairman, the other directors were Daniel Krowpman Sr., who participated in the fraud; Joyce's father Harold Lipman; Hal Berman, Barry's former weight-lifting instructor; Neal Dem, a stationery and gifts manufacturer who owned the building ZZZZ Best rented for its generators; and Vera Hojecki, whose previous experience was in telephone sales.

Rooney, Pace was unperturbed by this motley collection of trustees, but it was disturbed that ZZZZ Best had pledged Charbit a total fee of about $520,000 in May for his fund-raising on behalf of the company. The National Association of Securities Dealers regulates underwriting fees, and Rooney, Pace worried that Charbit's, on top of Rooney, Pace's standard 10 percent plus expenses, would be too high. Rooney, Pace wasn't about to take less, so the payments to Charbit were delayed and spaced out. When he persisted in meddling, an exasperated Griffin finally just blew up. "Get out!" she yelled at a meeting one day. "Get out and don't come back!"

Charbit should have counted himself lucky. The underwriting process involves endless meetings, including interminable "all-hands" sessions in which the lawyers, accountants, investment bankers and so forth shut themselves up in a conference room all day, order in for food when they get hungry and try to hammer out an S-1, the detailed SEC filing that will contain the prospectus and other relevant documents.

For Barry to go through all this rigmarole must have required him to plumb the depths of his self-discipline. He did not go quietly. One of his most painful experiences during the whole process was having to turn down an invitation to appear on "The Tonight Show" with Johnny Carson. Barry was just dying to do it, but the lawyers were adamant; there is a "quiet period" before an offering becomes effective, when a company and its executives must be very careful not to seem that they're hyping the stock. All the information is supposed to come from the prospectus. But Barry never came to resent the lawyers the way he did Faith Griffin. "Hey, can't you get that bitch off my back?" he would plead to Bob Grossmann. Barry even called Randy Pace, her boss, to assert that Griffin was ruining his business, but Pace, to his credit, never interfered.

On the contrary, the more Griffin looked, the more she wanted to know. She took the not-altogether-unusual step of having a private investigator look into several of the ZZZZ Best principals, to no particular avail, and she and Grossmann kept asking to visit the major restoration job sites. Barry always said, "No problem."

But Barry actually had plenty of problems. As if he didn't have his hands full fooling the world and keeping Faith Griffin at bay, Barry also had to keep Morze and Padgett on an even keel.

Morze was fast becoming a nervous wreck. By now he realized the full scope of the fraud, and was terrified of getting caught, but he lived on the hope that the offering would succeed and ZZZZ Best could then sidle over into legitimacy. "Let's only worry about what we can control," Barry would say soothingly, and Morze would calm down a little. His condition was aggravated by sleep deprivation and too much caffeine, a stimulant which he knew from experience he couldn't handle comfortably. As a result, he was tense and irritable all day. Morze was having trouble sleeping anyway, because he was so worried. He drank coffee because he was always having to stay up all night creating the impeccable forgeries that Barry depended on. The lawyers and accountants and bankers were driving him crazy with requests for records, and since there were no authentic documents, Morze had to create them.

"There were nights when I looked like the Pillsbury Doughboy, I had so much 'Wite-Out' on me," he recalls. Other times he likened himself to the abominable snowman, noting that despite Griffin's demands, "No one in the restoration end of it *ever* saw an original document. They always got Xeroxes."

But the quality of his work was truly exceptional. Bank statements, checks, invoices, contracts, whatever was needed would spring forth from Morze's clever hands. It was really artistic, and Arrington later testified that Morze actually had the help of an artist—his sister Minta (although she was never indicted and no other proof of her involvement has been revealed). Morze had many long meetings with Barry to plot tactics and strategy, and these usually ended in gales of laughter as exhaustion and absurdity finally overtook the two of them. As anxious as he might have been, Morze managed to muddle through.

Padgett was a special problem. Barry and Morze both considered him crazy—he has seen *Platoon* nine times—and Barry told him that when dealing with Jews he should turn his gold ring around so the swastika wouldn't show. At one time or another Padgett headed the Los Angeles Odinist Fellowship, which he likens to a Norse version of the Black Muslims. The fellowship worships Odin. "When I first tumbled into this, it was like an ancestral memory," says Padgett, who was baptized a Methodist. "This is in my genes." Thus the ring, a solid gold casting of Odin complete with winged helmet and ruby eyes. On one side is a swastika, and on the other the dual lightning bolts of the Waffen S.S. Padgett says these are Viking runes. Morze, who shocked and revolted Padgett by sleeping with a black woman, saw a picture of Hitler in Padgett's office.

The trouble now was that Padgett was in love.

Like many people, Tom Padgett made the same mistake in this department twice. He was wildly in love with a slender, pretty young woman named Debbie in 1976, lost her and was devastated. As if joining the French Foreign Legion, Padgett re-entered the military. Now history was repeating itself. To Padgett, the Debbie working in his outer office at Interstate Appraisal was practically a clone of the earlier one—same name, same looks, same sort of person. Unfortunately, there was more or less the same outcome. He was insanely enamored of her, but this Debbie had another man. Padgett might have stood it if his rival were a sensitive, intellectual type. But Debbie's boyfriend Nick was a handsome and muscular martial arts expert who was bigger and perhaps ten years younger than Padgett. So on top of everything else, he felt himself out-machoed.

If there is a focus to all of Padgett's sprawling paranoia, it is his manhood, and it didn't help when he heard that Debbie supposedly preferred her new boyfriend because she considered Nick more manly. Faced with losing Debbie, Padgett did what anyone else in his shoes might do. He went nuts.

He would wake up at six A.M. and start out with a six-pack, deteriorating further as the day—and the drinking—progressed. Padgett laid aside his insurance studies, bought some books on investigative techniques and launched an anonymous terror campaign against Debbie's suitor. He made so many threatening phone calls that the guy finally had to leave his apartment.

As for Interstate and the ZZZZ Best scam, Padgett lost the will to keep up. One Friday in July, he realized that Debbie was preparing to quit, and he spent the weekend in drunken despair. Sure enough, on Monday she resigned, saying she had another job, but Padgett was convinced her boyfriend made her leave. That night Padgett slept in the office, and then went home to his apartment in Hollywood for an early-morning six-pack. Later he began wandering the streets with a loaded gun, just looking for trouble, which is normally relatively easy to find in Hollywood.

If Padgett was almost deranged with despondency, Barry was absolutely frantic that Padgett would do something stupid—such as shooting his rival for Debbie's affection—and thereby destroy ZZZZ Best. Barry and Morze did everything they could to prop up their colleague—Barry's perspective was that no woman was worth it—but Padgett was just hanging on by his fingernails.

The man who may have saved him—and thus saved Barry—was Mark Moran Roddy, a voraciously appetitive albino whom Padgett had met through Sandra. Roddy occasionally dated her.

Gradually, he and Padgett became phone friends, and during the depths of Padgett's despair over Debbie, Roddy took to calling virtually every night, often talking with his friend for two solid hours. For a while Barry really worried that Padgett would crack up altogether, but Padgett is a born follower, and his leader finally managed to say something that had an effect. Barry told Padgett that the only way to deal with the whole thing—and to have any hope of getting Debbie back—was to pull himself together, if only to prove to her that he *could* pull himself together. "Show her what you can make of yourself," Barry urged. "Show her what she's missing."

Barry and Morze were relieved to see that Padgett seemed to be coming around. He was drinking less, immersing himself again in the insurance business, and most important, starting to look like someone they could once again rely on.

Roddy was about to rely on Padgett as well. After listening since perhaps February as Padgett poured out his soul over the phone, the two men changed roles. On Saturday, August 30, 1986, Roddy was arrested by the federal Drug Enforcement Agency in Albuquerque, where he had been staying at the Marriott Hotel under an assumed name. He was charged with possession of more than a kilogram of cocaine with intent to distribute, as well as aiding and abetting and interstate travel in aid of racketeering.

Released on bail, Roddy called Padgett and laid things out. He was unemployed, he was facing serious narcotics charges, he didn't have much money and life was just generally a bitch. Padgett was filled with sympathy. When Barry asked him to fly out to Oklahoma during the week of October 6 and take some pictures of the flood damage the state had lately suffered, Padgett recalled that Roddy had spent some time in Tulsa and figured he'd take his friend along. Padgett introduced Barry to Roddy on the telephone, and Barry agreed to pay both their expenses for the trip. Padgett and Roddy spent about a week in Oklahoma, and had a great time. They shot roll after roll of flood-damage photos.

Delighted, Barry soon got to meet Roddy in person, and at the appointed hour found himself staring at two of the strangest-looking men he had come across in quite some time. Roddy was big, fat and milky-looking, with white hair and pinkish white skin. He brought with him an utterly emaciated accountant named Norman Rothberg who seemed to consist entirely of a hawklike nose and large, even teeth. Everything about Rothberg was gray, including his skin. The two men made a strange pair. They seemed as opposite emotionally as they were physically. Roddy was gregarious, Rothberg retiring. The only thing they seemed to have in common was their thick eyeglasses.

Roddy and Rothberg actually had a little more in common. Rothberg was a certified public accountant and law school graduate who had worked as a field auditor for the IRS during the 1960s. More recently, he and Roddy had worked together in a futile effort to raise money for a couple of screwy business ventures, and they figured they'd try to interest Barry in one of their deals. Rothberg in particular was hoping something would turn up. He had just gone through a divorce and was so broke he was about to be evicted from his apartment.

Barry announced that he would lend Roddy the money for none other than Arthur Barens, who had represented Barry during his contacts with federal authorities over Catain. Barry also hired Roddy for $500 a week in cash to help Padgett at Interstate Appraisal, and then told Rothberg to set up the books at Interstate, for which Mark Morze paid him $1,000 cash and a $2,000 check. Barry later sent Barens $16,000 on behalf of Roddy.

Like many of the players in the tragicomedy of ZZZZ Best, Mark Roddy was big, strange, funny, fast and dishonest in a breezy, guilt-free sort of way. Born in 1951, he is about the same age as Padgett and Morze, and is yet another of the hyperactive types that Barry routinely managed to attract. (The affinities between these men are a little scary. Mark Morze and Tom Padgett were even born on the same day: October 14, 1950.) Roddy is described by two of his friends as a thoroughly manic rogue who is fun to be around but insensitive to the consequences of his actions. He will make an appointment and then never show up, or leave a friend with a $15,000 telephone bill. He would pay his respects at his mother's grave and then swipe some flowers from the cemetery for his date later that evening. Roddy loves beautiful women, fine food and expensive clothes, and when he has money he spends it freely on the high life he so enjoys. He used to take Padgett down to the bar in some fancy hotel, pick out a couple of women and tell them he and his companion were in the movie business: "You saw *The Color Purple*, didn't you? I financed it."

Hypersensitive to sunlight, which could be lethal to him, Roddy is a fanatical movie buff who liked to spend sunny days at multiplex theaters, sneaking from one picture to another just for the fun of it. Those who know him say that, like Barry, he could charm the skin off a snake if he set his mind to it. Physically powerful but not violent,

Roddy has a keen mind and plays a tough game of chess, but he never finished college. He is a master of trivia with a great facility for names and numbers, an inveterate gambler and an unregenerate prankster. One friend recalls driving down the Hollywood Freeway at 100 miles an hour with Roddy behind the wheel.

"Listen Mark, you're gonna lose your license driving this way."

"They can't take my license away."

"Oh no? Why not?"

"Because I don't have one."

"What?! What happened to your license?"

"They'd never give me one. See, I'm blind."

Roddy wasn't entirely sightless, but his pupils quivered enough so that reading and driving were difficult. With his white beard and great girth, Roddy strongly resembles Santa Claus. His sister is a psychologist, and at Christmas he used to dress up in a Santa suit and hand out gifts to mental patients.

Roddy was the consummate wheeler-dealer. Before Barry met him, he was in the commodities business, but he has also dabbled in pay phones, energy, Christmas trees, real estate and candy. Generally, he would buy and sell anything to make money. Herb Weit, Roddy's former lawyer and roommate, says Roddy wasn't really an active drug dealer, but that he was caught in Albuquerque with six kilos of cocaine hidden in an air-conditioning duct. Roddy had run afoul of the law before; in 1979 he was sentenced to sixty days in jail and three years' probation on an amphetamines charge, and he did some more jail time in 1983. A judge once sentenced him to some Alcoholics Anonymous meetings.

Roddy was an important addition to Barry's coterie, because he could provide help where it was most needed—with Tom Padgett.

Even at his best, Padgett was no criminal mastermind. Interstate Appraisal was a sham that needed to look real, but Padgett never even established secure banking or credit relationships for it. Here was a company supposedly giving ZZZZ Best millions in new business, and Dun & Bradstreet, the credit-reporting firm, had no record of it. For a while Interstate had a paltry account at Valley National Bank in Van Nuys; when Rooney, Pace wanted to see a bank statement, Padgett was in trouble. His statements from Valley National would show minute balances and little activity, instead of the thriving insurance-adjusting firm they were supposed to reflect. So while Barry and Padgett were driving along in Barry's BMW, Barry picked up the carphone and called a woman Padgett knew on the bank's staff.

"Hey, Lynn, this is Tom Padgett, how you doing?" Barry said heartily.

Padgett could barely contain himself as Barry persuaded her to write a letter attesting to some innocent facts, such as how long Interstate Appraisal had been with the bank and its typical balance. Morze later doctored it, typing in a high balance, for example, to impress Rooney, Pace and make Interstate Appraisal into a cherished Valley National customer. Actually, Valley National soon grew suspicious of all the fishy activity in the Interstate Appraisal account, which customarily had a balance of, say, $80, but would occasionally swell to $180,000, all of it withdrawn the very next day. A couple of checks bounced and the bank closed the account, leaving Padgett and Roddy to scramble for a replacement. The result was that for a while when the bankers and lawyers were scrutinizing ZZZZ Best for the upcoming public offering, the company that was giving ZZZZ Best 86 percent of its business didn't even have a bank account.

To remedy this potentially fatal oversight, Padgett and Roddy tried Trans World Bank, also in Van Nuys. Trans World asked for their business-registration statement. This document, filed with the county clerk and known as a "d/b/a," or "doing business as," still showed the name of Michael Vecksler, Padgett's original partner, because no one ever got around to filing a new one. Things were getting desperate; Barry was screaming that Interstate Appraisal just *had* to have a bank. Padgett and Roddy decided to dash downtown for a new d/b/a, but for some reason they were using a borrowed compact with a stick shift, which Padgett knew how to drive only theoretically. The trip was maddening. They sputtered and lurched along in traffic, cursing, sweating, stalling and so thoroughly aggravated that Padgett split the dashboard by pounding it in frustration. Eventually they got the Trans World account—but it was soon closed too, thanks to five large, rubber checks. Barry, near despair, finally sent Padgett to see Bob Turnbow, his boyhood banking friend, at Sterling Bank.

Despite their antics, Padgett and Roddy made a good team. Both would do almost anything, and they shared a sense of humor about what they were up to. Padgett tried to get Roddy interested in racist politics, and through another ZZZZ Best sham company, Roddy gave a little money to Metzger's White American Political Association. Like Padgett, Roddy was above all an outsider, mocked as a child and noticeable wherever he went. Weit says money had no meaning to him except as a way of getting in, and the same was probably true of Padgett. Like Mark Morze, they were clever and a little manic, down on their luck when Barry found them, and displaced persons generally, without wives, children or satisfying careers.

Barry was a master at making people feel important when in many cases defeat and disaster had been their main accomplishments before. It's odd and distasteful how often the people around Barry compare him to Jim Jones, who led a mass suicide in Guiana, or even to Hitler. Barry wasn't really like those men, and to blur such distinctions is a pernicious habit of mind that reduces the importance of everything. But he had that one quality: the ability to make people believe.

14

Barry and his friends had hoped the ZZZZ Best stock offering would be complete in the fall of 1986, but when the fall rolled around and evenings in the Valley finally began to cool, it was clear that the cash was still weeks away. This realization brought on another crisis. The Ponzi scheme had to be fed. Where was the money to come from?

Barry rounded up the usual suspects. In September, he called Perry Morris Corp., claiming he needed to lease still more Cornwell equipment. Bill Dolby, a former minor-league pitcher who was handling the ZZZZ Best account at Perry Morris, remembers that Barry was in a tremendous hurry this time. Proud of its reputation for efficiency, Morris quickly handed Krowpman and his company $250,000. After all, ZZZZ Best had a terrific payment record, and everybody was impressed with Barry. Over the coming months, ZZZZ Best and Perry Morris developed a beautiful relationship. Morris laid out another $200,000 or $300,000 to buy a bunch of electrical generators it would lease to a ZZZZ Best subsidiary. Morris also spent $40,000 or $50,000 to buy computers for lease to ZZZZ Best. Some of this equipment actually might have been real.

Also during October, Barry told Pavia and McHugh of FFC, another leasing company, that he had landed a big restoration project in Goleta, California, which presented another golden investment opportunity for them. FFC promptly put up $200,000.

Peter Strauss, who had done well with Barry and grown very fond of him, lent ZZZZ Best another $1 million at 10 percent interest, plus warrants entitling him to buy 175,000 shares at $2.00 per share. Strauss's experience with the company weighed heavily with

Grossmann. Strauss was a sophisticated investor who wasn't addicted to OPM, and he had always scored with ZZZZ Best. As it turned out, the investors who kicked in the $1.5 million for the private placement were able to do likewise, given the company's stock performance for a while.

Another natural thought for Barry was First Interstate Bank. ZZZZ Best had been paying the bank on time, and so Barry talked to Steve Monchamp again. But Monchamp was insistent: unless First Interstate could visit some job sites, it wasn't willing to lend without Strauss's guarantee. In early October Barry said he'd like Monchamp to come and work for him. A week later they had dinner, and Monchamp soon quit his $35,000-a-year bank job for one paying $47,500 (plus bonus and $500 a month for a car) at ZZZZ Best.

Meanwhile Barry arranged a meeting with Monchamp's boss, Richard Motika, to discuss additional borrowing. It was the first week of October, and Barry was piloting his white BMW through rustic-looking Coldwater Canyon to reach the Beverly Hills office of First Interstate. Driving with Barry was an adventure; his friends had first-hand experience of his lengthy motor-vehicle record. He once borrowed neighbor Rob Byers' brand-new Cadillac and banged it up so badly he finally had to buy the thing.

Padgett, in the passenger seat beside him, knew that today they were going to a vitally important meeting.

"Listen, Tom, are you over Debbie yet?"

Padgett said no. In fact he was still making anonymous phone calls to her boyfriend.

"Look," Barry said, "Ken Pavia's thinking of selling his house in Newport Beach. How about if I buy it for you?"

Padgett was flabbergasted. Pavia had a beautiful house on the ocean, and Debbie had said she always wanted a beach house. Padgett told Barry that would be fantastic.

When they arrived at First Interstate, Barry, Padgett and Morze tried to persuade Motika and another bank executive to lend ZZZZ Best more money without Strauss's guarantee. (They didn't say that one of the reasons they needed the money was to repay Strauss.) Motika really wanted to help. An intelligent Navy veteran who joined the bank in 1975, he found Barry "a dynamic young person" with "vision" and "charisma." First Interstate preferred not to rely on third-party guarantors like Strauss anyway. So the bankers tried to satisfy themselves that ZZZZ Best and its principals were a really good risk.

"Is Interstate Appraisal bonded?" they asked.

"Sure," Morze replied.

"Okay, could we get the name of your bonding company?"

"Well, we got a little problem there," said Padgett, thinking fast. "A lot of times the bonding comes through the insurance company. But if you guys wait a week, I'll get hold of some people and you can talk to one of my bonding companies."

Barry and his friends also showed the photographs Padgett and Roddy had taken in Oklahoma, but Motika was most interested in visiting a ZZZZ Best restoration site. Barry wouldn't budge; the confidentiality rule was hard and fast. As a result, he didn't come away with any money, but it looked like progress had been made. Later, Barry and Morze hurriedly incorporated Liberty Western Bonding and rented a suite on Wilshire Boulevard, where many insurance companies have their offices. Then Padgett gave the name of Liberty to First Interstate. When the bankers phoned, their call was forwarded to Morze, who posed as a Liberty executive and assured them that Interstate Appraisal had been bonded for some time with no problems. When First Interstate asked for a copy of an actual bond, Morze had to create one from a thirty-year-old library book.

First Interstate was being finicky, but the public offering was moving ahead. The amount to be raised had already been increased to $13.2 million, from the $8 million Barry originally requested. Rooney, Pace planned to sell 1.1 million ZZZZ Best units at $12 each. Each unit was a package of three common shares and a single warrant enabling the holder to buy another share of ZZZZ Best common from the company at $5 between September 9, 1987, and December 15, 1989, when the warrants would expire.

While the prospectus was being drafted, Barry was supposed to tell Rooney, Pace about anything relevant to his business or any shady characters that had been associated with it. He was also supposed to disclose any lawsuits. Yet that October, in the middle of the underwriting process, one of the Rooney, Pace lawyers talked to a friend at one of Barry's former banks. The lawyer, Mark Klein, asked a question: Why didn't they bank Barry anymore? The banker couldn't exactly say, but he disclosed on deep background that the bank's records relating to ZZZZ Best had been subpoenaed.

Barry was still haunted by Jack Catain. When it all came out, Griffin, who happened to be in Los Angeles, was like the wrath of God. Barry showed up late for a meeting, and when he walked in she started screaming. "You lied to us! How could you do this? What else is there you haven't told us about?"

Barry was mortified; it had been some time since anyone had addressed him that way publicly, and Griffin kept at it until finally Moskowitz, the lawyer, stepped in. He took Barry aside and talked to him privately for about an hour, after which he reported that Barry was deeply embarrassed but had been a victim, had fallen into Catain's clutches as a very young man and had thought the whole thing was over with. Catain was already under indictment. Arthur Barens bore all this out; Barry had been a victim and was cooperating with federal authorities in their investigation of the mobster. All that was necessary was to disclose Catain and his lawsuit in the prospectus.

On October 29, ZZZZ Best announced that it had filed a registration statement with the SEC for its upcoming securities offering by Rooney, Pace. ZZZZ Best also announced a 1-for-2 reverse split of its common stock effective the next day. The move would cut the 15.5 million ZZZZ Best shares in half while doubling their value. The result would be a $4 stock after the offering, instead of a $2 stock. Investors don't like very low-priced stocks, the exchanges have certain rules for listing and some underwriters won't even take part if the stock doesn't sell for a certain minimum per share.

Finally, in the same press release the company announced sharply higher sales and profits for the year ended April 30, 1986—the figures Greenspan audited—and the unaudited quarter ended July 31 of the same year. These figures were also contained in Rooney, Pace's preliminary prospectus, known as a "red herring" for the red type on the cover warning of the document's tentativeness. One of Barry's lawyers said later that as the prospectus was being printed, Barry stood by and juggled oranges while wearing a Ronald Reagan mask.

The prospectus described a company experiencing explosive growth. Revenue seemed to increase exponentially, from $575,117 in the twelve months ended April 30, 1984, to $1.24 million the following year, to $4.85 million the next.

The profit picture was equally attractive. Pre-tax profit was $152,192 in the twelve months ended April 30, 1984, a mere bag of shells compared to what lay ahead: $357,814 in the following year, and $1.81 million the year after that.

ZZZZ Best's performance during the three months ended July 31, its fiscal first quarter, was absolutely eye-popping. Revenue was an astounding $5.4 million—more than the entire preceding year! more than *eight* times revenue in the year-ago first quarter! And profits! Profits before taxes were $1.83 million, again exceeding the entire previous year and outstripping the year-ago quarter by eight times.

ZZZZ Best was unbelievable—literally. But too many people wanted to believe, even though the red herring was filled with red flags: for example, although ZZZZ Best was known as a carpet-cleaning concern and planned to use much of the offering proceeds to open new cleaning outlets, 86 percent of its business in the most recent quarter came from insurance restoration contracts. And all of these were assigned by a single customer, who wasn't identified until the SEC insisted that Interstate Appraisal be named in the final version of the prospectus.

ZZZZ Best was also deep in hock, although this wasn't entirely reflected on the balance sheet because much of its borrowing occurred after July 31, when the first quarter ended. Nevertheless, buried in the prospectus was the disclosure that the company's short-term borrowings exceeded $6.2 million, on top of nearly $1 million in long-term debt. Stockholders' equity—assets minus liabilities—was a mere $3.1 million by comparison. (These numbers were bogus too; short-term debt was much higher, and stockholders' equity was nonexistent.)

The prospectus also disclosed the lawsuit by Catain, his usurious lending and Barry's cooperation with the federal investigation. On top of everything else, ZZZZ Best was entirely dependent on Barry, who the prospectus says was all of twenty years old. "Although the Company has a $2,000,000 insurance policy on the life of Mr. Minkow, which the Company intends to increase to $5,000,000, his loss would have a materially adverse effect" on ZZZZ Best, the prospectus says.

ZZZZ Best's enormous debt load, the company's utter dependence on a single customer, Barry's ridiculous youth and his dealings with a mobster all should have raised serious questions in the mind of any potential investor, but Barry and his story were compelling, and he was making a lot of people a lot of money.

Besides, new offerings like ZZZZ Best's are always risky, and prospectuses always sound like they were written by Chicken Little on a fixed income. A characteristic of many Ponzi schemes is that they give people faith—while they last. Investors want to believe, and Rooney, Pace helped convince them, partly with a nine-stop road show for Barry and his minions to acquaint the investment community with ZZZZ Best. Beginning and ending in New York, Barry visited Boston, Atlanta, Minneapolis, Chicago, Beverly Hills, San Francisco and Dallas between November 11 and November 20, 1986.

Barry's performances were always remarkable. He seemed semiliterate at times, but he was also astonishingly intelligent. Investment bankers, accountants and other professionals marveled at how quickly this unschooled kid grasped their specialties and seemed versed in all the Talmudic complexity of securities law and investor psychology.

Yet traveling with Barry every day was an adventure. He was afraid of flying and weirdly childish; for his handlers the experience was like shepherding an unruly twelve-year-old who is uncomfortable in a suit and tie, or perhaps a chimpanzee dressed up as a corporate executive. Barry would fire spitballs across the aisle in first class, and Grossmann or some other father of the moment would have to tell him to stop. Even the chairman of a public company can't carry on that way aboard an airplane.

Stock offerings take awhile, and Barry needed cash now. He still hadn't managed to borrow from First Interstate without Strauss's guarantees, but one of his greatest skills was using each new sign of legitimacy to wheedle more money out of someone new, which would gain for Barry still further legitimacy—and still more money.

In late October of 1986, he sent Susan Russell at Union Bank a copy of the ZZZZ Best red herring, brimming with official-looking information about his company. Russell was startled by the rapid growth and phoned Barry. "Congratulations," she said. As a banker she was now interested, but mainly in getting a nice healthy deposit. The prospectus, after all, indicated a major fund-raising in the offing, and ZZZZ Best had retained a Big Eight accounting firm as well. On November 4, Russell and Union Bank colleague Vanessa England drove out to Reseda.

"You know," Russell said, "I really don't know if anything is going to come of this, but we'll give it a shot."

They met with Barry, Arrington and Andersen. Predictably, Barry did most of the talking. He spoke convincingly about how his age had kept him from establishing a banking relationship on his own, forcing his resort to costly joint-venture partners. Now that his company was stronger financially, he wanted to go it alone. Russell and England in turn described various investment and cash-management services their bank offered to businesses. For example, Union Bank can tell a customer what his balance is every day, which can be useful in helping a business manage its cash. Barry soon brought the conversation around to borrowing. He said he needed money to pre-pay suppliers for carpet and other goods in order to get the deep discounts he depended on for ZZZZ Best's great profitability. The stock offering would be completed soon, and Barry asked if Union Bank would provide financing in the interim. He gave the two women an in-depth report on his fire- and water-damage restoration activities, and made it clear that although he was young, he was in charge.

"My parents work here at ZZZZ Best, but believe me, if they weren't doing the job, I'd fire them just like anyone else," he said. Russell and England told Barry Union Bank might be interested in lending ZZZZ Best some money until the offering was completed, but they'd have to get back to him. Then they got a tour of the company's facilities.

Back at their office, the Union Bank executives contacted Rooney, Pace, First Interstate, Ernst & Whinney, Hughes Hubbard and George Greenspan. Moreover, Union Bank was more comfortable with ZZZZ Best now that the company had found a second source for its all-important restoration work. It seemed that ZZZZ Best had picked up one or more jobs from Crawford & Co., a large, well-known insurance concern.

This was crucial. Padgett had asked a friend at Crawford's offices in Northridge, near Reseda, if he had any work for ZZZZ Best. Padgett's friend was in a different department, but he sent Barry to another Crawford official, whom Barry sized up over dinner. Padgett told the FBI that Barry gave the man $23,000 as a down payment on a house, and Crawford gave ZZZZ Best a few small jobs. More important, the man allegedly verified that Crawford was working with ZZZZ Best. When Griffin called, for example, he confirmed that Crawford was giving ZZZZ Best some work and said a $7 million job wasn't all that unusual. He even sounded jealous when he told her he knew of Tom Padgett by reputation.

The Crawford job was enough for Russell and England. On November 7, Union Bank loaned ZZZZ Best $600,000 in desperately needed "gap financing" to tide the company over until the offering proceeds came in. That same day, to Barry's great satisfaction, Jack Catain was convicted of conspiring to sell part of a $3.3 million cache of counterfeit $100 bills. The mobster who supposedly took advantage of Barry, whom Barry actually conned and then discarded, was now licked. Convicted at last and in broken health, he didn't have time to worry about the kid who had screwed him.

Barry Minkow Day dawned the next morning. Saturday, November 8, 1986, was dedicated in his honor by Mayor Bradley, again thanks to busy, busy Jeri Carr.

15

The ZZZZ Best road show went well despite Barry's antics, and the Crawford job went a long way toward assuaging the fears of the investment bankers and lawyers. But Faith Griffin would not rest until someone had walked through a couple of restoration jobs, and the accountants from Ernst & Whinney were also starting to insist. Larry D. Gray, the partner-in-charge of Ernst & Whinney's San Fernando Valley office, noticed that the Sacramento contract had had a major impact on the ZZZZ Best financial statements for the quarter ended July 31. He wanted to see that job in particular.

Cynics might have fun with his name, but it's not fair to laugh. Larry Gray may well be the world's unluckiest accountant, even if he does still have his health. Plump and affable, he was the Ernst & Whinney partner in charge of ZZZZ Best, and although he isn't necessarily the sharpest guy in the world, what happened wasn't really his fault. I know a senior partner at a rival Big Eight firm who is known around Los Angeles as a very savvy guy.

"It could have happened to any of us," he says over and over, shaking his head as if considering a healthy colleague felled by lightning on a Palm Springs golf course. Sooner or later, in any discussion of Larry Gray, this man will cast his glance skyward in mute acknowledgement, as if to say: "There but for the grace of God . . ."

When Gray asked to inspect the important Sacramento job, Barry responded characteristically: he stalled and he lied. Barry claimed his contracts with insurance companies restricted access to the jobs for liability reasons. This didn't strike Gray as unusual, but he remained curious, and on October 27, 1986, a Monday, he took advantage of a happy coincidence: he had to be in the state capital on other business. He didn't have an address for the ZZZZ Best job, so he just drove around. Eventually he noticed construction activity at the eighteen-story 300 Capital Mall building, and assumed that was the secret ZZZZ Best job in the city.

The pressure to visit a site soon became irresistible. Griffin was threatening to hold up the stock offering unless a Rooney, Pace representative got to see one, and Ernst & Whinney wasn't going to certify his company's financial statements unless they got to go along. After much stalling, Barry finally agreed to let them walk the Sacramento site.

It is a measure of both Barry's faith and his audacity that he agreed to such a visit, since he knew very well that there was no Sacramento job site. To his subordinates, Barry seemed as calm and confident about this little difficulty as he did about all the other crises that forever threatened him and the future of his carpet-cleaning empire. If there was no Sacramento job site to show the auditors, one would just have to be found.

Around the second week of November, Padgett and Roddy flew up to look for one, and quickly discovered there was only one building in town that could possibly harbor $7 million worth of damage: the 300 Capital Mall building. Gray, feeling clever, had already questioned Padgett about it: "It's the Capital Mall building, isn't it?" he had asked slyly.

Padgett and Roddy took a deep breath and went in to see the building managers. Padgett and Roddy said they needed to lease a considerable amount of space, "but our investors can't come except on a weekend."

In fact, the visit was scheduled for November 23, a Sunday. ZZZZ Best told Gray this was in order to avoid interfering with ongoing work at the site, and to avoid accidents. But the truth was, the ZZZZ Best gang chose a Sunday because they wanted the place as empty as possible to avoid trouble. They noticed that someone was indeed doing a little construction work at the building, and even a casual washroom conversation could do them in. To Padgett's and Roddy's immense relief, the building's management agreed to provide keys for some vacant space in the building over the weekend.

On November 17, a Monday, Mark Morze, Tom Padgett and Mark Roddy went to one of those instant-office places, laid out $2,000 in cash and overnight Assured Property Management had an office, furniture, file cabinet, phones, copying privileges, etc. Assured existed only on paper, of course, but it was supposedly in the business of looking after the interests of the insured party in one of these restoration jobs. It enabled Roddy plausibly to stand in for the building's owners, managers and insurers. Roddy and company put up a big map with pins in it, signifying all the jobs Assured was assuring, and the place suddenly looked convincing. If anyone asked how Interstate was getting these big claims, the story would be that Roddy and Padgett went to Boston University together, fell out of touch and renewed their acquaintance at a reunion. Roddy, who'd lived in Boston for a while as a kid, wasn't completely ignorant of the city, and the story had just the right mix of serendipity and old school tie to be plausible.

Things were coming together, but before Gray and Moskowitz headed for Sacramento, Barry demanded written promises of secrecy from both. On Friday, November 21, in order to satisfy ZZZZ Best's secrecy requirements, Hughes Hubbard drafted confidentiality letters. Moskowitz and Gray agreed in writing not to disclose the location of the site to anyone, even at their own firms. More important, the letters said: "We will not make any follow-up telephone calls to any contractors, insurance companies, the building owner, or other individuals (other than suppliers whose names have been provided to this firm by the Company) involved in the restoration project. . . ."

With promises from two such men of honor not to make the slightest objective effort to determine what was going on, the outlandish Sacramento scam was beginning to look like it had an outside chance, a very long outside chance, of working. On Saturday, Morze flew up to check things out. All seemed well; Barry's men had even had the foresight to memorize the route between the airport and Assured's offices and the Capital Mall building, because they knew they'd have to seem as if they'd made the drive many times before.

Barry called frequently.

"This is the Super Bowl," he told Padgett. "It's like a field goal with no time left on the clock."

"Barry," Padgett would say, "I'm going to center it, and Morze is going to kick it."

Saturday night, Padgett, Roddy and Morze went out to dinner and drank Moosehead beer at the Sacramento Inn. Roddy played poker for part of the evening, while his colleagues in crime drank themselves into a stupor. Then Padgett got up at five AM and drove Morze to the airport. It was Sunday morning, and Morze had to go back to Los Angeles to meet Moskowitz and Gray.

"You guys are working me to death," he kidded them when they arrived. "I was in Arizona all night on a job."

Meanwhile, Padgett woke Roddy. It was time to put their plan into action. A key moment came at around 10:20 AM when Roddy approached security guard Tom Myers at the Capital Mall building.

"Listen, would you like to make an extra fifty dollars for yourself?"

"What do I have to do?"

"Just be nice to some people I've got coming through here later on, guys named Mark Morze, Larry Gray and Mark Moskowitz."

"Well," said Myers, accepting a $50 bill, "being nice is part of the job."

Roddy explained that there was a "big deal" going on, and he wanted his guests treated like important people. An honest man, Myers nodded and then filed an incident report with his employer, Burns International. He also turned in the $50.

Upstairs, Roddy and Padgett were taking care of things. They put up ZZZZ Best signs wherever they could, left a ZZZZ Best T-shirt in one of the empty rooms and swiped a set of blueprints to make things look official. Then it was only a matter of time. Roddy sat down in the conference room of his fake offices and watched a football game on television.

Back in Los Angeles, Gray, Moskowitz and Morze caught a flight north. In Sacramento, they rented a car at the airport and drove to the supposed office of Assured Property Management, where they visited with Roddy for about half an hour. Larry Gray had been led to believe Roddy was sort of the building manager, hired by the insurance company to protect its interests by overseeing the restoration work and leasing space.

Then all four men—Morze, Roddy, Moskowitz and Gray—piled into a car and drove over to the 300 Capital Mall building. Padgett stayed out of sight, at the hotel. As far as the lawyer and the accountant were concerned, he wasn't even in Sacramento.

It was a Sunday, and the place was deserted. Moskowitz and Gray were wearing plastic ZZZZ Best badges with their pictures on them.

"Every time I talk to accountants and lawyers, I get into trouble," Roddy joked.

"Hey, we're on your side," they replied jovially, and Roddy, who was free on bail at the time, laughed.

In the lobby, security guard Myers dutifully exchanged pleasantries with Roddy and Morze, who seemed completely at home. Roddy signed in at 1:15 P.M.

"We were informed that the damage occurred from the water storage on the roof of the building," Gray wrote in a memo to the ZZZZ Best file at work the next day. "The storage was for the sprinkler systems, but the water somehow was released in total, causing construction damage to floor 18 and 17, primarily in bathrooms which were directly under the water holding tower, then the water spread out and flooded floors 16 down through about 5 or 6, where it started to spread out even further and be held in pools."

The memo says the tour first went up to the seventeenth floor, which was occupied by a law firm, and Gray later told police that they also visited five lower floors chosen at random.

"ZZZZ Best's work is substantially complete and has passed final inspection," he wrote. "Final sign-off is expected shortly, with final payment due to ZZZZ Best in early December."

Gray added that "The tour was beneficial in gaining insight as to the scope of the damage that had occurred and the type of work that the Company can do."

Roddy and Padgett couldn't believe it. Gray and Moskowitz had walked through a building that had absolutely nothing to do with ZZZZ Best, and were completely fooled. Padgett eagerly called Barry to report their success but was disappointed to learn that Morze had beat him to it. Everybody wanted to be the first to tell Barry they had won the Super Bowl.

But in a Ponzi scheme, there is never any rest for the weary. On November 28, just five days after the hair-raising Sunday Barry spent worrying himself half to death during the Sacramento job-inspection, he was working hard to raise more cash. On that day he once again met with Union Bank executives in Reseda.

As in so many of his relationships, the balance of power in this one had subtly shifted; now they were coming to him. The bankers, Russell and two other women, treated Barry to the results of a cash-management study they had performed on ZZZZ Best. Then Barry told them what he really needed to improve his company's cash management: more cash. They lent him another $300,000. Barry and the other ZZZZ Best executives made their own presentation as well, giving the bankers their road show for the stock offering. As usual, Barry was clearly in command. He narrated a slide show and spoke on the restoration business. His comments and slides showed that that business had grown fast, would eventually peak and then would diminish in importance to the company. Arrington spoke on the carpet-cleaning business, which supposedly held the company's future.

Andersen spoke on the company's finances. The ninety-minute meeting concluded with another plant tour.

Barry knew he was about to hand Susan Russell an enormous deposit, and he intended to get a lot out of her in exchange. He also knew enough not to ask for it all at once, but rather to proceed in increments. He had already borrowed $900,000.

On December 4 he, Andersen and Moskowitz met with Russell and other Union Bank executives. Barry was in fine fettle. He had initiated the meeting to introduce Moskowitz and the bankers, after which he said ZZZZ Best had just been awarded an $8.2 million restoration job in San Diego, as well as several other insurance jobs. He gave them copies of the contracts and outlined how much money ZZZZ Best would make on them. Barry's speech, as usual, was masterful.

Suddenly he noticed that while he was talking to the bankers, Andersen and Moskowitz spoke to one another. Annoyed, Barry stopped in midsentence and glared until the room was quiet.

"Excuse me, I'm speaking here," he said pointedly. "I've got the floor."

The Harvard-trained lawyer and the certified public accountant looked at each other sheepishly and said nothing. They sat in embarrassed silence as Barry resumed. He went on to say that publicity surrounding his stock offering had brought in "more business than I know what to do with," and as a result he needed more money to capture these opportunities without resort to costly joint-venture arrangements. He asked to borrow $1.3 million, again to pay for supplies in advance and thus gain very low prices. He also said he wanted a $7 million line of credit. The bankers came away impressed.

December 4 was a busy Thursday for Barry. According to the police, that was the day he personally showed Moskowitz two more supposed restoration sites. First he took the lawyer to visit a two- or three-story Pasadena office building, where they saw carpet work in progress in a couple of offices. Moskowitz later told police he saw Barry's old high school friend, Tony Scamardo, working there. Then Barry drove Moskowitz to a Thousand Oaks shopping mall, where he showed the lawyer some stores that had supposedly suffered water damage from a leaking roof.

On Tuesday, December 9—not a minute too soon for Barry's ravenous money-eating enterprise—the SEC declared the ZZZZ Best offering effective, meaning that seven days later Rooney, Pace would officially be permitted to sell all that stock. Barry was thrilled; the check was practically in the mail. Two days later, Russell had lunch with Oscar Jimenez, an Ernst & Whinney partner who confirmed his firm's work for ZZZZ Best. Union Bank granted the $1.3 million loan, but the $7 million didn't come as easily. Barry had to wait nearly another week.

On the following Monday, December 15, the marketing executives at Union Bank held their regular twice-monthly meeting. Marketing is important in a country like the United States, where there is basically plenty of everything, including purchasing power. You have to get people to buy whatever you're selling. Union Bank's marketing people met to trade tips, gripes and so forth. To gain inspiration, they occasionally heard a guest speaker. On December 15, the speaker was Barry.

His topic was telemarketing and rejection, and they could not have chosen a better man. He gave a galvanizing performance, using a marking board to illustrate his points and speaking from direct personal experience: Barry really did know what it's like to make cold calls. He told the two dozen bank marketing executives not to fear rejection. "Face the fear," he urged, "and the fear will disappear."

The next day, Tuesday, Russell met Barry and Moskowitz at the Beverly Hills law offices of Freshman, Marantz, Orlanski, Cooper & Klein. Mark Klein presented Barry with an $11,555,000 check from Rooney, Pace for the offering of 1.1 million units. (Total proceeds had been about $13.2 million.) Delighted, Barry handed the check to Russell for deposit at Union Bank, which granted his company a $7 million line of credit later the same day. The atmosphere at the offices of Freshman, Marantz was celebratory. An arduous process was complete, and the rewards were rich. It's kind of sad Maurice Rind couldn't be present, even if he had opposed the public offering. It was his forty-eighth birthday.

The money started flowing out as soon as the offering check was deposited at Union Bank, if not a little sooner. First of all, $1.5 million was used to pay off investors in the Rooney, Pace private placement. According to Mark Morze, another $5.5 million was disbursed to Bank Hapoalim, First Interstate Bank, Charbit, Pavia, Rozario and her investors, entities controlled by Rind, Schulman or Victor. Morze says Barry got $1 million personally. He estimates that that left roughly $3 million of the offering money. But much of what was paid out was recycled or reinvested.

December of 1986 seemed like a time of unmitigated triumph for Barry. The day after Union Bank approved the $7 million line of credit, Barry emptied it. His company got a $3 million credit facility from First Interstate, at long last without Strauss's guarantee. And of course, all that stock was sold to the public. All in all, Barry's company had hauled in more than $21 million, and Morze estimates conservatively that ZZZZ Best began 1987 with $29 million in all. Grown-ups weren't just taking Barry seriously. Now they were treating him with respect.

On Saturday night, December 20, Barry and his friends celebrated in style. ZZZZ Best held a Christmas party for between 500 and 1,000 guests at the slick Bonaventure Hotel in downtown Los Angeles. The event was a combination revival meeting, sales rally and Academy Awards ceremony. As usual, no expense was spared, but the carpet cleaners and their dates, all dolled up for the occasion, made the proceedings feel like a fancy wedding on Staten Island.

So it might have been, if not for Barry. His employees were grouped at tables by store location, and as Barry cited each of their outlets, they whooped and hollered. Their regard for their leader seemed to border on worship, and he worked the crowd masterfully, shining larger than life in a snow-white tuxedo, white shoes and black tie. His hair was cut razor sharp, and there wasn't the slightest trace of nerves about him. When the crowd chanted in unison, "Bar-ry . . . Bar-ry . . . Bar-ry . . ." he seemed once again at the center of some sinister personality cult, and his exalted position before the adoration of his minions sent him into ecstasies. Vanessa England would later grope for words: "He was like a master of ceremonies, a circus barker—the center of attention."

The highlight of the evening was a prolonged and in retrospect macabre awards ceremony, in which Barry heaped elaborate praise on flunkies, dupes and co-conspirators alike, handing each an outsized trophy as they embraced him, some in embarrassment, others with their lips quivering, their emotions spilling over.

16

One of Barry Minkow's biggest mistakes was running afoul of a cheerful young mother named Robin H. Swanson, who did as much as anyone to destroy him.

"I think it's the only thing I've ever been obsessed with," she says now with a certain awe.

Robin Swanson is not at all rich and powerful. She works as a secretary in Burbank, lives in a modest house and sounds crisp, orderly and bright-eyed on the phone, as if she's had enough sleep and couldn't engage in any duplicity if she tried. Swanson is busy with her family and her job, but on January 15, 1986, when ZZZZ Best was still a corporate stripling, she took the time to do something nice.

"I was buying flowers for my boss's wife," she says in her cozy living room. "She had had a hysterectomy and I wanted to send her flowers in the hospital. I looked in the Yellow Pages and picked a place close to the hospital."

The place was Floral Fantasies, in Canoga Park, and Robin ordered a bouquet by phone. It cost $23.95, and she charged it on her Bank One Visa card. But when she got her February 20 statement, the Floral Fantasies charge was for $601.11. And Bank One was charging 21.6 percent annual interest on her outstanding balance. On March 6, Robin called Floral Fantasies to complain, and they told her to call Barry Minkow, who was supposedly the owner.

"He said, 'Oh, I'm so glad you called,' " she remembers. "He said he'd put through a credit right away."

But Swanson's next Visa bill was even worse. Not only had Barry failed to expunge the $601.11, but Floral Fantasies had added $23.95 as well. Exasperated, she called Floral Fantasies and Barry Minkow on March 31, April 3, April 4, April 7 (twice), May 7 and May 9 (twice again). Either he wouldn't come to the phone or wouldn't speak to her when he did.

On May 9 Swanson wrote her bank, which wrote back on June 16 to say that they had ordered a copy of the sales draft from Floral Fantasies in order to investigate further. Robin was pleased. Consumers who use credit cards are protected by stringent federal laws that give them the right (with some exceptions) not to pay charges that they legitimately contest, at least until their bank investigates. But in the third week of September, Bank One wrote back from Columbus, Ohio, to say that because Robin hadn't notified them within sixty days of the disputed charge, she was out of luck.

She was also incensed. Minkow or someone had had over $600 in ill-gotten gains for months. He had lied and then ducked her, and now he was going to keep her hard-earned money, which she felt he had stolen. But Robin Swanson was not alone. More than $100,000 in similar bogus credit-card charges were submitted by Floral Fantasies in early 1986, enough to arouse the interest of Gil Lopez, the investigator at First Data Resources, who knew Barry from the last round of credit-card fraud at ZZZZ Best. But this time the financial institution on the line—California Overseas Bank, where Floral Fantasies had its account and deposited the fraudulent credit-card slips— was a client of First Data, so Lopez was serious.

He talked to Barry ten or fifteen times about the Floral Fantasies charges, to no particular effect. Unable to recover his client-bank's money, Lopez began building a case. Floral Fantasies had abused the charge-account numbers of 300 to 400 customers, mostly Asian-Americans living in San Diego. He contacted twenty of them, obtained detailed statements and made ready to submit his findings to law-enforcement authorities for criminal prosecution.

"Out of the blue," Lopez says, "Mr. Barry Minkow calls up the bank and calls me up and says, 'I will pay the entire amount back.' And he did. It took him about three months."

Swanson didn't know about any of this, and it mightn't have helped her anyway, since she had missed the sixty-day deadline. But she wasn't about to give up. On September 23, 1986, she went to Small Claims Court; the sequence of events in her case is so clear and the dates are so precise because she assembled an impeccable paper trail, including credit-card documents, phone bills, time cards, copies of all correspondence and even a running diary of events.

When Robin filed suit, her husband, a strapping, easygoing sandblaster who'd advised her to forget the whole thing, went out to serve the papers on Barry. It was the morning of September 25, a bright, beautiful Thursday. Bill Swanson called first and identified himself as Bill King, owner of 400 apartments all around the San Fernando Valley. He talked to Robert Minkow (he didn't really understand that this was a different person than Barry) and told him he needed some carpets cleaned. The elder Minkow seemed eager for the business, so Swanson headed over.

"I walked into this multiunit industrial complex and all I see are a bunch of people talking on phones, facing the wall," Bill recalls.

After some discussion about Mr. King's vast apartment holdings and their acres of soiled carpets, Swanson realized that Robert Minkow was not Barry Minkow, and so told the truth—that he was Bill Swanson, and that somebody owed his wife 600 bucks.

Bill Swanson firmly believes that the squeaky wheel gets the grease, and soon he was raising such a ruckus that the ZZZZ Best telephone sales force had to stop making calls; it was just too noisy. Barry's father tried to make him calm down and read his son's autobiography until Barry turned up, but Bill kept at it until a couple of big guys came in. "They were firm but pretty nice, so I quieted down," he says. When they left he started up again, and the elder Minkow was beside himself. He tried to give Swanson a cup of tea, but Bill kept suggesting that he call the police. Finally Swanson got thrown out, and just as he was leaving, a white BMW came screeching around the corner and a solidly built, dark-haired guy jumped out, all dressed in white. A second guy, blond-haired, jumps out as well.

The dark-haired guy said, "I'm Barry Minkow."

Swanson immediately handed him the court papers.

"All you guys are witnesses," Swanson said to those assembled.

"Fuck this!" Barry said scornfully. "Six hundred fucking dollars, that's chump change!"

Then someone with blond hair slugged Swanson hard enough to knock his glasses off. (There were indeed witnesses.) Swanson is a big guy who doesn't look like he would run from a fight, but he was surrounded by what he later termed "shaved gorillas," and therefore retreated toward his El Camino. Suddenly he realized he was missing something—his eyeglasses—and so he walked back to get them.

"Barry stomped them," he says. "Then the blond guy chased me to my car."

When Robin heard about all this, she went a little crazy, and soon she was almost as obsessed with ZZZZ Best as Barry was. She won a default judgment for $628.73—as usual when someone sued Barry, he didn't show up in court—but she was infuriated that the judge didn't award interest on the ground that she should have notified her bank sooner. Even after a collection agency finally succeeded in getting the money (and deducting a hefty fee), Robin remained obsessed. She kept a Barry Minkow scrapbook, with all her records of the case and any clippings she might come across in the newspaper, and at one point she got into her old Chevrolet (a hand-me-down from her mother) and drove over to Barry's house in Woodland Hills. She had to sneak through a hole in the fence—it's a gated community—and she noticed a Porsche and a Cadillac in the driveway. The house was beautiful, with lovely grounds and a nice pool, and her visit made her even angrier. "As far as I'm concerned, he's a crook," she told anyone who'd listen. "He and his pals beat up my husband."

Robin couldn't let go. She looked up some other cases against Barry and found a host of judgments in 1984 and 1985, obtained by individuals and companies. And she badgered people: the Los Angeles Police, the Los Angeles County District Attorney's Office, and the state Attorney General's Office, among others, all to no avail. On Monday, November 17, 1986, she called the *Los Angeles Times*, where somehow she got me.

Coincidentally, I had just finished a piece about ZZZZ Best for the next day's paper. Not long before, a colleague on the metro staff, Ted Rohrlich, had written a major profile of Jack Catain that mentioned Barry deep down toward the end of the lengthy story. Now I had just written a highly skeptical business story about ZZZZ Best's plans for a public stock offering, reporting in greater detail on Barry's relationship with Catain. The story stressed the company's huge debt, its founder's strange ties to a notorious gangster and its reliance on a single customer—Interstate Appraisal—for almost all its business, which was damage restoration rather than carpet cleaning.

The story was all set, and Robin Swanson's call didn't change much. I had my hands full with other things, and a single credit-card dispute is of no interest to the *Los Angeles Times*. Nonetheless, at some point I asked Moskowitz whether ZZZZ Best had had any credit-card problems and he answered with a lawyerly "Not to my knowledge." I didn't pursue it, and my piece ran the next day the way it was. To my consternation, though, it only ran in the *Times'* Valley edition, which is seen by about one-sixth of the paper's total circulation. Our more flattering profile of Barry a year earlier had run in all editions, with the result that most of our readers were still shielded from the earliest bad news about him.

Barry was in for a little more unaccustomed bad publicity, in a place where it ought to have hurt. In December *Barron's* mocked the ZZZZ Best offering outright.

"Mr. Minkow, for all the traces of down that still might be on his cheeks, is wise beyond his years in investment acumen," Alan Abelson opined in his best Eustace Tilley style. "While John and Jane Q. will be forking over $4 a share for their stock, Mr. Minkow paid two cents for that same stock. Thus, after the offering, Mr. Minkow's six million shares will be worth on paper $24 million, the same six million shares for which he paid the equivalent of $120,000 five years ago."

Indeed, for Barry and his cohorts, completing the stock sale was an unbelievable coup that left all of them jubilant. First and foremost, it brought ZZZZ Best a large, desperately needed infusion of cash. The offering went so well that on January 8, 1987, Rooney, Pace exercised its option to market another 165,000 units, gaining ZZZZ Best an additional $1.7 million the following week. That brought the company's take from the whole process to $12.4 million after expenses, not counting what the offering had made it possible to borrow.

Rooney, Pace hadn't done badly either, garnering about $2 million in badly needed commissions and fees. Rooney, Pace also got warrants to purchase up to 110,000 additional ZZZZ Best units, which would have been great except they weren't exercisable for another year. All told, about 21 cents of every dollar that investors pumped into ZZZZ Best went to lawyers, accountants, underwriters, consultants, etc.

Looking ahead, the offering widened the currency of ZZZZ Best shares beyond the hardy band of 160 stockholders who had owned them before any new shares were sold (actually, the number was even smaller; many of the 160 were nominees). By increasing the liquidity of ZZZZ Best shares, bestowing a certain legitimacy on the company and getting it a little investor attention, the offering helped immeasurably in launching the stock upward.

Just as important, it allowed Barry to arrogate to himself the enormous aura of legitimacy surrounding not only firms like Ernst & Whinney and Hughes Hubbard & Reed, but any company whose stock is publicly traded on a major U.S. exchange. Being such a company implies that you operate under the watchful eye of the SEC, as well as of the exchange itself. Both are perceived to act as stabilizing influences, and they make investors more confident in putting their money down.

Such was the case with a British investment consortium called Plushcell Ltd. Peter Strauss, Barry's great financial rabbi, knew Plushcell from the movie business, in which the firm had invested. He had told Plushcell about ZZZZ Best before the stock offering, but its management was unwilling to lay out any money until afterward, believing that it thereby derived some greater level of assurance. Now Plushcell decided to invest. Strauss agreed to function as Plushcell's agent with ZZZZ Best in exchange for a share of the profits arising from restoration jobs Plushcell financed. The British company's lawyers were so careful that they demanded that Interstate Appraisal sign the restoration contracts directly with Plushcell itself, instead of ZZZZ Best. Plushcell would then subcontract with ZZZZ Best to do the work. During the first few months of 1987, Plushcell reportedly plowed more than $5 million into Barry's business.

But there really isn't any free lunch, as Barry's investors would someday learn, and Barry too was realizing that the blessed offering that had dumped so much cash into ZZZZ Best was not without its drawbacks.

For example, Barry continued to own 5,925,000 shares of ZZZZ Best, but now they represented just 53 percent of the total, instead of 77 percent. More important, Barry's shares were again restricted, this time under a federal securities law commonly known as Rule 144, which says that someone in Barry's position cannot dump his stock in the open market immediately after his company has just sold a raft of new shares. Barry would have to wait until January of 1988, after which he could only sell in the securities markets gradually.

Barron's had wisely sneered at Barry and his company, and that publication is a powerful force among investors. But the ZZZZ Best offering didn't suffer much from the weekly's sensible warnings. Assuming no value for the warrants, ZZZZ Best stock came out at $4 a share in December, sagged a bit until after the new year and then soared into the stratosphere like a ballistic missile.

17

Sitting in his baroque office above the Rainbow Room atop Rockefeller Center, Steve Greenberg had never heard a story like ZZZZ Best before. It was fantastic, it was incredible. It gave him goose pimples.

Greenberg first heard about ZZZZ Best from his old friend Bob Grossmann at Rooney, Pace, who correctly guessed that Barry and Steve would make a good match. One of New York's most colorful and successful stock promoters, Greenberg was just the man to help ZZZZ Best realize its full potential on Wall Street.

Once I flew to New York and took the subway in from the airport. In the 57th Street station beneath Sixth Avenue, I passed a group of urine-drenched men with no other shelter from the cold; the mezzanine reeked of them. I dashed up another flight of steps, and when I emerged into the night air I ran right into Arthur Miller.

That story, with its rapid movement from the base to the exalted, goes in the category of "only in New York," where it belongs right next to Steven A. Greenberg. Paunchy, whimsical and crowned with gray, shoulder-length hair surrounding an increasingly naked scalp, Greenberg resembles nothing so much as a sybaritic Ben Franklin. Born in 1944, he grew up in Brooklyn and attended graduate school in economics at New York University. Since then he has been a securities analyst, a fast-food restaurateur, the owner of a roller-skating rink, a partner in a rock club, the founder of a slick magazine and a man about town whose name regularly crops up in the society and gossip pages. He is seen at the trendiest places with the most beautiful women, who must look sort of comical beside his double chin, potbelly, and unusual haircut, which comes with sideburns. He stays out late so often that he never schedules early-morning appointments, and he has a large and expensive collection of Art Deco artifacts, including a massive half-moon desk at the rear of his cluttered office.

Greenberg's real claim to fame is the stock market: since 1973 he has been associated with a number of notable success stories. During the early 1980s, for example, he made a killing in Edgcomb Corp., a steel company. But Greenberg is best known for his role in Commodore International. Commodore was one of the earliest and highest-flying of home-computer companies, and its Commodore 64 made a shambles of the low-priced marketplace. Greenberg helped promote the company, whose stock soared (it would later plummet as it struggled to cope with changing realities in its industry).

Greenberg was moving away from financial public relations at the end of 1986 when Grossmann told him about ZZZZ Best, a company that was too good to pass up. For Barry the connection was fortunate. In January of 1987, the SEC finally drove Rooney, Pace out of business for dealings unrelated to ZZZZ Best (Randy Pace insists the company closed voluntarily). The agency found that the firm had willfully violated federal securities laws in connection with three separate stock offerings. Pace himself was suspended for a year, followed by five years of harsh restrictions on his activities in the securities business.

The collapse of Rooney, Pace meant it could no longer help support ZZZZ Best stock in the investment community, but Greenberg could easily pick up the slack, and Bob Grossmann wouldn't starve either. He joined the New York-based securities firm of Ladenburg, Thalmann & Co., where he would continue to provide strong backing for ZZZZ Best. Faith Griffin also went to Ladenburg.

Ladenburg is another firm that specializes in what are often known as emerging growth companies, and Ronald Koenig, Ladenburg's chairman, had already heard about ZZZZ Best through Steve Greenberg, for whom Koenig had great regard. Greenberg had helped Ladenburg prosper mightily on Commodore. When Grossmann was hired, he told Koenig: "This company is ready to explode."

To Koenig, an intelligent man who kept up with developments in the world of business, a twenty-year-old entrepreneur didn't seem so far-fetched. He thought of Steve Jobs and Apple Computer, as well as Bill Gates, the youthful founder of Microsoft Corp. During a visit to Ladenburg's Los Angeles office, Koenig took the opportunity to meet Barry, who impressed him as nothing short of a dynamo. Barry was at once driven and respectful. He seemed to know everything about his business down to the number of paper clips it used, and, addressing the Ladenburg chairman as "Mr. Koenig," excitedly told him about ZZZZ Best, stressing that its future was not in the restoration business.

"That's just to make money now," Barry said. "The future of this company is in carpet cleaning."

Before long, Ladenburg became a major backer of ZZZZ Best stock. Grossmann wrote a highly favorable research report, and Ladenburg began pushing ZZZZ Best with its clients, some of whom made a lot of money as a result.

Greenberg, who works through a private company called Anametrics Inc., also saw a golden opportunity. He often takes a position in the companies he touts, and in the case of ZZZZ Best he received warrants to buy 250,000 shares at $4 a share, exercisable immediately. Anametrics was also to provide financial counsel, in exchange for which ZZZZ Best promised it 1 percent "of the gross valuation of any financing, acquisition, divestiture or similar transaction initiated during the two-year term of the agreement."

Steve Greenberg is not addicted to OPM. He puts his money where his mouth is, in this case spending $1 million out of his own pocket to exercise his warrants and buy ZZZZ Best stock. Greenberg really believed.

He was excited and maybe even a little moved during his first encounter with Barry. The young chairman of ZZZZ Best listened hard, leaning forward and occasionally placing a hand on the older man's knee. He was like a respectful sponge, soaking in every word. He called his latest mentor "Mr. Greenberg" instead of just Steve, and he bent over backward to show humility and gratitude. When Greenberg corrected him on, say, a particular financial ratio, Barry said "thank you," and didn't make the same mistake again. Greenberg was struck by Barry's intelligence, which stood out all the more against the backdrop of what Greenberg perceived as his client's functional illiteracy.

Nor was Greenberg particularly suspicious. He lived in a world in which people calmly paid $7 million for a little townhouse. Why should it be so strange that anyone would spend $7 million to restore the interior of an enormous building damaged by fire or water?

Back home, of course, hardly anyone saw the angelic countenance that Barry showed Greenberg. Barry's successful manipulation of so many mature, well-educated professionals during the public offering, and the wealth and attention that resulted, did nothing to increase his humility or make him more honest. Everything seemed to be breaking his way: on February 21, for example, a Saturday, Jack Catain died of natural causes at Encino Hospital. He was fifty-six.

Anyone who looked carefully—like Mark Morze, for instance—could see that Barry's view of the people around him, including those he claimed to love, was completely selfish and cynical. He regarded most of them as weak, greedy and foolish, a collection of puppets to be manipulated by someone wealthier and smarter. This attitude pervaded everything Barry did, including some things he seemed to do altruistically. While coaching the local girls' softball team, he routinely had his flunkies pay people $10 or $20 each to sit in the stands and cheer. Records of a ZZZZ Best slush fund kept by Barry's neighbors, Jack and Janet Polevoi, show that he spent $2,050 for this purpose on April 11, 1987, but still wasn't happy.

"There's not enough people," he complained. "I want fanfare. I want pompons. I want placards. I want bullhorns."

So two weeks later, $4,250 was spent to hire more fans, the way professional mourners are hired in some cultures to bewail a death for a fee. At one point Barry hired some Moorpark College cheerleaders to egg his girls on.

"He would spend three or four thousand dollars on a Saturday like it was nothing, just to have someone cheer," marvels Eugene Lasko, who knew Barry and once hollered himself hoarse for $100.

The increased outlays generated such roaring for his team that one of the parents from the other side came over to complain. He seemed to be arguing with Barry, but the argument didn't last long, because Barry's bodyguard soon flattened him.

Rod Paulson had a glimpse of the real Barry Minkow at a restaurant in Glendale where they had gone to talk business. Barry treated the waitresses like peons, barking orders and then waving them off while Paulson sat and fumed. Barry was unhappy too; Paulson, who owned A-1 Carpet Cleaning, a leading ZZZZ Best competitor, was refusing to sell Barry his business for $10 million, a stunningly attractive price. But Barry wanted the official price to be $5 million. He wanted to give Paulson the other $5 million in a briefcase, in unmarked bills. Paulson knew his business wasn't worth $10 million, and knew there was something illegal about the deal Barry was offering. He had long suspected ZZZZ Best's books were cooked; the rapid growth and profitability Barry was claiming just weren't possible, he felt. Paulson had had problems with Barry before. When they met for the first time, at a Society of Cleaning Technicians convention in Savannah, Georgia, he had complained to Barry about raiding his carpet cleaners;

Barry had been offering a bounty to any who came over to ZZZZ Best, and Paulson lost thirty or forty trained individuals that way.

A-1 is based in the San Fernando Valley, and Barry wanted both to eliminate the competition it posed and acquire for ZZZZ Best a strong, money-making carpet-cleaning business, since his own company's carpet-cleaning operations were a shambles. By December of 1986, ZZZZ Best had thirteen locations, and in its prospectus pledged to open ten more within twelve months—even though each of the existing outlets was nothing but a money pit. One day Mark Morze went over their monthly reports, shaking his head in despair. "If we could just get one of these places to show a profit," he pleaded. "Just one!"

One way ZZZZ Best hoped to make something of its carpet-cleaning operations was by getting the concession to do such work for the major department-store chains. The Broadway, for example, offered carpet-cleaning services, which it contracted with outsiders to provide. Somehow, in June of 1986, ZZZZ Best had won The Broadway contract for metropolitan San Diego, and it was trying to gain other such contracts elsewhere. In January of 1987, Barry told Arrington that he had talked to someone at Sears, Roebuck & Co. who said the Sears contracts weren't available—but the company that held them was. The contractor, it turned out, was for sale.

Barry learned that this company was known as KeyServ Group, but its formal name was Flagship Cleaning Services Inc., based in Newtown Square, near Philadelphia. The company was owned by London-based Northern Foods PLC, which was eager to get rid of it. KeyServ was hardly a plum; other than the deal with Sears, which covered forty-three top U.S. markets, it had few assets and wasn't even profitable. Annual sales were about $70 million.

"All they had were old trucks and middle-aged men," says Steve Storti, the former KeyServ marketing executive. "Mostly what buyers wanted was the Sears name."

KeyServ got bids from several interested parties and the highest approached $20 million. Bidding had ended when Barry called one day and said he would pay $25 million. Better yet, unlike the other bids, which involved notes or some other wrinkle, Barry was offering to pay the full amount at closing. Northern Foods reopened the bidding.

Barry, Greenberg and an unknown investment banker showed up in Newtown Square soon after and the KeyServ executives, who had barely ever heard of Barry Minkow, went into their usual dog-and-pony show. Before they got very far, Barry cut them off and started telling the KeyServ executives why he was successful—and they weren't. He talked about how he would turn things around at KeyServ, and how he had built a success in the hotly competitive California market, where KeyServ was doing poorly.

"He came across as a very smart-assed young kid," Storti says. "He was going to tell us what we were doing wrong and how to run our business. We couldn't say anything because Northern wanted to sell the company."

The KeyServ people were taken aback; they couldn't believe the person they were listening to could come up with $25 million. They were wrong, of course. In the early part of 1987 it seemed that Barry could get millions just by tapping a rock. Thanks to Greenberg, his latest father and guide to wealth, he was about to tap the renowned investment banking firm of Drexel Burnham Lambert.

For Barry, though, one of the unfortunate side-effects of Grossmann, Greenberg and the stock sale was a much higher level of public scrutiny for ZZZZ Best. Barry relished the spotlight, for himself and for his company, but what he wanted was attention, not analysis. Having people look too closely at ZZZZ Best could only spell trouble, as his many headaches during the offering process had proved. The Sacramento scam had been hard on everyone, and dealing with Griffin was a nightmare. But now that Barry had left the sordid ranks of penny-stock companies and burst upon the national investment stage—during the first three months of 1987 its stock rose 331 percent, making it one of the biggest gainers on Nasdaq—he would have to live with all kinds of outsiders poking around his company and telling him what he could or could not do. Drexel would only make things worse.

ZZZZ Best had always been a charade; now Barry stepped up his efforts to put a legitimate face on things. He had Roddy take Padgett out and clean him up. Roddy spent nearly $3,000 of Barry's money on stuff for Padgett to wear, including a Brioni suit, and Barry later gave Padgett a gold Rolex wristwatch to go with his new image. (Padgett's thinking was harder to change: a believer in reincarnation, he attributed Barry's financial precocity to his earlier lives, which Padgett felt contained a great deal of business experience.) Barry felt the corporate image of Interstate Appraisal was similarly in need of burnish. He sent Roddy and Padgett out to rent classy offices in Century City or Beverly Hills, but they couldn't find anything suitable that didn't cost a fortune. Finally they took something mundane in Culver City and hired a few employees to try to drum up legitimate claims. Interstate didn't get many, and so ZZZZ Best remained its life-support system; Interstate was costing Barry $40,000 a month just to cover expenses.

Barry was wise to take these steps; all the ZZZZ Best players would have to take the field in a much bigger league now. Ernst & Whinney, for example, seemed to be with Barry for the duration. Public companies can't just fire their auditors. Doing so raises questions and requires a public filing with the SEC, which wants to know if there was any disagreement over accounting. The spurned auditor must soon file likewise, so everyone can see if the company lied. Then, after all that, another firm of similar stature must be hired to suppress investor suspicions.

During the public-offering process, Ernst & Whinney had merely conducted a "review" of the ZZZZ Best financial statements for the quarter ended July 31, with the promise of an audit to come. This allowed the name Ernst & Whinney to appear in the prospectus without meaning very much. A review "is substantially less in scope" than a full-blown audit, Ernst & Whinney noted in its review-report letter, which was included along with audit opinions for the previous years from Greenspan & Co. and a guy in Bakersfield, California, named Larry G. Baker. My first instinct was that Baker was a fiction, but he turns out to be real.

The accountants of Ernst & Whinney are not careless. When the firm was retained by ZZZZ Best in September of 1986, it hired a private investigator to conduct a background check, as it often does for new clients. ZZZZ Best and its principals came up clean.

During the course of Ernst & Whinney's work at ZZZZ Best, Larry Gray noticed that the company had a big restoration job in or near San Diego. Gray demanded to see it. Barry soon realized that the Sacramento scam would have to be repeated in San Diego, and in January of 1987 he dispatched Padgett and Roddy south. The idea was to rig up some office space so it looked like someplace ZZZZ Best had been paid to refurbish. Padgett and Roddy had done it before, with a little help from their friends, and so at first they were reasonably confident. ZZZZ Best always chose far-flung places for its supposed refurbishing jobs, because that way they couldn't be checked as easily. The trouble was, Barry for some reason had told the lawyers and accountants that the $8.2 million restoration job in question was in

National City, just outside San Diego. When Padgett and Roddy got there, there weren't any buildings that could even remotely pass for a structure in the midst of an $8 million face-lift.

Others might be daunted, but Minkow's men were made of sterner stuff. You could tell that just by looking at them. Roddy and Padgett, for example, cut a memorable figure during their trips to San Diego.

"It was like watching Laurel and Hardy," says one man who dealt with them. "Roddy would do all the talking while the Nazi would walk around looking at a gun catalogue, looking at machine guns and bazookas. He had the thing highlighted in yellow ink."

These two partners in crime looked funny, behaved strangely and believed weird stuff, but they had two things strongly in their favor: money and chutzpah. They checked into the swank old Hotel del Coronado, across the bay from San Diego, found themselves a commercial real estate broker and then laid out $22,560 for a year's lease on a small office and industrial space by the Miramar Naval Air Station near the city. As for the little discrepancy about where the job actually was; they'd just say, "well the *supplies* are in National City, but see, the *job*, that's actually in San Diego." To fill the warehouse, they ordered in $168,000 worth of the cheapest carpet they could get. By now it was early February, and time was getting short. This warehouse was to be the local outpost of Roddy's Assured Property Management. They put up a map and circled all the San Diego-area jobs that Assured was, uh, assuring. They even threw popcorn all over the floor—Padgett was a notorious popcorn freak—to make the place look lived-in. Then they went over to see Christopher M. Penrose, who figured they were nuts but who still had a building to lease.

Penrose is a handsome, cheerful, sandy-haired guy who was in training for a triathlon when Roddy and Padgett stumbled into his life. He was working for Merrill Lynch Realty at the time, representing the Federal Savings & Loan Insurance Corp. in its sullen receivership of the brand-new eight-story structure at 1551 Fourth Ave., at Cedar St., in San Diego. The federal agency never wanted the place, but got stuck with it when a thrift institution in Pine Bluff, Arkansas, failed and Uncle Sam had to cover the losses, seizing any assets in the process. For FSLIC, the building was just another headache in the ongoing collapse of the nation's savings and loan industry. For ZZZZ Best, it was a godsend.

But there was no longer time to waste; Larry Gray had signed another confidentiality letter, and would soon be on his way. Roddy and Padgett were ready. When the time came, they told Penrose they were set to lease much of his building.

"Our investors are coming in this weekend," they said, remembering their lines from Sacramento. All they needed was the keys, so they could show their backers around the place. As expected, they got them.

From here on events moved fast. On Friday night, February 6, Gray and his family arrived in San Diego and checked into the local Marriott, combining his visit to the job site with a family outing. Early the next morning, a sunny Saturday, the ZZZZ Best gang went into the building and put up ZZZZ Best signs and phony contractors' permits, just as they had in Sacramento. They took down any realtor signs showing the building to be for rent.

"Poor Larry Gray," one of the conspirators said later. "They'll ask him, "How do you know this is a courtroom, Larry? How do you know you were working for an accounting firm? How do you know you're you?' "

Soon Mark Morze collects Gray and drives him over to the Assured office, where there is a ZZZZ Best truck parked out front. Gray sees rolls and rolls of carpet and padding; Morze explains that the broadloom is intended for a building damaged by both fire and water, which they will visit next. Gray takes notes so he won't forget anything. Then he and Morze drive over to Fourth and Cedar, where they are greeted by Roddy.

"How're you doing, Larry?" Roddy asks jovially. "Gee, looks like you're following me all over the state.

At that very moment, Roddy must have experienced the scrotum-tightening sensation which James Joyce associated with the sea, because suddenly the *real* contractors drove up to the building, threatening to ruin everything by their mere unthinking presence. Now, Mark Roddy is not perfect. He has a criminal record, he eats too much and he can have a nasty temper. But at that particular moment he was impeccable. He immediately ran over and told these contractors that he and his party were buying the place. He even found out what floors they were working on and made sure to avoid them. Then everybody went inside.

"This building was vacant. . . ." Gray wrote the following Monday. "Per Morse (sic) the building is about 4 years old, and a fire on one floor spread to other floors through a faulty trash drop (where retaining doors had not been closed properly). Also, building had much water damage. . . ."

Gray went on to say that "Building was ready for inspection on Monday. Following this, the wallboard was ready to go up (wallboard was on site), ceiling could be installed and carpet laid . . . in the common area of each floor, painting was done, carpet down and basically this looked complete."

No wonder it looked complete. ZZZZ Best hadn't done a thing to it. Apparently Gray saw some finished space—he was told this was done for prized tenants who got first priority—and lots of unfinished space, and he also saw various ZZZZ Best signs and permits on the walls. "It was a very clean job site," he wrote.

Gray has no background in architecture, engineering or private investigation. He was expecting to look at some kind of half-finished office space, after all, and that was just what he saw. Larry Gray seemed satisfied.

As Barry approached his twenty-first birthday on March 22, the gap between fantasy and reality continued to widen. On Monday, March 9, the same day Ladenburg, Thalmann issued a glowing report predicting fast growth for ZZZZ Best, Barry went to Dr. Lovitz complaining of acute stress and vomiting. Barry was hospitalized the next day, and wasn't sent home until Friday. (Dr. Lovitz never made a positive diagnosis of bleeding ulcers, but he was convinced that was the problem.) On Sunday Barry was readmitted for a couple of more days as a result of severe nausea, vomiting, diarrhea and dehydration. While he was in the hospital, ZZZZ Best filed its fiscal third-quarter report with the SEC for the period ended January 1, 1987. It showed tremendous sales and profits, and in a press release announcing the results Barry was quoted as saying, "our insurance restoration work also continues to expand rapidly. . . ."

Indeed, in April ZZZZ Best was claiming it had finished the San Diego job. Accordingly, Larry Gray demanded to see it again.

For ZZZZ Best, this was perhaps the biggest crisis yet. It was one thing to walk some people through a little empty office space, but now Barry and his friends would somehow have to get control of the San Diego building and complete its interior in time to show the place once more to its auditors. Even if they could do this, it would cost a fortune, but an even bigger problem had arisen: for some reason the people in charge of the building wouldn't grant Barry's men a lease. Everyone was frantic. The world was about to end.

18

Brian Morze saved the day. Brian was Mark's older brother, a man to whom the word "philosophical" applies in much the same way "wealthy" applies to the Sultan of Brunei. But Brian came to Los Angeles not for reasons of the mind nor even of the spirit, but rather because his leg hurt.

It was December of 1986 and Brian probably would have stayed on in Pittsburgh had it not been for a stint with the Marine Corps in Vietnam, where he suffered a leg wound that left him miserably uncomfortable in the cold. But Brian also knew about all his brother's recent troubles—the health clubs, the bankruptcy—and so was susceptible when Mark told him on the phone what a wonderful thing he had stumbled into, what an exciting opportunity there was with this ZZZZ Best outfit, and how great it would be if Brian would come out and help.

Brian came out. On January 9, 1987, he left freezing Pennsylvania and arrived in sunny California. The difference was striking, and he was further startled to find his brother waiting at the airport in a chauffeur-driven limousine. Mark had brought a cold, dry bottle of Dom Perignon champagne.

If Brian arrived with any illusions, they were very soon dispelled. Mark had already shown his willingness to embroil his family in the machinations of ZZZZ Best. Perhaps he was even motivated partly by some strange vision of family togetherness that the Morze clan could share through ZZZZ Best. Roddy later told the FBI that on the day Brian arrived he was taken to a meeting with Mark Morze, Tom Padgett and Barry Minkow, where "the fraudulent part of the scheme" was laid out for him. Roddy says he knows because he was there.

In the sad saga of ZZZZ Best, Brian Gene Morze is a more peripheral and perhaps more tragic figure than his younger brother. How this pipe-smoking, jazz-loving intellectual ever got involved in such a mess is a story whose outlines would probably be familiar to Cain and Abel. It is also difficult to avoid a certain rhetorical flourish in writing of Brian, because of the way he speaks.

Brian is the only person involved with ZZZZ Best who can use the word "cognitive" in a sentence. He can tell you what Jainism is, too, and about the weak force in physics. Brian is only four years older than Mark, but the difference feels so much greater that he seems almost a 19th century ancestor of his slick younger brother, a brooding and disheveled polymath with no formal training—he never even finished high school—who can speak subtly of Schopenhauer, Nietzsche and Goethe, as well as Melville, Einstein and God. And his speech is a locomotive of rumbling refinement, a learned growl of perfect diction bordering on affectation; "*That*" is writing, he will say of a particularly beloved author, giving "that" two syllables, the last a delicate and airily enunciated explosion of tongue and palate that gives its maker the air of a grizzly bear eating with his pinky raised. Mark speaks perceptively of the people around him. Brian speaks cogently of abstractions, of the unity of spirit which all of us share, of the Kafkaesque nightmare that faces the innocent in a criminal justice system of greatest advantage to the guilty.

Both brothers are physically powerful, but where Mark is huge above the waist, Brian is gigantic at it. He is fat, bald and diabetic, with a scraggly red beard and piercing eyes set halfway back into his head. Both brothers are smart and look a little alike, but Mark is formally schooled and somewhat fastidious. Brian, by contrast, is an autodidact possessed of a towering intellect and a physical appearance so bedraggled that, coupled with his oracular speech and terrifying breadth of learning, it makes him seem ready for the part of a prophet, should Hollywood return to Biblical epics anytime soon. Indeed, Brian delivered more than one late-night jeremiad to his younger sibling.

The Morze brothers come from the area around Detroit, but have spent much of their lives in Los Angeles, and are close in the ways that brothers close in ages can be, especially when they have shared the loss of their father while they were young. Both are divorced.

Both love sports. And larceny lurks in both their hearts. Despite all appearances to the contrary, Brian fit in with the rest of the ZZZZ Best gang better than even he would acknowledge. He was just as rootless and just as resourceful, and was marked by the same weird sort of coincidence: like Mark Morze and Tom Padgett, Brian Morze and Mark Roddy also share a birthday, in this case May 29, although Brian is five years older.

The Morze brothers both like cats, although Mark probably talks to his more. In his very darkest hours, with no one else he could let in on the scheme, Mark Morze unburdened himself to his two cats. Before long these felines knew more about ZZZZ Best and Barry Minkow than anyone else outside the company, and if they had Social Security numbers it wouldn't surprise me to find brokerage accounts in their name, fat with profits from shorting the stock.

Brian was the one who saved Barry's bacon in San Diego. The idea was to complete the unfinished interior of the building at Fourth and Cedar streets so Larry Gray could see a finished job. Mark Roddy tried to lease the building under the company name MRI, but something made the building's prospective owners—Broe Co. of Denver—suspicious, and they backed out. Broe Co.'s Val Wheeler had good instincts. Aside from the immediate scam, Roddy, in exchange for the dropping of the more serious charges arising out of his August 1986 arrest in New Mexico, had recently pleaded guilty to the lesser charge of using a phone to distribute narcotics. He was trying to lease the building while awaiting sentencing.

"Don't get too attached to that beach house," he told Padgett on the phone one day.

"What do you mean?"

"We're having trouble down here. That building's in receivership. They just won't lease it to us."

Actually, there were a couple of problems. First, the Broe Co. found that it took months to close on a real estate purchase from the Federal Asset Disposition Association, which handled properties orphaned by savings and loan failures. And second, Wheeler and leasing agent Chris Penrose found Roddy incredibly suspicious.

Roddy had come around in February eager to do business, and then suddenly disappeared (after showing Larry Gray through the place). Now all of a sudden he was back, hotter than ever to rent even more space in the San Diego building. Wheeler couldn't understand it. There was plenty of vacant space in metropolitan San Diego, and this guy was fishier than a trout. Wheeler told Penrose to demand financial statements and other information useful in proving Roddy's authenticity. It wasn't forthcoming, and that seemed to be that.

Barry, Roddy, Padgett and the Morze brothers argued over how to proceed. Roddy had already offered to rent the entire building either for one year or just several months, meeting the asking price and doing all interior construction at or above the local building-code standard. His pleas were unavailing.

"Well, just blow it up!" Padgett finally declared in exasperation.

But Barry would not hear of failure. Finally Brian Morze flew to Denver to "come clean" with the Broe officials, figuring that when all else had failed, Barry and his men might as well resort to the truth. Basically, Brian Morze told them, "Okay, guys, you win. The truth is, Padgett and Roddy work for ZZZZ Best, and ZZZZ Best is the party that really wants the building. We wanted to keep the whole thing secret because of some unusual activity in our stock lately," etc.

The Broe people called Barry to confirm all this, which of course he did, and a Draconian lease was finally negotiated. ZZZZ Best had to take the place for seven years, put down $500,000 as a security deposit and pay a month's rent in advance. It hurt, but Larry Gray, in his plodding way, had made it unavoidable.

Now that the building was leased, the men from ZZZZ Best faced an even bigger hurdle: getting the interior finished in time for Gray's anticipated May 11 visit. It seemed almost impossible: ZZZZ Best didn't take possession until around May 1, so it had roughly ten days to wire, dry-wall, paint, carpet and otherwise complete six floors of office space (two were already done). Because ZZZZ Best was incapable of changing a light bulb on its own, no less renovating an entire building overnight, it had already hired Pals & Associates, a contracting company based in Alhambra, California, to which Barry's men had promised at least $200,000 a day plus unlimited access to a bank account across the street from the work site.

Time was of the essence; Gray was due in a matter of days. Roddy, Padgett and Brian Morze set up a command post at the Intercontinental Hotel, looking out across the water, and immediately sent out for some $200-an-hour call girls. They were gorgeous. "Look, I'm under a lot of tension," Padgett told one. "Let's start with the massage and go from there."

Working round the clock, the construction crews attacked the unfinished building interior with a passion. Everybody was worried, but also pretty excited; they couldn't quite believe they had managed to get things this far. At one point Barry himself came down to see how the work was going, touring the facility like Churchill visiting his men at the front.

The place was a madhouse, but there were signs of progress every day, and at one point, thinking ahead, Roddy handed out some ZZZZ Best T-shirts and got the workers to pose momentarily while he took pictures. Meanwhile, since Gray had been promised a visit to Dallas, Barry and his men moved to take care of that as well. On Saturday, May 9, John Meyer got a call from Mark Morze in the middle of the "Sky's the Limit" conference at the Century Plaza Hotel, where Barry was doing his best to cement relations between KeyServ and ZZZZ Best. Meyer used to make cleaning chemicals, and sold the business to ZZZZ Best, where he continued to run it. On the phone, Morze told him to ship a truckload of supplies to Dallas pronto.

"What kind of supplies?" Meyer asked. "What should I ship?"

"It doesn't matter," Morze replied. "Just get them there."

Meyer, an ornery, overweight old guy who would never call Barry anything but Barry, told police that's when he realized the restoration jobs were fake. He shipped the supplies anyway. ZZZZ Best had already rented a warehouse in northwest Dallas, where it had sent all the carpet and padding from the San Diego warehouse.

The following afternoon, May 10, less than twenty-four hours before Larry Gray was scheduled to visit, Padgett, Roddy and Brian Morze toured the six floors their contractor had worked on so frantically. It had cost ZZZZ Best $1 million, but the job was basically done.

"This is ZZZZ Best magic," Padgett said. "This is a miracle."

The next morning, Monday, May 11, the Morze brothers walked Larry Gray through the building. "Job looks very good," he wrote in a memo to the file the next day, not noticing that some ceilings were dropped so low that the closet doors wouldn't open. "Per Morse [sic], they expect full acceptance on the job later this week."

Gray didn't bother to look at the San Diego warehouse again, since Morze told him it was pretty much empty by now. Instead Gray, Morze and Dennis Harris, a certified public accountant working for ZZZZ Best who had also toured the San Diego building, flew directly to Dallas. At the rental-car counter, Morze intentionally caused some kind of time-consuming snag—perhaps he tried to use an expired credit card, perhaps he claimed to have a reservation and didn't—with the result that when he, Gray and Harris drove to the ZZZZ Best warehouse, they were somewhat pressed for time.

Morze told Gray there had been little movement of supplies at that facility since a recent ZZZZ Best inventory, a copy of which Harris seemed to have on hand—"except that as we were there, a small shipment of chemicals and cleaning compounds arrived," Gray wrote Tuesday in the inevitable file-memo. Also while Gray was present, Morze took a phone call in which he supposedly learned that ZZZZ Best had won two more building jobs in the Dallas area totaling $10.1 million.

As for the existing jobs in Dallas, Gray wrote, "I was informed that the contracts are in hard-hat stage and outside spectators were not allowed." Morze was taking a huge chance with this, because no other arrangements had been made in Dallas. But time was short anyway, and Gray, who was accustomed to things being in order at ZZZZ Best, said this was fine. Everybody flew back to Los Angeles. Barry and his friends had done it again.

19

The miracle of San Diego was only the beginning. So many other grand things were happening to Barry in the spring of 1987 it's hard to know where to begin in describing them.

April seemed an especially good month. He stopped paying Irv Rubin of the Jewish Defense League, for example. Better yet, on April 6, ZZZZ Best shares peaked at $18.375, giving Barry a paper fortune of roughly $109 million. His stock wasn't legally salable yet, but he was already taking steps to unlock some of its treasure. Through his girlfriend's brother-in-law, a stockbroker named Jim Manuel, Barry applied for a $20 million line of credit from P-B Finance Ltd., a unit of Prudential-Bache Securities Inc. in New York. On April 13, a Monday, P-B executive Sharon W. Elowsky approved a line of up to $5 million secured by 1.4 million of Barry's restricted ZZZZ Best shares. Barry's stated net worth at the time was between $75 million and $100 million, and the 1.4 million ZZZZ Best shares were worth more than $20 million. But since the stock wasn't completely liquid, it had certain flaws as security, and P-B would lend only up to 30 percent of its value. Furthermore, most of the borrowing was to be used for buying other stocks through Pru-Bache, and those other shares were to remain in the securities firm's vault. Such transactions were a way for Pru-Bache to generate trading commissions. They also helped entrepreneurs like Barry to diversify.

Barry told associates he had also talked to Pru-Bache about financing the proposed KeyServ acquisition. He planned to acquire KeyServ by borrowing, but Pru-Bache didn't work out, so ZZZZ Best moved over to Kidder, Peabody & Co. In early March, when Barry asked Susan Russell if Union Bank would increase the ZZZZ Best line of credit to $10 million, she heard from Kidder that a debt restructuring was being planned for ZZZZ Best that would include repayment of all the Union Bank loans, according to her account to police. She rejected Barry's request anyway, and the ZZZZ Best line of credit stayed at $7 million.

A month later Russell was glad she'd said no. Her trust in Barry was shaken when her colleague, Vanessa England, read his company's quarterly report for the three months ended January 31. Third-quarter profits were up fivefold on eleven times higher revenue, but the balance sheet indicated $8.2 million in debt. ZZZZ Best owed Union Bank only $7 million. It had borrowed the rest from First Interstate.

Russell and England were amazed. Their loan agreement with ZZZZ Best specifically barred other bank lenders.

"Steve Greenberg of Anametrics says these agreements are made to be broken," Barry scoffed. When Russell persisted in chastising him, Barry cut her off: "Listen, no one's going to tell me what to do."

He was right; Russell wasn't happy, but she didn't do anything about it. Nor did Barry much care; Kidder soon dropped out or was pushed out, and the aggressive firm of Drexel Burnham Lambert took its place. Drexel says it got involved thanks to Steve Greenberg and some of his associates. Drexel had had several prior dealings with Greenberg, including his successful investment in Edgecomb.

Drexel laid out a deal that, to Barry, Mark Morze, Padgett, Rind and all the others, was absolutely eye-popping. Not only was Drexel going to raise the $25 million needed to buy KeyServ. It would also raise $15 million more for working capital, and according to Morze, planned to arrange $40 million in additional financing soon after. Morze says this was only supposed to be the beginning. He says Drexel told ZZZZ Best, "If you can earn one million a month for nine months, we'll get you six hundred and fifty million and you'll do a hostile takeover of ServiceMaster."

Based in suburban Chicago, ServiceMaster L.P. seemed like a good match. It mainly does housekeeping for hospitals, colleges, factories and the like, but it also cleans up fire- and flood-damage and provides a range of residential services, including housecleaning, lawn-care and pest control. It even cleans carpets. But ServiceMaster is a well-established New York Stock Exchange company that is just a little bigger than ZZZZ Best: 1987 revenue was $1.5 *billion*. Drexel says its talk of a ServiceMaster takeover was "strictly conceptual," but the idea nevertheless reflects Drexel's hubris in the spring of 1987.

On April 15, less than a month after Barry's twenty-first birthday, ZZZZ Best officially hired Drexel to finance the KeyServ deal by raising $40 million through a private placement of the junk bonds for which the firm was famous. Junk bonds were the brainchild of Drexel's Michael Milken, a financial genius who realized that the high yields of low-rated corporate debt far outweighed the risk, especially in a diversified portfolio. The explosion in such high-yield corporate IOUs during the 1980s changed the rules of the game altogether. Milken made it vastly easier to borrow staggering sums, fueling a vicious takeover binge and helping debt drive out equity.

For ZZZZ Best, junk bonds meant it might be possible to go legit. By buying KeyServ, ZZZZ Best could get off the Ponzi treadmill, take advantage of the revered Sears name, pay off its other debts, do away with the nonexistent damage-restoration business, and (theoretically) live happily ever after. To Barry Minkow and Mark Morze, who had been through so much, it hardly seemed possible.

Two days later, on April 17, 1987, ZZZZ Best announced the signing of a definitive agreement to acquire Flagship for $25 million. That same day, Barry was the subject of a timely—and flattering—profile in *The Los Angeles Herald Examiner.*

The KeyServ deal would mean a whole new round of scrutiny for ZZZZ Best, and whatever else one might say about Drexel, its well-paid investment bankers were very far from naïve. (Drexel itself was no paragon of business ethics. The firm would later plead guilty to six counts of fraud and pay $650 million in fines and restitution as the result of a federal insider-trading probe unrelated to ZZZZ Best.) In March or April, Drexel's investment bankers had warned Barry that he better reveal any skeletons in his closet, because they would find them anyway. Barry told them about ZZZZ Best's credit-card problems, which he blamed on others, and about Mark Morze's bankruptcy. They had seemed satisfied, and with Drexel's extraordinary fund-raising abilities working for him, the future seemed unlimited. Barry was at the very pinnacle of his powers. On April 27, ten days after the KeyServ agreement was announced, he appeared on "The Oprah Winfrey Show."

This television appearance was a watershed for Barry, a vintage performance capturing his desperate need for attention, his inability to sit still, his astounding capacity to lie with a straight face and the extent to which he succeeded at fooling the world. The show itself is heedless advertising for the ignoble idea of dedicating one's youth to the pursuit of money, and as a preview of the young-entrepreneurs' segment, Winfrey makes the ridiculous promise that "Later in the show you're going to learn how you can do exactly what they did."

Barry relished the national exposure, boasting on the Winfrey show that "I could sell frozen yogurt in a blizzard." He had been a fixture for some time on Southern California television, and a new $2 million TV advertising campaign was making Barry Minkow and ZZZZ Best household names. David Marchese's clever commercials were working, even if they did infuriate the competition. Commencing in February of 1987, they showed cretinous and dishonest carpet cleaners ruining people's rugs or making dubious offers. Then Minkow would appear looking neat, clean and honest. Nobody could have seemed more straightforward.

Barry's commercials contrasted sharply with his performance on "The Oprah Winfrey Show," because on the talk show he was out of control. Winfrey introduced him with these words: "By the eleventh grade, this whiz kid was making more money than his high school principal." When Barry appeared on camera, he looked bored, as if fulfilling an obligation, although his characteristically heavy-lidded, thick-lipped appearance may have contributed to the impression of ennui. As usual, he wore no necktie.

As the discussion began, Barry's evident boredom quickly gave way, and he could barely stay in his seat. He didn't get to speak until after a commercial break, but he stood out almost immediately from the other young entrepreneurs, most of them polite, mature and in one case even literate. By contrast, Barry interrupted repeatedly as the others spoke, openly mocked one or two of his fellow guests and did everything possible to gain and keep the spotlight for himself, including talking when he wasn't on camera. "The stock that I own in ZZZZ Best right now is worth ninety million dollars," he said at one point. "Ninety million dollars is nothing. You got people like Mike Milken who are worth between five and ten billion." Barry was exaggerating, as usual. In 1989, *Fortune* magazine estimated Milken's wealth at 1.2 billion.

When the group was asked for advice, several gave practical tips and recounted their own difficulties in getting started. Barry said, "Think big, be big," and "Tough times pass, tough people last," and "Face the fear, the fear will disappear." Winfrey's studio audience seemed excited by all this. When they cheered Barry, he acknowledged the applause by quickly shifting to comedy: "Thank you— that's my mother," he said of those who clapped.

Barry continued in a more serious vein: "Life is a movie," he said. "You're the actor, you're the director, you're the writer. And if you don't like the way your life is going, you'd better change the script, because it's your life and you have complete control over it."

Finally, Neil Balter interrupted. The founder of a Southern California company that organizes closets, Balter is another much-heralded young businessman in the local press.

"Barry, a lot of your clichés, that you use so articulately, are good, but it's not where the rubber meets the road. . . . These people want to know how they can be successful." Balter warned that young people tend to fail in new businesses because they are undercapitalized and overly optimistic.

Barry cut him short.

"Excuse me, Neil, your sales were seventeen million dollars. Mine are fifty million. End of story."

Barry's apotheosis had reached its zenith. Thanks partly to Jeri Carr, partly to the times, and partly to his own shameless self-promotion, Barry's story reached virtually every corner of the land. The Associated Press said he was the most successful of the 100 young tycoons honored by the Association of Collegiate Entrepreneurs. The *American Banker* quoted him prominently about banking services for start-up companies. *Newsweek* led an article about new stock offerings: "Twenty-year-old Barry Minkow got a check in the mail for $13 million one day last month." (Barry was quoted as saying, "Getting $13 million makes you feel pretty good.") *Inc.* magazine regurgitated the entire legend.

There is no harm in the pursuit of wealth. Personal freedom, good health and civilization itself would be diminished if not impossible without it. Economists going back to Adam Smith have observed the extent to which enlightened self-interest benefits everybody. Some go so far as to say that pursuing personal gain is the most highly moral thing you can do; that it brings the greatest good to the greatest number, without any pointless and ineffectual heart-bleeding. There is much truth to this, but it is not the only truth, and it is a mistake to elevate money-making to the level of a sacrament. During the 1980s the economists extended their hegemony far beyond the narrow realm of dollars and cents to claim dominion over political science, ethics, and philosophy, much as theologians ruled the intellectual roost in the Middle Ages. People in casual conversations talked about market solutions to problems in their love lives. Youth and wealth went hand in hand to form a new idealism. It was kind of Gatsbyesque; even the good people were studying the bond business, and a sense of entitlement was in the land. People were no longer abashed about things. Hypocrisy itself had come to seem archaic. Guilt—healthy, civilizing, ennobling guilt—was out, yet our sheer grasping selfishness didn't interfere at all with our obsessive need to feel wholesome, to love ourselves. Echoing across the decade were the words of Ivan Boesky, that consummate crook, who proclaimed: "Greed is healthy. You can be greedy and still feel good about yourself."

Ronald Reagan's eight years in office were a second Era of Good Feelings, but his presidency should also be remembered as the age when fantasy and selfishness took their rightful places side by side. The two are cousins anyway. Our fantasies are just projections of ourselves onto a stubborn and untidy outside world, and any selfishness, good or bad, was exalted during the Reagan era. Our poor stewardship of the environment, our willingness to accumulate massive deficits, our refusal to invest (in education, transit, roads, bridges and low-income housing) all reflect this me-first attitude, and tomorrow be damned. There is evidence that the President himself lived in a dream world, and it is hard to say whether his outlook was a reflection of the nation's or vice versa.

I think everybody pretty much understood that Reagan's demagogic braying about getting "big government" off the backs of the people was really just a cover for attacking aspects of government that hindered the affluent from growing more so. But it also implied an attack on the rule of law, I think, and perhaps predictably, official corruption flourished in government while financial chicanery bloomed on Wall Street. Junk bonds, Drexel and the takeovers they financed nurtured massive insider trading, which contained all the requisite elements for popularity in the 1980s: it was lucrative, socially unproductive and extremely class-conscious.

Given all that, it's not surprising that Barry and a bunch of other young businessmen and -women should capture something in our imagination. Horatio Alger is one of the most famous 19th century Americans, and during Barry's dizzying rise his own version of an Alger rags-to-riches saga stood out from among a whole spate of stories about young people who had made tons of money despite their tender years. Few actually went from rags to riches; most had been comfortably middle-class, the better to identify with. Our susceptibility to such stories mirrored other phenomena in society: many Americans were downwardly mobile, and a tide of the homeless flooded our streets. Life felt a lot less secure: the Japanese seemed to be buying everything in sight (a grossly exaggerated perception, actually), and the words "compete" or "competitive" bombarded us daily. Commerce became a preoccupation, as if everyone suddenly decided that business really was the business of America. Some of this was even healthy. But some of it was absurd, and there was always a quality about Barry that suggested he held an MBA from the Dada School of Business.

Barry's spending, for example, wasn't merely free; it was hysterical. Dissatisfied with his old Ferrari, he bought himself a new one, a $150,000 top-of-the-line Testarossa. He bought Joyce a fur coat, jewels and three consecutive German cars starting with a Volkswagen and ending with the Porsche. He went on gambling sprees to Lake Tahoe and Las Vegas, where he bet thousands and put himself and his friends up in the schlock splendor of Presidential suites, with pianos and room service. Barry would order two bottles of Dom Perignon at $125 apiece, and then pour one down the drain. "The second bottle is always the best," he'd explain. Back home, Barry bought everything in sight, including, of course, people. He bought them not just as co-conspirators, admirers and softball fans, but also as servants and sexual partners. He picked up every check, and he let nothing stand in the way of his own gratification. Once Barry went out to a lake and wanted to rent a small powerboat. They were all taken, so he bought one on the spot. It cost $5,000. When he needed suits, Joyce had a tailor come out to Reseda. Barry owned the house, the condominium, a multimillion stock portfolio ranging from IBM to Art World, tax shelters and of course his shares in ZZZZ Best. He got his pal Scamardo, an experienced carpenter, to build a ludicrous little replica of Barry's own home, complete with windows, carpeting, paneling and a vaulted ceiling, for Louie. Louie was Barry's dog.

Barry's documented personal expenditures totaled $415,000 in 1986, not counting thousands in undocumented cash. In 1987 the total exceeded $2.3 million, again not counting cash, and that was just through October. Barry saw money as more than the solution to every problem. By now it was how he defined himself. He talked about his wealth constantly. Barry would say things like, "ZZZZ Best was up half a point today, that's another three million I'm worth." At the end of an evening out with Rob and Jan Byers, Barry would even joke about his self-absorption. "How'd I do? What was the percentage?" He was asking how much of the time he had talked about himself. Rarely was the answer less than 90 percent.

On "The Oprah Winfrey Show," Barry never said anything about the fraud, the gangsters, the betrayals or the temper tantrums. Yet in some large sense it was the genuine Barry who appeared, and sadly enough that same Barry was a hit with the Oprah Winfrey audience.

Alas, Barry's good fortune wasn't enduring, and his great successes in April proved merely a clever disguise for the month's signature cruelty. Barry's betrayer wasn't even one of his victims.

Norman Rothberg had found the freeway of life pretty well paved with potholes. In the spring of 1987 he was a fifty-one-year-old chain-smoker thrust deep in poverty by a variety of mishaps, marital and otherwise. Thrice-divorced, Rothberg couldn't pass the California bar and lost $140,000 (all borrowed) trying to finance a real estate deal with Offshore Investments Ltd. of Decatur, Georgia. OIL, as the company was known, claimed in newspaper ads that "We can creatively solve almost all your financial problems." OIL's creative solution was to take your money. By claiming to arrange billions in loans from overseas banks, OIL bilked investors out of $1.5 million in up-front fees, which it charged for its nonexistent service, and the ringleaders eventually went to prison. Norman Rothberg sent a cashier's check.

Bankruptcy ensued, but Rothberg was undaunted. He plied his accounting trade on his own, and his tax returns showed a loss for every single year during the 1980s. He got caught up with ZZZZ Best because he and some other creative business-types used the same San Fernando Valley psychic. One thing led to another, and Rothberg was working with Mark Roddy.

In March of 1987, Rothberg moved his offices from his apartment into the Culver City office of Interstate Appraisal, for which he had been doing some accounting to work off the $8,000 he'd got from ZZZZ Best. He was soon on a weekly retainer of $400. Toward the end of March or the very beginning of April, Rothberg overheard a strange conversation involving Padgett or Roddy or Mark Morze or all three. It had to do with tricking a couple of fellows named Mark and Larry, and there was much laughter.

"We sure pulled the wool over their eyes," Padgett or Roddy or Morze gloated.

Not long after, Rothberg claims, he got hold of a ZZZZ Best prospectus, spotted the names of Mark Moskowitz and Larry Gray, and put two and two together. Rothberg had noticed strange doings in the Interstate Appraisal bank accounts; there were substantial sums deposited and then immediately withdrawn. Sometimes the withdrawals even *preceded* the deposits. He asked Padgett what was going on, and Padgett told him not to worry about it.

Early in April—just about when ZZZZ Best stock was hitting its all-time high of $18.375 per share—Rothberg called Howard Levy. Levy was a partner with Ernst & Whinney in Century City, on the west side of Los Angeles, and Rothberg had known him since the early 1970s, when Levy's old accounting firm was engaged to audit a client of Rothberg's former employer. Levy found that Rothberg would crop up every now and then as the years went by.

This time Rothberg wanted to meet about what he described as a "matter of mutual interest." Curious, Levy probed for details, but Rothberg was mum: "We'll talk about it when I get there."

On April 13, the same day Sharon Elowsky approved Barry's $5 million Pru-Bache line of credit, the two men met in Levy's office for an hour, during which Rothberg posed a hypothetical case.

"What if," he said, "a client's financial statements are materially misstated by as much as eighty percent?"

Levy told him the accountant could consult the Code of Professional Ethics of the American Institute of Certified Public Accountants. Or he could call a lawyer.

"Is this a client of yours?" Levy wanted to know.

"No."

"Is it a public company?"

"Yes."

A light went on in Levy's head.

"Is it a client of Ernst and Whinney?"

"Yes."

Alarmed, Levy pressed: "Is it a client of our office?"

"No."

"Is it a client in the area?" Levy persisted.

"Yes."

"Well, who is it?" Levy demanded.

Rothberg wouldn't say. He merely reached into his vest pocket.

"I got proof," said Rothberg, brandishing a microcassette. "I got it on tape."

Eleven days later, at Rothberg's request, the two men met in Levy's office again. This time Rothberg demanded $25,000 to $30,000 in return for the name of the fraudulent Ernst & Whinney client. He claimed his own client was doing business with the company in question and he would probably lose that much in fees if he revealed the wrongdoers.

Levy tried to contain his indignation. He told Rothberg that if the allegations were true he should terminate his relationship with the client anyway. He also said it was unlikely Ernst & Whinney would make any such payment, but that he would check with someone and get back to him.

Rothberg still wasn't naming the company, but he provided further clues: it had recently held a public offering, was about to sell more securities and used to borrow money from an unsavory character. Levy was especially alarmed that another securities offering was in the works.

After this meeting, Levy talked to William Dudley, Ernst & Whinney's regional director of accounting and auditing for the western U.S. Dudley said the company was probably ZZZZ Best.

Levy subsequently called Rothberg and told him Ernst & Whinney would not pay for the information. But it still wanted it, and so Levy set up another meeting for his office. This time, on May 19, Dudley was present, and suddenly, Rothberg blurted out, "The company is ZZZZ Best."

He went on to say that the big Sacramento restoration job was fake and Larry Gray's tour of it had been staged, with phony signs and so forth. He said the San Diego job might be fake as well, and that overall the ZZZZ Best financial statements were off by up to 80 percent. That very morning, *The Wall Street Journal* reported ZZZZ Best's announcement of a $13.8 million restoration contract from Assured Property Management and Interstate Appraisal in Dallas. Rothberg said he didn't know if that job was real or not.

(Others knew. "A $14 million contract would be the biggest contract ever to be let. That we wouldn't know about a deal like that in our backyard would seem incredible," scoffs Kurt Blackmon, president of Blackmon-Mooring Steamatic Catastrophe Inc., a forty-one-year-old restoration concern in Fort Worth. "We monitor that day and night. That's our business.")

Rothberg says he was just trying to get the truth out, but his actions say otherwise. Was it the hope of personal gain? Revulsion at Padgett's politics? Whatever the case, Levy and Dudley were flabbergasted as he explained that Barry and his friends were merely circulating the same money around and around, to make it look like they had a going business. Rothberg said he knew all this because his client was Interstate Appraisal, which was supposedly giving ZZZZ Best the insurance jobs. Rothberg never said anything more about wanting money for his information. He just spilled his guts and left.

20

Rose Schindler had been to prison before, so she was without fear as she arrived at Wayside Honor Ranch, on the northern outskirts of Los Angeles County. Schindler is learned, pretty and small, got her law degree at De Paul University after several years as a social worker, and had been an attorney with the Securities and Exchange Commission for less than two years when she went off to Wayside to see Dirk Summers on April 7, 1987.

Much to Barry Minkow's subsequent misfortune, Dirk Summers and Maurice Rind had been locked in a blood feud ever since September of 1984, when they got into a fight over a show they were producing with comedian Jonathan Winters in Las Vegas. The production was a disaster, and the two men, who'd met a few months earlier in some kind of real estate transaction, became sworn enemies.

Picking sides in this dispute is like choosing between Iraq and Iran. Rind, of course, is an ex-convict. It's hard to say who Summers is. Authorities have three different birthdates for him, and as many different names. A State Department agent investigating Summers for possible passport fraud was quoted in the *Los Angeles Times* in 1985 saying that Summers' fingerprints prove he is actually Ronald W. Kelly, born in 1931 in Chicago. The same man, apparently, has used the names Ronald Wayne von Werbe and Dirk Summers in several scrapes with the law. Summers also tells interesting tales: about his supposed secret marriage to actress June Allyson; about his alleged exploits with George Raft in pre-Castro Cuba; and about his family's theatrical history, which supposedly includes performances at the Globe Theatre in Shakespeare's day.

Summers doesn't convey nearly the impression of toughness that

Rind does, but he turned out to be an unfortunate opponent. He was somehow caught up in the First City debacle in Texas, and when he was good and mad at Rind he went to see William Belzberg, whose family controlled First City. Summers spilled the beans on September 12, 1984.

"Rind is a convicted stock swindler who is now manipulating First City's stock," Summers warned. He also burdened poor Belzberg with the saga of the ill-starred Jonathan Winters show, and claimed that his own ancestors had been actors since the 16th century. When he left, Belzberg called his lawyers and demanded that they figure out who was this "wild man." He also told them to see what Rind was up to. Not content with talking only to Belzberg, Summers also went to the SEC, which took a dim view of the whole First City mess and put a stop to it several months later, about as fast as the agency can move. By that time—a federal judge signed the consent decree February 13, 1985—the First City scheme had been underway for more than two years.

Infuriated, Rind by now had launched his own personal investigation of Summers, and on November 24, 1984, Summers was arrested for stealing Rind's Cadillac. The prosecutor was a deputy Los Angeles County district attorney named Michael Edward Consiglio, and before long Summers was facing twenty-two counts in five different cases, including grand theft, receiving stolen property, passing bad checks at the supermarket and using someone else's credit card to charter a jet. (Summers pleaded guilty to grand theft and was sentenced to three years. In return, the prosecution dropped the other charges.)

Meanwhile, Consiglio had become friendly with Rind, according to the police. Rind himself says the two men had lunch a few times and went to a boxing match together. Rind says he even gave Consiglio investment advice, and that the prosecutor made a few thousand dollars buying stocks, commodities and art at Rind's recommendation. But the police say Consiglio also helped Rind. In a search-warrant affidavit, police asserted that Consiglio, forty-seven, warned Rind and Schulman they were under police surveillance, and that Consiglio tapped into a law-enforcement computer network to get information for Rind. Consiglio's name, the name of his bank, and his phone and Social Security numbers were later found in Rind's ledger books, the affidavit says. (Consiglio hasn't done anything improper, his lawyer asserts.)

Rose Schindler arrived at Wayside Honor Ranch by a route more circuitous than the Golden State Freeway, which actually delivered her to the facility on the Tuesday of her visit. Still feuding with his arch-enemy Rind, in late 1986 Summers contacted an SEC lawyer at the agency's Fort Worth office, whom he knew from the First City case. Maurice is up to his old tricks again, Summers said, only this time with the stock of an outfit called ZZZZ Best. The SEC lawyer in Texas referred the case to an SEC investigator in New York, where Rind was thought to be living. This investigator considered Summers flaky but credible because of First City, and since Summers was in Los Angeles, the investigator called Schindler, who began making inquiries.

She did not know Norman Rothberg, and had never heard of Robin Swanson. The name Barry Minkow didn't mean anything to her. But she reached Summers by phone in late February through Consiglio, who asked a lot of questions. She also "blue-sheeted" the various securities firms serving as market makers in ZZZZ Best stock. Official SEC questionaires—they are printed on blue paper—were sent out requiring the firms to name the buyer and seller of ZZZZ Best shares in every transaction they had handled. Blue-sheets tend to scare people. The SEC may be slow, but it has the power to destroy any securities firm, and its scrutiny of the ZZZZ Best trading was duly noted.

Schindler does her homework. She holds a master's degree in education and completed the course work for a doctorate in social work, and before driving to Wayside she had learned something about ZZZZ Best. When she arrived, she found Summers mannered but full of allegations about Rind and ZZZZ Best. He told her the stock was being manipulated, and she naturally asked if Barry, the chairman and chief executive, was involved. Summers said yes.

It's not clear how he knew all this. Summers told the SEC he had hired a couple of crackerjack private investigators to get the low-down on Rind. The accusations seemed wild, as did Summers, and Schindler asked if he had any proof. Summers said he had documents.

But time went by and no documents appeared. Schindler meanwhile studied the various ZZZZ Best SEC filings. It was hard for her to say why, but the company looked funny. Some things were obvious: the phenomenal growth, for example, or the three outside accountants.

Summers kept calling Schindler and she kept asking for the records that would lend credence to his allegations. Summers seemed frightened, and despite the two or three names he already seemed to use, he asked about a new identity under the federal Witness Protection Program. Schindler, who didn't have such authority, had no interest in that. Eventually, Summers would get in touch with the Los Angeles Police.

Mike Brambles first picked up the ZZZZ Best trail indirectly. It was on March 3, a Tuesday night he spent in Malibu at a popular restaurant called Splash. Brambles hangs out in some classy places for a cop because he is a D3—a sort of senior sergeant—in the Organized Crime Intelligence Unit of the Los Angeles Police, and he goes where the mob goes. He was in Splash, for example, because he'd heard there was a New Jersey fugitive warrant outstanding for a man named Ronnie Lorenzo, who was expected to be meeting someone at the restaurant.

Lorenzo was forty-one at the time. He is five feet eleven inches tall, weighs about 220 pounds and talks with a New York accent. According to an affidavit Brambles filed in support of a search warrant, he is a "made member of the Bonanno organized crime family and is allegedly involved in cocaine smuggling and trafficking."

At eleven-thirty P.M. Brambles and Detective Frank Skrah arrested Lorenzo at Splash. Brambles asked Lorenzo what he had to do with Splash, and according to Brambles' report, Lorenzo answered that he was a hidden owner and was managing the place for Harold Fischman (the New York attorney who helped ZZZZ Best go public). Both Lorenzo and Fischman denied repeated requests for interviews for their version of events, but according to Brambles' report, Lorenzo and Fischman had recently bought Splash in a sale handled by something called Richman Financial Services of Encino, out in the San Fernando Valley. In police parlance, "Lorenzo made further statements which were indicative that he was skimming profits from Splash Restaurant." Brambles also ran the plates on his 1986 Pontiac, which Lorenzo said Fischman had bought for him as an employee benefit. But the car was registered to Richman Financial Services at 17824 Killion Street Apt I, Encino, and the name Harold Fischman didn't appear anywhere. Instead, the purchaser and applicant for registration were listed as Maurice Rind.

Rind was identified in the motor vehicle papers as Richman's president, and Brambles learned all about him by punching his name up on the FBI's national computerized records system. Brambles also learned that on March 5, Rind filed a grand theft report with LAPD, claiming $13,000 in cash was stolen from his briefcase at the offices of Art Auctions Inc., a schlock-art company in an industrial section on the city's southwest side. Acting on a tip, on April 2, a Thursday, Brambles and Detective Steve Sewell staked out the place. They arrived at around four P.M. and parked across the street. During the next hour people who worked in the surrounding buildings headed for home, and the two detectives watched Bowcroft Street gradually drained of cars. At about six-thirty P.M. they saw Ronnie Lorenzo arrive in a 1985 BMW registered to Richman Financial Services. Soon after, a Cadillac limousine pulled up, and Brambles noticed immediately that it didn't have any license plates. Maurice Rind and his driver both got out and went inside Art Auctions. The limo had been driven by Joey Mangiapane, "a reputed Lucchese organized crime associate" whose background includes several run-ins with the law in New York, Brambles later told Congress. Mangiapane, whose name means "loafer," subsequently pleaded guilty to two extortion-based charges unrelated to ZZZZ Best.

Anyway, Brambles and his partner heard shouting inside and went over for a closer look. It was a balmy night, and they found a couple of windows open. So they listened. A loud argument was apparently in progress, with Lorenzo particularly agitated. The lawmen couldn't make out everything, but according to Brambles' report, "Ronnie Lorenzo was arguing about 'cleaning and investing the money . . .'" He also said that somebody in New York whose name the detectives didn't catch " 'wants answers to his questions about the money.' Ronnie Lorenzo yelled loudly that he does not 'want to face the boss without an answer about what to do with the money.' "

All this yelling and screaming apparently gave Mangiapane, Rind and Lorenzo an appetite, because about an hour after arriving, they drove to a restaurant in Beverly Hills to get something to eat. Brambles and his partner left them there.

The impression was rapidly forming in Brambles' mind that he was onto something. Mike is sleepy-eyed, sometimes wears a droopy mustache and has sloping shoulders that make his medium height look even more medium. He has a square lawman's jaw, rides horses in the Santa Monica Mountains, and used to work as a lifeguard, but he's not physically imposing, and his partners are often bigger than he is. Nor is Brambles from the typical police officer background. His family had a copper-mining business in the Philippines, and his parents met there during World War II in a Japanese concentration camp, where they spent four years living mostly on rice and bugs.

"My mother ate my father's dog," Brambles likes to say.

He lived in the Islands until he was nearly twelve. Back in the

States, he became an avid surfer and attended Cal State-Northridge, where Barry would someday address the collegiate entrepreneurs, but he went into the Army before finishing and became a tank soldier in Vietnam. Eventually he got a degree from the University of California at Los Angeles, with a major in geology. His senior thesis was entitled, "The Disruption of Sea Kelp Beds in Palos Verdes." The problem was sunlight filtered by the heavy pollution of Santa Monica Bay.

Brambles is very smart and very smooth. He is forty-one, and became a cop at twenty-two. He is good at it by now, with just the right mix of youth and experience. If Brambles has a flaw as an investigator, it's probably that he tends to get a little carried away by the labyrinthine nature of his work, but that's understandable, and sometimes even useful. ZZZZ Best, for example, was a paranoiac's dream, and Brambles, who doesn't usually seem paranoid, just kept making connections.

Take Richman Financial. The mailing address was to Richie Schulman at his Killion Street condo. By now Brambles knew that Schulman was an ex-convict and figured he'd better take a closer look at the condo. He learned that the utilities were listed in Schulman's name at B&M Insurance, 16661 Ventura Blvd., also in Encino. Checking corporate records, Brambles learned that B&M was formed September 25, 1985, wasn't licensed to do any insurance business and that the registered agent was listed as—Barry Minkow.

That's not all. Now that Barry was comfortably established at his fancy new home in Woodland Hills, he had a house-sitter to take care of his condo at 7211 Cozycroft Avenue, #25, in Canoga Park. It was none other than Joey Mangiapane.

Brambles was hot on the trail. It emerged that B&M had moved from Ventura Blvd. out to 19860 Nordhoff Pl., Northridge, where the 4Z Equipment Co. was located. As its name implies, 4Z was a unit of ZZZZ Best.

Brambles was getting excited. Here was a nest of what he likes to call "OC," for organized crime, and they were all up to something new and wonderful in conjunction with Barry Minkow, the famous young entrepreneur whose television ads by now were everywhere. He certainly had the best-known carpet-cleaning company in Southern California.

Starting in March, detectives sat and watched the Nordhoff Place address and "established that Richard Schulman, Maurice Rind, Joseph Mangiapane and Robert Victor/Viggiano, among others, were conducting business within the premises." Throughout April and

May, detectives from the organized crime unit also took turns watching the Killion Street condominium, which was Schulman's home and the business address of Richman Financial. They saw Barry, Rind and Mangiapane come and go.

Meanwhile, Brambles was asking around about Lorenzo. His informants told him, as he put it in his report to Congress, that "Ronnie Lorenzo is involved in cocaine trafficking and the laundering of drug profits through Splash Restaurant. The same two informants further advised that Ronnie Lorenzo, through organized crime associates, is laundering money derived from cocaine transactions through Barry Minkow and ZZZZ Best."

This seems to be where Brambles took something of a wrong turn. He got hold of the main ZZZZ Best SEC filings and dived in, learning what he could about the company. Eventually his informants told him that what he was reading was lies, that the restoration jobs were false and that the revenue being booked from insurance companies was actually from mobsters, who made it selling illegal narcotics. Brambles then drew the reasonable but mistaken conclusion that what he had was a giant money-laundering case (rather than a colossal securities fraud), and at this point, late in April, he went in to see his boss.

21

Different people place the beginning of the end for Barry Minkow at different times. If you believe in original sin, the question is easy, but for the rest of us there are so many choices. Who can sort out the unique combination of nature, nurture, free will, airborne pollutants and who knows what else that causes someone to take a particular course in life?

The location of Barry's nativity and upbringing might be crucial, for example. It may be sheer chance that he sprang up from soil enriched by the mulch of decades of fraud before him. Then again it may be that something about Southern California, some extreme promise of paradise, is especially conducive to people like Barry. Law-enforcement authorities say the area has far more than its share of telephone-sales rip-offs, investment cons and other traps for the unwary. Los Angeles was also home to Equity Funding Corp., probably the biggest financial scam of the postwar era. When this high-flying insurance and investment concern collapsed in 1973, investigators discovered that two-thirds of its $3.2 billion life insurance portfolio was nonexistent. Investors lost more than $260 million.

Lesser scams abound in L.A. Maybe a place that's always sunny is different from other places, encouraging optimism and belief. Certainly in their day-to-day encounters with one another Southern Californians are the nicest and most trusting of people, and despite the naked materialism of the place, class-consciousness seems lower than elsewhere. In Boston or New York, a person's background reveals itself instantly in speech, clothing, etc. Such distinctions are far subtler in Los Angeles. Barry would seem much more obviously a hustler in New York, yet working from L.A., he had New Yorkers fooled.

Angelenos are notoriously open to new ideas, and ideas are like people—some are good, some are bad and some are crazy. Historian Carey McWilliams quotes *Life* magazine as complaining decades ago that Southern California "is corrupted with an odd community giddiness . . . nowhere else do eccentrics flourish in such close abundance. Nowhere do spiritual or economic panaceas grow so lushly. Nowhere is undisciplined gullibility so widespread."

Far-out religions thrive, and money usually plays an important role. Southern California may itself be such a money-making theological outcropping, a giddy expression of faith by millions in the goodness of life and the remoteness of earthquakes. Sunshine, land and water were the overt themes in the region's development, but money—and fraud—were the fuel. The history of Barry's San Fernando Valley tells the story.

The Valley was first spied by white men on August 5, 1769, when a Spanish exploration party led by Captain Don Gaspar de Portola reached the top of the Sepulveda Pass, a fortuitous gap in the Santa Monica Mountains that now accommodates the San Diego Freeway. From the account of Father Juan Crespi, it's clear that the trusting, openhanded character of Californians goes way back.

"We saw a very pleasant and spacious valley," he wrote. "We descended to it and stopped close to the watering place, which is a very large pool. Near it we found a large village of heathen, very friendly and docile; they offered us their seeds in baskets and other things made of rushes. . . . Each of them brought some food with which to regale us."

Southern California had great weather, but it wasn't on the way to anyplace and didn't have a natural port. The place as we know it is really an act of will born of some remarkable men who saw the potential for profit in its sunny, breezy climate. Propaganda, cheap train tickets, plentiful open land and a vast, speedy streetcar system attracted people in droves, until the region ran up against the limits of its water supply around the turn of the century. This problem was solved by the legendary William Mulholland, chief of the city's water department, and a group of local citizens who perpetrated one of the century's great land swindles.

Mulholland's secret plan was to siphon water to the city by means of a $25 million, 250-mile aqueduct from the hapless Owens Valley to the north. When the plan was well underway, but before word got out, a syndicate of powerful Angelenos led by Harrison Gray Otis, publisher of the *Los Angeles Times*, bought the 16,200-acre Porter Ranch in the northern San Fernando Valley. That was in March of 1905. On June 29, when news of the water plan was made public (in Otis' *Times*, of course), land prices in the Valley soared. The conspirators then pulled out all the stops to get voter approval for an initial bond issue to finance the project. The aqueduct never even reached Los Angeles, terminating instead in what was portrayed as the only sensible place to store all that water—the San Fernando Valley. McWilliams says speculators bought up vacant properties for $5, $10, or $20 an acre and then sold for 100 times as much, making an estimated $100 million in profits. A fictionalized version of the story, set a generation later, is told in the movie *Chinatown*.

Roughly the same bunch of conspirators got together for an even bigger Valley land deal soon after. Their Los Angeles Suburban Homes Company bought 47,500 acres for $53 each and eventually sold most of them for $150 to $600 each. This company is noteworthy in the tale of Barry Minkow because in 1911, roughly in the center of the Valley, it created a new town named Marian, for General Otis's daughter. Since there was already a Mariana in California, the community adopted the name used by the local Southern Pacific Railroad station—Reseda, the botanical name of the blue-green mignonette flower that grew there. Reseda thus used to call itself the Flower of the Valley.

In the spring of 1987, it still seemed that Barry was the Flower of the Valley. But sometime during the week of May 18—the week when accountant Norman Rothberg made like a canary at the Ernst & Whinney offices in Century City—Barry called Peter Griffith, a senior audit manager at Ernst & Whinney in Woodland Hills. He told Griffith that the *Los Angeles Times* would likely publish an article soon about credit-card fraud at ZZZZ Best. Barry explained that the *Times* had got hold of some old news about some former employees who misused customers' credit-card numbers. ZZZZ Best had made good on any losses and got rid of the bad apples, he told Griffith. The story was being dredged up now only because a certain *Times* reporter had an ax to grind against Barry personally.

I ground no such ax; I like everybody. In fact I was even a lame duck. I had already told the editors at the *Times* that I would be leaving for *The Wall Street Journal*, where I would begin work June 1, and figured on leaving Barry behind forever. As I hurried to tie up loose ends in order to squeeze a small vacation between jobs, I came across the material Robin Swanson had sent me. Despite my fervent promises, I had never even checked it out. I decided to dispose of the thing one way or another before I left.

Tenacity, thy name is Robin Swanson. The world turned out to be full of customers whose credit cards were abused by ZZZZ Best—and full of bankers who wanted to "nail that little prick," as one so eloquently put it. I was able to show massive fraud, and when I called Barry with the evidence, he admitted through Moskowitz that ZZZZ Best had submitted $72,000 in phony credit-card charges from November 1984 to March 1985. In an earlier, less guarded conversation, Barry admitted $150,000 to $200,000 in false credit-card charges. In any case, he blamed them all on twelve unscrupulous carpet-cleaning subcontractors whom the company had been paying an immediate 50 percent commission, and who therefore had an incentive to submit bogus charges even if those charges were credited to the ZZZZ Best account and not their own.

This might have been plausible, except I also discovered $91,000 in Floral Fantasies forgeries. Barry claimed he repaid those charges only to help his friend Arrington, who had bought the shop and inherited the problem from a prior owner. Barry was lying. City tax records showed that Arrington acquired the place in October of 1985; the phony charges were submitted months later.

The result of all this, on May 22, 1987, was a 1,200-word story headlined BEHIND "WHIZ KID" IS A TRAIL OF FALSE CREDIT-CARD BILL-INGS. It portrayed Barry as a liar, laid out the bogus charges, recounted his meteoric rise and mentioned his past problems with mobster Jack Catain.

On Wall Street, ZZZZ Best stock was immediately pummeled. It lost 28 percent of its value in active trading during the day to close at $11.125, down $4.25. May 22 was the normally slow Friday at the beginning of the Memorial Day weekend, but news of the credit-card allegations was carried throughout the investment community by the Dow Jones News Service.

Barry and his followers were as shaken as the company's stock. The timing couldn't have been worse. Drexel was in the middle of arranging financing for the crucial KeyServ acquisition, and less than two weeks earlier ZZZZ Best had held the lavish "Sky's the Limit" conference, leaving people like Jeri Carr breathless with enthusiasm for the company. Carr's husband, who usually rises first in the morning, woke her with the news.

"Guess what?" he said. "Your boy's in the paper."

DANIEL AKST

Carr looked at the headline and gasped. Her reaction was fairly typical. Many of the people around ZZZZ Best who thought the company was clean—or at least figured it wasn't unusually fraudulent—were shocked. Outsiders, who had been led to believe that Barry was some sort of entrepreneurial Messiah, read for the first time about his seamier side. Barry himself tried not to show much distress, even though the story plunged his Ponzi scheme into turmoil. Bankers, lawyers, board members, investors and most of all Drexel would demand an explanation. On top of everything else, Sharon Elowsky arrived that very day from New York.

Barry had been sweet-talking Elowsky for weeks in the hope she would give him some more of Prudential-Bache's money. They had met in New York, when Barry invited her to one of his slide-and-chart performances there in connection with the planned Drexel funding. Elowsky found him enthusiastic, knowledgeable, and "very, very friendly." After that he called her once or twice a week. Sometimes they talked about business—"get someone with a better name than Drexel," she urged, alluding to the firm's legal troubles—but often they discussed personal matters. Barry and Elowsky became friends.

At one point Barry told her he was seriously considering buying the Seattle Mariners, maybe by borrowing money and then selling shares in the baseball team to the public. Barry wanted Pru-Bache to consider putting together a deal, so Elowsky set up a meeting with the firm's investment bankers in Los Angeles. Then Barry asked Elowsky to attend, all expenses paid. She hesitated at first, but he sent her a first-class plane ticket with hotel and car reservations. Elowsky's resistance crumbled.

Shari Elowsky graduated from the University of Michigan and has a law degree from Boston University. She grew up in Jericho, Long Island, and when she met Barry she was living in Brooklyn Heights, that elegant enclave bound by ties of subway and spirit to New York's financial district. Quick, dark and attractive, Elowsky is five feet four inches tall and begins every day with three Diet Cokes or Tabs, consuming can after can throughout her waking hours. These no doubt contribute to her intensely alert appearance, but Elowsky is not merely besotted with caffeine. She is almost palpably bright, perceptive and articulate, under certain circumstances even a bit of a wiseguy. Elowsky had met many rich men in business, but they were all older and had grown wealthy by more conventional means. Barry was very different, and very charming.

Elowsky had already let him borrow some cash from his Pru-Bache line of credit when she arrived in Los Angeles on May 22 to meet with Barry, the investment bankers and Arthur Barens, Barry's lawyer, who owned the minor-league Palm Springs Angels. Barry had already provided Pru-Bache with the Mariners' financial statements.

The credit-card allegations spoiled the meeting. Barry was so busy putting out fires that he was able to attend only briefly—he talked about getting the people of Seattle behind the team—and later he apologized to Elowsky, saying that had he known what the day would be like, he would have canceled her visit. Elowsky accepted his elaborate explanation about the subcontractors, and concluded that Barry's handling of the fraud was a sign he was a good manager: "There was a problem, he found out what it was and he solved it," she said later in court.

Barry expected everyone to react this way, and he remained outwardly cool despite hours of tense strategy sessions with insiders like Mark Morze over how to control a crisis that threatened to engulf the company. Barry had been through tough times before, and really, why should news of a relatively insignificant credit-card snafu make such a difference? Compared to what was really going on at ZZZZ Best, it was nothing, and the sums were relatively minor. The sound and fury could be handled if nobody panicked. Barry was besieged by calls and fielded most of them deftly. Elaine Orlando's was typical.

"Barry, what does this mean?" she asked worriedly. "I'm nervous."

Barry reassured her the same way he reassured all the others: by blaming dishonest ex-employees or subcontractors, and by citing the personal vendetta of a single embittered newspaperman. Everything was going to be all right.

"Don't even think about it," he urged.

"Well, should I be nervous? Are there any other secrets or anything that I should know about?"

"Don't be ridiculous," Barry said.

The next day, at eight A.M., he called her back. Kay Rozario was also on the line. "Now is the time to show support," he said, and thus Orlando was one of the many people prodded into writing letters to the *Times* on Barry's behalf.

"Has the reverent *Los Angeles Times* stooped to the level of the weekly tabloids?" demanded Milton L. DuBane of Canoga Park.

"I am amazed at the lengths a newspaper will go to sell papers," thundered Barbara Ayash of the Concerned Businessmen's Association of America, whatever that is.

"Let's not convict Minkow before all the facts are in," urged David Jackson of Van Nuys.

"I am proud to know Barry and would venture to say he will lead us to a brighter future," Orlando wrote in concluding her paean. "Light the way, instead of reaching for the switch."

The switch was unfortunately near at hand, and despite his unruffled public posture, Barry sensed that darkness was beginning to descend.

At Union Bank, the May 22 *Times* story shocked Vanessa England. Her boss, Susan Russell, was on vacation, but England and several other bank executives met that day to discuss the $7 million question: is our money safe? ZZZZ Best had borrowed its entire line of credit, and would have taken $3 million more if Russell hadn't refused to raise its limit. Everybody was pretty worried, despite whatever assurances England had managed to elicit from Barry over the phone. The group, which included Union Bank's legal counsel, drafted a letter to Barry and then England drove out to Reseda to deliver it personally. Barry kept her waiting, and when she finally got to see him she briskly summarized the letter, which he had to sign. It required ZZZZ Best to assign directly to Union Bank any proceeds of Interstate Appraisal contract 0147 for the $8.2 million restoration job in National City. This contract—a fiction, of course, like the job itself—had supposedly begun in December and ended in May, but the bank hadn't been paid. Barry said ZZZZ Best hadn't been paid either. Padgett later told Union Bank that payment had been delayed by the insurance company, but would be forthcoming within fourteen days.

Mike Malamut was also among the worried.

"It's old news," Barry insisted. "I don't even know why they're bringing it up now. The lawyers knew all about it, it was just some former employees taking advantage. We fired them, and we repaid the customers. Case closed. Drexel knew all about it, and they considered it too small to be material."

"What about Catain?" Malamut asked. "Are you involved with a guy like that?"

"Mike, I was eighteen years old and I needed money to start my business. I would have borrowed it from anyone. No one else would loan me the money." Barry insisted that this too wasn't material. "In fact, I was a witness for the government against Catain."

That same day, Barry summoned Arrington home from a KeyServ operation he was visiting in New Jersey. Arrington, who was miserable about being named in the article, met with Barry soon after landing.

"We're in danger of losing the company over this, Chip," Barry said. "Drexel wants to know exactly what happened. If the truth comes out, we could lose this company in a matter of days."

Arrington agreed to tell anyone who asked that the credit-card problems at ZZZZ Best were caused by former subcontractors, and that the problems at Floral Fantasies were inherited from a former owner, who had left Arrington with some receivables that for some reason had to be deposited gradually over time. That would explain why the forgeries were dated after Arrington became legal owner of the store.

This was the same old story with a clever twist, but investors weren't buying. After the long weekend the news reached a much wider audience: *The Wall Street Journal*, which doesn't publish on Memorial Day, carried a five-paragraph item in Tuesday's paper. *Barron's*, in a lengthier account, said Barry blamed subcontractors even though the ZZZZ Best prospectus specifically stated that the company never uses any. When trading resumed on Tuesday, May 26, ZZZZ Best shares continued their free-fall.

That same day, Barry had to face Ernst & Whinney. Larry Gray and Howard Levy were very unhappy about the *Times* article. Levy hadn't credited Rothberg's allegations at first, and Ernst & Whinney even hired a private investigator, just as it had when it first accepted the ZZZZ Best engagement, with equally blank results. Then all of a sudden the *Times* was calling Barry a liar and accusing his company of fraud. Maybe there was something to what Rothberg had said. The prospect was almost nauseating.

So as ZZZZ Best shares were losing value and the company's phones rang off the hook, as Drexel's lawyers met ominously with Mark Morze in the other room, Barry and Moskowitz sat down with Gray and Bill Dudley of Ernst & Whinney to thrash out the Rothberg allegations. Dudley had already told Moskowitz about them, but this was a chance for the accountants to get their answer from the horse's mouth. The horse denied everything.

"Who's Norm Rothberg?" Barry demanded. "Why are you listening to a crank like this?"

The men from Ernst & Whinney said they wanted the matter put before the ZZZZ Best board of directors. Barry said he knew for a fact that some of the board members were out of town, but Moskowitz said they would be rounded up for a meeting as quickly as possible.

Barry was enraged, and he turned his wrath on Rothberg. That same day, Rothberg found himself in a room in the Culver City offices of Interstate Appraisal with two hulking individuals: Mark Roddy, who had celebrated his thirty-sixth birthday just the day before, and Brian Morze, who barely knew Rothberg. Together, they outweighed him four to one.

"Did you tell Ernst and Whinney the Sacramento job doesn't exist?" they demanded.

"I never said any such thing," Rothberg replied.

"Well, we're told you did, and you also told Ernst and Whinney the San Diego job might be fake, and the ZZZZ Best books might be off by as much as eighty percent. You didn't say any of that?"

"Look, I'm the only person in this room who knows if I went to Ernst and Whinney, and I say I didn't. We can argue about it all day and never accomplish anything."

Roddy's face was turning a nice carpaccio red as his anger increased. He pounded the desk and jabbed his finger at Rothberg, insisting the latter had "blown the whistle" on his friends. At 138 pounds, Rothberg was getting worried.

Ernst & Whinney hadn't been shy about taking his complaint to ZZZZ Best, which in turn wasn't shy about taking it right back to Rothberg. So much is written about corporate culture these days; here was the ZZZZ Best corporate culture at its best. There was a handgun on the table.

"We have a problem," Brian said at last, lifting the pistol and placing the business end momentarily in his own mouth. He was taking the role of good-cop. "If we can't do something here, I might as well blow my brains out."

Rothberg realized before long that they were in no position to kill him. His meeting with Roddy and Brian Morze broke up after a while. Then the two big men would huddle together or talk on the phone, and Rothberg would be summoned again. He was becoming numb; the day seemed to stretch on forever. Finally Brian Morze demanded that he recant. Rothberg, a law school graduate, literally didn't know the meaning of the word.

At one point Rothberg had to listen to Barry scream at him over the speakerphone, ranting and raving about how he was destroying ZZZZ Best. The tension lasted until the next day, but the talks soon turned into a negotiation. Rothberg learned what it means to recant, and agreed to take $1,000 a week in return for doing so.

Meanwhile, the bloodletting on Wall Street continued. When the stock market closed on Wednesday, May 27, ZZZZ Best stock stood at $6.75, which meant that the 11.5 million shares outstanding had fallen by $8.625 each since the credit-card article the preceding Friday. (Ironically, a *Washington Post* story that day about young entrepreneurs featured Barry, without mentioning his troubles.) The decline of ZZZZ Best stock seemed out of all proportion; what was a little credit-card fraud, after all? Again and again, corporations had been caught raping the environment, selling harmful products and stealing from the government. While their stock prices often suffered commensurate with any penalties imposed, the punishment inflicted by Wall Street on ZZZZ Best seemed cruel and unusual. It made me a little giddy. I have never earned more than a modest living, and it tickled some deep, anarchic funny bone within me to think that I had wiped out $100 million, just like that. On paper, at least, Barry had lost about half.

The ZZZZ Best stock plunge had Bob Grossmann, Steve Greenberg, Maurice Rind and perhaps 1,000 investors frantic with worry, not to mention ZZZZ Best employees and suppliers. The stock had lost so much value that there had already been margin calls, meaning that buyers who had purchased ZZZZ Best shares with borrowed funds had to put up more cash or watch their position liquidated. ZZZZ Best investors were experiencing a one-stock crash.

Something had to be done. On Thursday, May 28, at 10:08 A.M. Eastern time, the Dow Jones ticker reported tersely, ZZZZ BEST PUTS YEAR NET AT $5 MILLION VS YR AGO $900,000.

Eighteen minutes later, the ticker followed with a fuller account of a four-page ZZZZ Best press release written, according to Jeri Carr, by Greenberg's Anametrics. The release boasted "record preliminary results" for the fiscal year ended April 30, in which ZZZZ Best said it expected to report profit exceeding $5 million, or about 50 cents a share, on revenue of more than $50 million.

In the preceding year, ZZZZ Best reported profit of $900,000, or 12 cents a share, on revenue of $4.8 million. The improvement was stunning.

The release was chock-full of good news. In it, Barry said that an independent investigation of the "reported" credit-card problems found no wrongdoing by the company or its management. Instead, Barry explained, the phony billings "were caused by six former sub-contractors and six of their employees, all of whom had been hired by ZZZZ Best as a group from another carpet-cleaning firm."

Barry also said ZZZZ Best had a backlog of $25 million in new restoration business and had won another $2 million contract just the day before. He projected "substantial growth" in sales and profits for the current fiscal year. He said the KeyServ acquisition would close within six weeks and would add to earnings per share, and that his company's investment bankers were expected to complete their due diligence within thirty days.

The release was a lie from beginning to end—ZZZZ Best had no earnings, Barry forged the credit-card drafts himself, KeyServ was unprofitable, etc.—and the figures were released without telling Ernst & Whinney, leaving Gray incensed. But the release worked. ZZZZ Best stock jumped $3.375 that day, closing at $10.125 on record volume of 2.1 million shares. Apparently with a little help from Anametrics, Barry had stopped the bleeding.

The patient was still very sick, however. Six days earlier, on the morning of May 22, I had been rousted from a hot shower by an anonymous caller who insisted, as I stood dripping onto the floor, that my story revealed only a small portion of what was happening at ZZZZ Best. He offered little to go on besides exhortation, and that one Titanic phrase common to all anonymous callers: "This is only the tip of the iceberg."

The SEC was getting similar calls, although it had little hard evidence until one day someone called with something more. He wouldn't give his name, but he seemed to know everything about ZZZZ Best, and he said its insurance restoration business was fake. On May 28, the same day ZZZZ Best issued the glowing press release that pumped up its stock, the SEC regional office in Los Angeles received a ZZZZ Best prospectus by Federal Express. Inside, someone had marked things that were false about the company, including passages on the Sacramento job, the generators and Interstate Appraisal. The knowing anonymous caller phoned again the next day to say he'd sent the marked prospectus. This time he was transferred to Schindler, whom he would subsequently call between nine and nine-thirty AM almost every morning during the rest of ZZZZ Best's brief and inglorious existence, describing to her in increasing detail the "massive Ponzi scheme" at the company. The caller sounded like a New Yorker, and refused to give his name because, he said, he feared for his own safety. He claimed to be motivated by vengeance and the desire to protect innocent people from further losses.

Less altruistically, he might have been a short-seller. These carnivores make money by finding stocks that will go down—or that they can drive down. Then they borrow shares in the company from a securities firm holding the stock in a margin account. They then sell the borrowed shares and wait for the stock to fall. If all goes according to plan, they can replace shares they sold at, say, $10 with shares they bought later at perhaps $5. Their funereal reputation notwithstanding, "shorts," as they are known for short, probably help keep the financial markets efficient. In any case, they had begun to circle around ZZZZ Best.

22

Mike Malamut is one of the more decent characters in the comic opera that was ZZZZ Best. When Barry invited him to join its board of directors, he offered Malamut 25,000 warrants as a perfectly legal incentive. Malamut was delighted to join the board, but steadfastly refused the warrants. He just felt it wasn't right.

When Malamut learned of the Rothberg allegations on top of the *Times* article, he was upset. Barry portrayed Rothberg as a kook, but Malamut could see that even if the allegations weren't true, they were taking their toll. Sometime late in May he and his friend and fellow board member, Neal Dem, met privately with Barry and told him it was imperative to extinguish the rumors swirling about the company by authorizing a thorough, independent inquiry into the whole mess. They wanted to call in a respected outside law firm.

"I'm sure there's nothing to all this," Malamut soothed. "But an independent inquiry would end the rumors, and ZZZZ Best could get back to business."

Barry wouldn't hear of it. "It's all been investigated over and over," he said in exasperation. "It's just a waste of money."

Malamut and Dem were among the few people who could stand up to Barry, and both said they would resign if he didn't go along. Recognizing that their departure would intensify the hurricane of questions already tearing up his venture, Barry was forced to agree.

On Friday, May 29, the ZZZZ Best board of directors met in what was probably the first such session in which Barry wasn't entirely in control. Larry Gray presented the Rothberg allegations to the assembled directors, who were visibly concerned by them. But then Barry had his say. He depicted Rothberg as a hard-luck character and perhaps a crazy man who was just angling for a job with a big accounting firm. As to whether ZZZZ Best actually performed the Sacramento job, Krowpman noted that he had supplied equipment for it, and Barry's response was unassailable: "Larry Gray and Mark Moskowitz *visited the site.* What better proof do you need?" None, as far as Malamut was concerned. The whole thing sounded bizarre to him anyway, and he was probably the smartest of the board members. As for the credit-card story in the *Times*, Barry said he just couldn't understand it. It was old news, it was former employees and it was all rectified. Barry added that Drexel had cleared him and the company, and that he believed the timing of the story was attributable to short-sellers attacking ZZZZ Best stock. Barry repeated that the author of the story was for some reason out to get him.

As planned, the board empowered Malamut and Dem to function as a special investigative committee, and appropriated $100,000 so they could hire outside counsel for an impartial, independent probe of the Rothberg and credit-card allegations.

"This will be the best thing you can ever do for yourself," Malamut told Barry afterward. "I know $100,000 is a lot of money, but this will show the world. This will be the best investment you ever made."

Barry insisted the whole thing was still a waste of time and money, but at least ZZZZ Best stock had held on to most of Thursday's gains, giving up only an eighth to close the week at an even $10 per share.

On Sunday, Steve Sanford, a West Coast consultant to Anametrics, talked to someone at the respected law firm of Kadison, Pfaelzer, Woodard, Quinn & Rossi about the problems at ZZZZ Best, and the firm was promptly hired by Malamut and Dem on behalf of the board to investigate four areas: credit-card fraud, the Rothberg allegations, Barry's former ties to Catain and whether Barry was abusing drugs. Kadison was probably a good choice. Robert Bonner, the local U.S. Attorney, was a former partner, and Richard Simon, the canny partner who would take the lead in the ZZZZ Best matter, had previously helped defend the law firm of Rogers & Wells in the J. David scam. (Rogers & Wells, whose role corresponded to that of Hughes Hubbard, settled an investor suit by agreeing to pay a staggering $40 million.) A bearded and affable miniature-train hobbyist, Simon would work the ZZZZ Best case with partner Jeffrey Riffer, who was a certified public accountant as well as an attorney, and with John

Murphy & Associates, a private investigations firm founded by former FBI agents. The Murphy firm specializes in forensic accounting—digging into a financial corpse in search of foul play.

Larry Gray had attended the ZZZZ Best board meeting on Friday, but Peter Griffith, his Ernst & Whinney colleague, spent the day poring over company records. He found things that made his hair stand on end.

Among them was a check for $5,000 dated December 15, 1986, made payable to Norman Rothberg. It was signed by Barry, whose posture so far had been, "Who's Norm Rothberg?"

Then there were the checks to vendors. These were supposed to cover supplies and equipment purchased by ZZZZ Best. But the endorsements—on the flip side, they were endorsed by ZZZZ Best employees! Furthermore, Griffith found that ZZZZ Best's records were unable to dispel the credit-card allegations in the May 22 *Times* story, and he wasn't the only one who was skeptical of Barry's explanation.

The people at Drexel Burnham Lambert were probably among the sharpest ever to take a close look at ZZZZ Best. They had known of the credit-card fraud at the company, but they hadn't known about the parallel incident at Floral Fantasies, which left them shocked and angry. Now they wanted some answers, and soon after May 22 they had grilled Arrington about the shop. As he had promised Barry, Chip told them he was its true owner, and had inherited the credit-card problem from the Lees, who had sold him the store. The Drexel people didn't believe him, and afterward Arrington reported fretfully to Barry that they were demanding paperwork to prove his story.

"Don't worry about it," Barry said. "Just call Mark Morze; he can do anything."

Morze asked Arrington for a blank check and his checking-account statement covering the time when Chip was supposed to have bought Floral Fantasies. Chip delivered these to Morze's condo, and later picked up the finished work: a cashed-looking check for $20,000, complete with Chai Lee's endorsement and bank stamps on back, and a bank statement showing an extra $20,000 passing through Arrington's account.

Chip signed the check himself, and lest there be any doubt about its purpose, the memo section said: "purchase of Floral Fantasies." He took these documents to Barry, who said he would get them to Drexel. Soon after, Arrington met with Drexel's lawyers again. They told him outright that they still didn't believe his story about the flower shop, and demanded that he write the numbers zero through 10 and 10 through zero on a piece of paper. They compared his writing to one of the forged credit-card drafts, looked at each other and then told Chip he could go.

Rothberg, meanwhile, began his about-face in a speakerphone conversation with Neal Dem. In the silent presence of Mark Roddy and Brian Morze, who sat with him as 500 pounds of insurance for the cause, Rothberg told Dem that he was sorry for going to Ernst & Whinney and causing so much trouble. He said he really had no firsthand knowledge of any wrongdoing, and didn't know anything for a fact. Rothberg similarly recanted to Mark Moskowitz over the speakerphone, with Barry and others listening in. When Moskowitz hung up, Barry said, "Great job, Norm."

But Rothberg had already let the genie out of the bottle, and on Monday, June 1, the creature's havoc became manifest. Anametrics was forced to issue a press release saying that Drexel and ZZZZ Best had terminated their relationship "by mutual agreement."

"ZZZZ Best Co. Inc. intends to pursue discussions with two other investment banking firms which have recently expressed an interest in arranging financing for the acquisition of KeyServ," the release continued hopefully. But it concluded on an ominous note: "The Company further stated that, it has not at any time been authorized to comment about any due diligence conducted by Drexel Burnham Lambert while it was engaged as advisor."

Drexel was filled with suspicion about ZZZZ Best, but the immediate cause of its resignation was Barry's comment at the end of a 345-word story in the *Los Angeles Times* on the preceding Friday. The last paragraph quoted him as saying that the "independent investigation" that cleared the company and its management of any wrongdoing "was conducted by Drexel as part of its normal procedure before arranging financing."

Drexel executives were outraged. Drexel hadn't completed its investigation, and the findings so far were anything but exculpatory. The firm's lawyers now felt that having Drexel's imprimatur erroneously broadcast in this way could leave Drexel open to enormous liability if things at ZZZZ Best really weren't in order and losses later resulted. Even Barry recognized his mistake, telling associates it was his own fault for "shooting off my big mouth to the media."

The market's punishment was swift: ZZZZ Best shares fell $2.125 to close at $7.875 on the day.

At eight A.M. the following day, June 2, Larry Gray called Bruce

Andersen to tell him that Ernst & Whinney quit. Later Gray told Moskowitz as well, and letters were delivered to the homes of ZZZZ Best board members.

"Hey, it's no big deal," Barry told Malamut. "With all the publicity, they're just not really comfortable with the engagement. Plus they're very expensive and we can probably do better. These accountants are a dime a dozen."

But that wasn't the way he really felt. Sometimes even Barry let down his guard.

"What are we going to do?" Padgett asked worriedly.

"I don't know, Tom," Barry replied. "I'm out of answers. You tell me." Padgett had never heard his commanding officer sounding so exhausted, and it left him deeply worried.

Fortunately for Barry, the law was on his side. Public companies normally have to announce important developments immediately. But in this case ZZZZ Best was able to put off issuing another negative press release, because federal law gives public companies fifteen days to disclose a change of auditors. Barry naturally took the entire fifteen days, which meant he would have until June 17 to find a new auditor and put a good face on things.

The auditor's resignation wasn't publicly known yet, but Rose Schindler's informant told her about it soon after. On Wednesday, June 3, Schindler had written ZZZZ Best asking that the company voluntarily provide certain documents concerning Interstate Appraisal, among other things. She wanted to see the documents, but she also wanted to test Barry's willingness to cooperate. Schindler was one of eleven children and used to work as a night social worker at a large public hospital in St. Louis. She is attuned to people's responses. She finally got the records, but not before fielding an inquiry from a renowned Hughes Hubbard partner in Washington.

By this time there were many, many people looking for the truth about Barry and his company, and it was increasingly a struggle for Barry and Morze to keep them all at bay. Reporters were starting to swarm, and the more press ZZZZ Best got, the more knowledgeable people questioned whether such a business was possible. The short-sellers were also active.

J. Patrick Dunn was a twenty-five-year-old analyst at Feshbach Bros., with $325 million under management the biggest short-sellers in the business. The Feshbachs are a trio of yuppie Scientologists with little formal education and a keen eye for crooked companies. Their specialty is small, sleazy companies with stocks hyped out of all proportion. Feshbach is based in Palo Alto, but Dunn saw the *Los Angeles Times* credit-card story and was intrigued. Barry's explanation sounded absurd, and Dunn, a rangy CPA from St. Paul, soon assembled a paper trail that smelled strongly of malfeasance. Checking around among companies that specialize in water- and fire-damage repair, he learned that ZZZZ Best's claim of a $7 million Sacramento restoration job was absurd. It looked like Feshbach had a live one.

ZZZZ Best stock continued to take a beating, closing the first week in June at $6.50. That was off nearly $12 a share—or 65 percent—from its all-time high only eight weeks earlier. Schindler was convinced something was seriously wrong, and Mike Brambles by now knew virtually the whole story, although he still thought the point was money-laundering. Personally, I was doing my best to forget ZZZZ Best. Reading *The Philadelphia Inquirer* on the stifling beach at Cape May, New Jersey, I watched the collapse of its stock with morbid interest, and when I returned to Los Angeles my beat at *The Wall Street Journal* was the entertainment industry. Imagining glittering Malibu soirees and wide-eyed starlets, I put Barry Minkow firmly out of mind.

23

Doug Galin and Mark Moskowitz were a couple of very unhappy lawyers early in June of 1987. Galin was counsel to
Ernst & Whinney, which had just quit as auditors for ZZZZ
Best, and he wanted Moskowitz to tell the world about what
was happening at Barry's company. Galin contended that when ZZZZ
Best filed the requisite Form 8-K with the SEC to explain its change
of auditors—a form whose contents are made public—Rothberg's allegations and the Kadison, Pfaelzer investigation ought to be disclosed.

Moskowitz, staunchly upholding the interests of his ludicrously
fraudulent client, thought any mention that the insurance jobs might
be fake was a terrible idea. He felt that to talk about the Rothberg
allegations in the 8-K would mean "an announcement to the public
that would cause the stock to plummet," resulting in losses over an
accusation that didn't even appear to be true. After all, Rothberg had
already recanted, and in Moskowitz's view Ernst & Whinney's stated
reason for resigning didn't relate directly to his finger-pointing.

"Ernst and Whinney—and they were questioned on several occasions—did not raise an issue of concern at that point in time concerning
management integrity," Moskowitz later told Congress in his best
post-Watergate style.

Remember that Moskowitz himself still had the 25,000 shares Barry
gave him for the IOU, and their value had increased considerably.
At one point they were worth more than $450,000. But it seems far-
fetched to say that this was on his mind. He probably just thought
he was doing a good job, and he really liked Barry.

The discussions between Galin and Moskowitz got pretty hot, and
Ernst & Whinney executive Leroy Gardner told Congress that

Moskowitz's firm finally used a club: "They threatened our firm with the financial responsibility in the event that the disclosure was forced upon the company by us, and that it should later . . . prove to be untrue." In other words, the accounting firm might get sued.

While Ernst & Whinney was urging Moskowitz to put some bite into the upcoming ZZZZ Best Form 8-K, the accounting firm itself was being more reticent. When Larry Gray was contacted by Arthur Andersen, Price Waterhouse, and Coopers & Lybrand, all Big Eight accounting firms that were considering a bid on the ZZZZ Best audit, he told them his firm quit because it was concerned by a lack of internal controls and supporting documentation on the restoration jobs; because of adverse publicity surrounding the credit-card issue; and because of the Rothberg allegations, which apparently weren't described in the direst terms. But he also said he had no reportable disagreements with management and no reservations about management integrity—pending the outcome of the Kadison, Pfaelzer investigation. "We just did not want to be involved," Gray told the other accountants. "We didn't want to become associated with the financial statements."

Unfortunately, the Kadison, Pfaelzer investigation was getting no help from what is known in the trade as the chief allegator. On June 8, Kadison attorneys Rich Simon, Jeff Riffer and David Eisen grilled ghostly Norm Rothberg about his earlier allegations to Ernst & Whinney. But to their dismay, the whistle-blower had grown silent.

The gravelly-voiced informant now claimed he had merely over-heard people at Interstate Appraisal saying that work on ZZZZ Best jobs was substandard, and that he conveyed this to Levy hoping Levy would tell ZZZZ Best, and ZZZZ Best would then give Rothberg a full-time job. The attorneys knew very well what Rothberg had ac-tually told Levy, and this was a very different story. They were questioning him closely on it when suddenly Rothberg announced that he had another meeting, got up and left.

It became clear to Norm Rothberg that a little more was going to be required of him than merely being vague on the telephone. Around June 9, he sat down with Barry and Brian Morze at Bakers Square in Reseda.

"Are you wired?" Barry demanded.

"I guess I've had a lot of coffee today, yeah," Rothberg answered defensively.

"No, no, no," Barry said in exasperation. "Are you wired for *sound?* Do you have a tape recorder?"

Rothberg demanded $100,000 at first but eventually agreed to accept $25,000 in cash and $1,000 every Friday for the next three years, also in cash. He actually got about $17,000 in all.

On June 11, Ernst & Whinney got a terrifying and mysterious letter signed only "B. Cautious." Well-written by someone obviously familiar with the world of accounting and finance, it stated baldly that the ZZZZ Best insurance jobs were fake and its earnings from them nonexistent. The detailed letter also said the generators ZZZZ Best supposedly purchased for $2 million were actually junk bought through intermediaries at vastly inflated prices to give the company an asset base; that checks passed between ZZZZ Best and its vendors were part of the cover-up, since they paid for no goods or services; and that the company's earnings in past years were also fabricated. "Confirmation of these allegations can be accomplished by a careful due diligence," the letter says, concluding chillingly: "Such due diligence on your behalf is imperative for your protection."

The letter was dated June 9, well before the Ernst & Whinney resignation became public. By this time Rose Schindler had formally requested subpoena power from the SEC commissioners in Washington, D.C. They didn't grant her request until July 2; the commissioners had unwittingly bought Barry more time. Schindler also wanted to halt trading in ZZZZ Best stock, but headquarters wouldn't go along. What did she have to go on, after all, besides a lot of suspicious activity and the ravings of an anonymous informant?

But little ZZZZ Best firecrackers kept going off all over the place. Susan Russell kept nagging Barry about the $7 million he owed Union Bank. They met three times in June, and each time she talked about his violation of their agreement by borrowing from First Interstate, whose debt she had been assured would be repaid long ago. Each time, Barry had to remain calm and placate her. Russell's colleague, Vanessa England, tried to talk to Padgett, but he was always "traveling." One day she talked to his associate, Brian Logan.

"When is our payment forthcoming?" she demanded.

"I wish I could help you," growled Logan, whose real name was Morze. "But I just don't have the file available. Tom Padgett took it with him."

Meanwhile, four separate class-action suits were filed in federal court between June 4 and June 10 by disgruntled shareholders accusing Barry and ZZZZ Best of securities-law violations for failing to disclose things like the credit-card problems, whose sudden emergence in the press had sent the stock into a nosedive.

Indeed, while Barry struggled in secret to keep things together, Wall Street quickly and viciously turned on its former favorite son. On Monday, June 15, ZZZZ Best stock was short more than 1.5 million shares, out of only about 5.5 million in public hands. Few stocks can hold up for long under such staggering short-interest, which hangs like a millstone around a company's neck. The Feshbachs accounted for most of the shorting. Based on Pat Dunn's analysis, they jumped ZZZZ Best with everything they had. When they couldn't find any more shares of ZZZZ Best common to short, they began shorting the company's warrants. When Schindler called Doug Galin that Monday, he did nothing to set her mind at ease. Galin finally confirmed that Ernst & Whinney had resigned as the ZZZZ Best auditor. He also told her about Rothberg's on-and-off allegations, and about the "B. Cautious" letter.

Galin told Moskowitz about the "B. Cautious" letter the next day by phone—was there an I-told-you-so tone in his voice?—and Moskowitz had him send it by telecopier. Tuesday, June 16, thus was not a great day for Mark Moskowitz. There was a ZZZZ Best board meeting that afternoon, and it was his unhappy duty to distribute copies of the "B. Cautious" letter.

June 17 was the deadline for ZZZZ Best to tell the SEC on Form 8-K why its auditors had quit. The world would know soon after; Dow Jones has someone stationed at the SEC in Washington full-time to sift all filings as soon as they come in. But the ZZZZ Best 8-K merely said Ernst & Whinney resigned June 2, and Price Waterhouse took over on June 5. With fussy legal particularity, it went on to say that "there were no disagreements between the Company and Ernst & Whinney on any matter of accounting principles or practices, financial statement disclosure, or auditing scope or procedure" that, if not resolved to the auditors' satisfaction, would have warranted mention in Ernst & Whinney's audit report. The 8-K also disclosed that "as a result of certain newspaper articles," the ZZZZ Best board of directors asked some of its independent directors to investigate with the help of Kadison, Pfaelzer. Then the shareholder suits were disclosed. Although this was not an 8-K to cheer the hearts of ZZZZ Best shareholders, it never mentioned that the ZZZZ Best auditors had been told the company's major business might be a sham.

To make sure that companies don't lie about why they've changed auditors, the SEC requires them to submit a letter from their former auditor giving the auditor's version of events. The auditor must provide this letter within thirty days of the company's 8-K filing. Naturally, Ernst & Whinney waited the full thirty days.

Without the Drexel fund-raising that was so crucial to keeping Barry's dream afloat, ZZZZ Best was once again about to sink for want of cash, even before all the short-sellers, regulators, reporters and others could manage to scuttle the company. Barry also must have sensed by this time that things were falling apart, but it's hard to say when he decided to pillage the company. ZZZZ Best had been through so much and emerged so often unscathed that I tend to think he still felt things would work out.

Indeed, Steve Greenberg was still trying to make the KeyServ deal work. With Drexel unwilling to help, Ken Pavia had made inquiries about getting someone else to sell the bonds, apparently without success. Greenberg, meanwhile, was going to assemble an investment group himself; there were plenty of people willing to put up millions sheerly on his word, but Barry was going to have to pay the price. "It's going to cost you some of your own shares," Greenberg told his protégé.

Perhaps at this point Barry considered the situation unsalvageable. ZZZZ Best was always notoriously short of cash, and he was going around saying the company really needed $7.5 million to cover the major insurance jobs it was supposedly working on. Around mid-June he asked Malamut for money.

"Mike, you never took anything for being on the board," Barry said. "Here's a way I can pay you back. You can be a joint-venturer."

Barry said he needed the money for a big ZZZZ Best restoration job in Texas. Malamut knew that previous ZZZZ Best joint-venture partners had made a lot of money. He talked to Peter Strauss, for example, whose experience had been exemplary. Closer to home, Malamut's friend Neal Dem had made a $600,000 profit on such a deal by lending ZZZZ Best just $500,000; to celebrate, he and his wife took the Malamuts and some other friends on a trip to New York.

"I can give you this chance," Barry said, "because you happen to be in the right place at the right time. We would have used the Drexel money, but until we arrange new financing, you have a chance to get involved in a very profitable project."

What Barry wanted was $1 million. Now, if I had $1 million I would probably put it in the bank, where it would generate enough interest and capital appreciation for me to live happily ever after without pushing a pen for a profit. But people who make $1 million tend to do so by taking risks in business, which is exactly how Malamut did it. Therefore, when Barry asked him for $1 million, Mike Malamut did not say, "Are you completely stark raving crazy?" Instead Malamut was excited and said things like "Thanks" and "Great."

It wasn't that simple, of course. Like most people with money, Malamut has lawyers and accountants and banks, and all had to be satisfied that he was making a prudent investment. Malamut is not so rich that he can afford to throw $1 million away. He doesn't even have it lying around. He borrowed the money from Sterling Bank, where Bob Turnbow worked, using some of his real estate holdings as collateral. These included the house his mother lived in, which they owned jointly.

Malamut did all this because he trusted Barry profoundly, and was told the returns would be enormous. Barry promised that the profits would be split 50-50 between Malamut and ZZZZ Best. Then Mark Morze came over to Malamut's office and laid it all out. He said ZZZZ Best anticipated a total profit of $750,000, half of which would be Malamut's. As the deal was structured, he was to borrow the money from Sterling and keep it in a separate account, disbursing it as needed for supplies. Malamut was to be very involved in the whole project.

As his lawyer, banker and accountant were going over the proposed deal—Barry had provided data from at least one prior job, and projections for the job in question, but they still had many unanswered questions—Barry began to press for the money.

"Mike, we're gonna lose this job if we don't fund it soon," he said.

Malamut tried to hurry things along. Finally, when the closing was just one day off, Barry called Malamut's lawyer and asked that the money be transferred directly to ZZZZ Best.

"That wasn't the deal," Malamut protested. He called Barry and told him the money was supposed to stay in a separate account, from which it would be paid out to suppliers as needed. For this, Barry succeeded in making him feel like a heel.

"Mike, with all the advance publicity, there's a lot of questions about the company right now," Barry said. "It'll look bad to our suppliers and everyone else if some third party was conducting business on behalf of ZZZZ Best. It would damage our credibility."

"Yeah, but that's not the arrangement—"

"You know, you've taken collateral," Barry persisted. "If for some crazy reason the deal doesn't work out, you have a second on my

house. You have stock as collateral. You also have my personal guarantee. Look, there's nothing to worry about. Give us the money and
we'll take care of business."

Malamut resisted and Barry finally said, "All the other joint-venture
partners just took my signature. Don't you trust me?"

As usual, this appeal turned the trick, and on June 24 Malamut
handed over the entire $1 million. He knew his money was secured
by one million shares that Barry owned in Art World, which Barry
said was worth $6 million, as well as a second mortgage on Barry's
house in Woodland Hills, which was already worth more than the
$700,000 Barry had paid for it. Of course at the last minute Barry
tried to avoid having to commit his house, but this time Malamut
insisted, not knowing that there were already two lienholders ahead
of him with claims on most of the equity.

Kadison, Pfaelzer meanwhile was still trying to figure out if ZZZZ
Best was a fraud. One of the things its lawyers did was to interview
individuals at the company. They talked to Mark Morze, who told
them that what Rothberg had overheard was probably just some "braggadocio" on his part. They talked to Chip Arrington, who lied about
credit-card fraud at Floral Fantasies. And of course they talked to
Barry, who said it was preposterous to wonder if the ZZZZ Best
restoration business was fake, but who still wouldn't disclose the
addresses of any job sites. Barry stuck to his story about the credit-
card fraud, but admitted having tried marijuana and cocaine. He even
had an answer ready when the Kadison lawyers asked him about the
beating administered to Bill Swanson, who had tried to serve Barry
with his wife's small-claims suit. Exuding filial devotion, Barry told
them he himself attacked Swanson (which wasn't true) because he
thought the man had threatened his father.

They also questioned Barry about a $42,000 loss for the Galleria
Fitness Center he had claimed on his income taxes. That had been
Morze's business, but Barry claimed the deduction. So Morze had to
forge a $45,000 check from Barry to prove Barry had actually invested.

Kadison wasn't getting very far, but it had had the foresight to hire
John Murphy and his people to go out and see what they could dig
up. At the end of June, the private eyes were beginning to piece things
together.

John Murphy is a big, hearty, ex-Marine and FBI man who founded
his own firm in 1981 but hasn't forgotten his roots. Murphy employees
dress in the conservative shirts and dark suits of FBI agents, even
though their clients these days are private companies. They do lots

of insurance work and even snoop around for the Los Angeles Rams. Their specialty is business investigations.

Unlike mere auditors, who are supposed to be skeptical but secretly wish everything would just add up, forensic accountants such as Murphy's eagerly look for trouble. In examining the ZZZZ Best Sacramento job, for example, Ernst & Whinney checked the company's paperwork, contacted vendors and even took the unusual step of visiting the site. Murphy's accountants may do all that, but they will also check for a construction permit, talk to the local public-safety officials, contact the building's owners and call around in the restoration business to see if anyone knows of this particular job—or if such large jobs are even plausible.

In setting out to investigate ZZZZ Best, Murphy assigned both investigators and accountants to the case. The investigators first prepared a written profile of all the key figures involved, including executives, employees and vendors. Murphy's investigators still do old-fashioned gumshoe work, but these days computers are just as important, and the firm relied heavily on vast data bases to assemble its profiles. These data bases are for the most part available commercially to anyone with a personal computer, and they allow the investigators to track things like driver and other licenses, property records, civil and criminal court cases and liens. There is so much information out there that Murphy's in-house computer specialist won't tell anyone his real last name; he knows what someone could do with it.

Using the profiles in conjunction with public records and the firm's extensive law-enforcement contacts, Murphy and his investigators quickly decided that Barry Minkow wasn't terribly honest—they learned about the forged Allstate drafts, for example—and that some shady characters were involved with ZZZZ Best.

Led by former FBI accountant Drew Maconachy, Murphy's accounting specialists then began poring over the ZZZZ Best ledgers, contracts and bank statements. Maconachy and his colleagues found thousands of ZZZZ Best checks, many of them highly suspicious: they were written by hand in large round numbers, for example, and were often payable to cash. To manage all the information these checks contained, Murphy's men again turned to computers. At the ZZZZ Best offices in Reseda, they entered information from every check into a Zenith laptop model with custom-designed data-base management software that permits a user to list and total checks by payee, bank-account number, endorser, amount or date.

The computer makes it easy to see who got what. Checks made out to different people but paid into the same account turn up right away, for example; such was the case with some big checks made out to Cornwell Tool by leasing companies who thought they were buying equipment for ZZZZ Best, which got the money instead. Murphy's men also compared suspicious checks to other documentation and the individual profiles prepared earlier.

Forensic accountants take nothing at face value. Instead of just checking with suppliers to confirm a company's payments, the Murphy firm checks out the supplier as well. Does it exist? Does the owner have a criminal record? If there is a contract between two companies, are there any suspicious ties between their executives? Might there be collusion or kickbacks?

One of the most important things Maconachy and his associates did was to analyze the flow of funds in and out of ZZZZ Best. They saw right away that an awful lot of money seemed to be moving between Barry's company and two others: Interstate Appraisal, which they knew was supposed to be providing the lucrative refurbishing jobs that accounted for nearly 90 percent of the ZZZZ Best revenue, and Marbil Management, a contractor they were told was working on restoration jobs on behalf of ZZZZ Best.

Murphy's accountants paid close attention to the amounts, destinations and timing of deposits and withdrawals. The probers became convinced that, as Murphy put it, "what we had was a monstrous check kite. It was a cash racetrack."

Murphy investigators soon visited Sacramento, San Diego, Santa Barbara and Dallas in search of supposed ZZZZ Best restoration jobs. They also talked to local fire and police departments. Nobody—but nobody—had ever heard of such projects.

24

In college Shari Elowsky studied women's history. During the summer of 1987 she relived a very old story.

When Elowsky first visited Barry in Los Angeles it was May, and he was coping with the credit-card allegations in the *Los Angeles Times*. But he and his visitor still managed to have lunch, and they didn't talk about business. Barry paid close attention to Elowsky, probed for information about her love life and told her how pretty and smart she was. She was so smart, in fact, that she was intimidating, he said. He also told her he might come to New York, and Elowsky said she would happily show him the city.

"You know, I like to spend money on other people but I'm pretty stingy about spending it on myself," he said. "Maybe I could stay at your place when I'm in town."

"Well, I only have a one-bedroom apartment. You can sleep in the bathtub."

They laughed. Later, after Barry made some phone calls from her room, he had to go.

"I really wish I could take you shopping."

"Barry, I don't like to be taken shopping."

"Well, I could buy you something and you could buy me something."

"I probably couldn't afford anything you'd want."

Still, he insisted on driving Elowsky to the mall—directly across the street—in his BMW. She didn't see him again that weekend, but they talked three or four times a week after that.

More important, between late April and late June, Elowsky let her new friend borrow cash from his $5 million line of credit at

Pru-Bache. It didn't happen all at once; as usual, Barry borrowed some, paid it back, borrowed more, etc., until the outstanding balance reached $1,775,000. Barry had said he wanted the money variously for real estate ventures and for pumping into ZZZZ Best. The credit was already approved; the only wrinkle was that Barry wasn't using the money to buy stock, which the securities firm would then have had as additional collateral. Instead he was taking away cash, and the only collateral for these borrowings was the 1.4 million restricted shares of ZZZZ Best stock, plus another 375,000 shares Barry provided to partially compensate for the drop in ZZZZ Best stock caused by the credit-card scandal.

No matter. Barry and his company seemed like a good risk, and Sharon Elowsky was pretty taken with both: after her first visit she bought shares of ZZZZ Best for her Individual Retirement Account. Barry seemed taken with Elowsky, too. He kept talking about coming to New York, although he never did, and finally, on June 25, a Thursday, he called and invited her to Los Angeles for dinner—for the next day.

"I thought he was crazy," Elowsky said later in court.

But Barry pleaded. He said he felt terrible about so often having to cancel his tentative plans to visit New York, and this time he wouldn't be distracted by such nonsense as the *Times* article. Her schedule was easier than his, after all, and he would gladly fly her out. Charmed and amused, Elowsky decided "it was a nice little lark," and that very night she flew to Los Angeles—again first-class, and again at Barry's expense. She arrived at the Warner Center Marriott Hotel to find a huge basket of fruit and a gigantic basket of flowers waiting in her room.

She spent the next day, Friday, looking things over at ZZZZ Best. Barry showed her a locked room that he said was used for credit-card processing, so careful had he become about any further problems in this area. She also talked to Barry and Andersen about the company's finances. The numbers were amazing: a $5 million profit for the fiscal year just ended, much higher than expected. "Are these numbers being audited? Are they holding up?" she asked. She was assured that they were.

Afterward Barry drove her to the nearby telemarketing offices, where she watched the telephone sales force in action. Barry said he had helped to write the script himself. He also showed her his training operations, chemical company and 4Z Equipment, home of the generators.

Elowsky drove back to the Marriott at around two P.M., giving Barry some time to deal with the other crises that kept erupting all around him. That day, for example, at around eleven A.M., Kadison lawyers Riffer and Eisen had met with Norm Rothberg, this time at a delicatessen in West Los Angeles. Rothberg wasn't much help concerning his prior allegations, and he continued to play them down. He said what he'd really overheard was just some "braggadocio" from Mark Morze. The lawyers looked at one another. It was the same unusual word Morze himself had used. Then they asked Rothberg about the $5,000 he had received from ZZZZ Best in December.

"That was for a square-foot analysis," Rothberg said, although he couldn't say what a square-foot analysis was.

"What about the tape you showed Levy?" the lawyers asked. "The tape you said was proof?"

"There was no tape," Rothberg said.

When Barry heard about all this, it couldn't have been much of a confidence booster for him. That night he picked Elowsky up for dinner in a Porsche (probably Joyce's car) and drove her out to Splash, the Malibu restaurant where Detective Mike Brambles had arrested Ronnie Lorenzo nearly four months earlier. On the way, Barry bought his date some roses from a roadside vendor, and when they arrived the maître d' greeted Barry warmly and put the flowers in water. Barry, explaining that he was a silent partner in the place, did all the ordering.

That night, in Elowsky's room, Barry wrote out three checks drawn on ZZZZ Best corporate funds. The first was for the expenses from her first trip, which he had somehow never got around to reimbursing. The second, signed but blank, was to cover expenses for the current trip. ("I trust you," Barry said. "Just fill in the amount, whatever it is.") The third was for $2 million, made out to "Prudential Basche."

"What's this?" Elowsky said. "There's only a million seven seventy-five outstanding."

"Shari, I really need another two hundred and twenty-five thousand," Barry replied. "Look, I only need the money for a little while. We've got some major insurance contracts coming in, but we have a cash shortfall right now, so I need to give the company a little money just to tide us over." He didn't mention that Mike Malamut had given him $1 million just two days earlier, or that the luminous set of ZZZZ Best financial statements she had seen masked a company that was dead broke.

"Barry, first of all why are you giving me a company check to repay your personal borrowing?"

"The company owes me this money," Barry said earnestly, explaining that he was due some kind of bonus. "This way is just easier."

"A wire transfer is better for two million. And, Barry—besides all that I haven't even decided to give you the loan yet."

On Saturday, June 27, while Elowsky was still in town and still convinced that everything at ZZZZ Best was terrific, Kadison, Pfaelzer attorneys Rich Simon and Jeff Riffer told ZZZZ Best board members Malamut and Dem that something definitely wasn't kosher in the restoration business. Malamut and Dem went pale. The question now, the lawyers said, is what's really going on? Were kickbacks being paid? Were the jobs merely inflated? Or was the entire restoration business a fake? Simon said he would have to know where the jobs were before the truth could be determined.

Shaken, Malamut and Dem reached Barry on his carphone and summoned him to Dem's office. Barry showed up in his usual workout suit. Participating by speakerphone was an experienced attorney named Fred Richman, who had been brought in by Steve Greenberg to help ZZZZ Best. Simon explained that he had serious concerns about the restoration jobs, and that the time had come to verify their existence.

Barry insisted he couldn't disclose the locations of these jobs and began his familiar confidentiality song when Richman cut him off.

"Barry, those days are over—the situation is too grave," he said. "It's now imperative that you be candid if you have any hope of going forward with KeyServ and Sears."

Barry resisted for about fifteen minutes, but Malamut and Dem added to the pressure.

"We have to have it," they insisted.

"Well, we could lose the business then," Barry replied.

"How do you mean we could lose the business?"

"Interstate might not want to give us any more business," Barry said.

But Richman wouldn't back down, and finally, looking defeated, Barry gave in.

"This may blow our insurance business, but I'm going to do it anyway," Barry said. "I need a day to talk to Padgett. I'll get back to you tomorrow and we'll set up an inspection."

Simon cautioned that this inspection wouldn't be like the others. He didn't intend to be driven blindfolded to some anonymous office building without the right to make a single corroborating phone call. But the truth was, at this point neither Simon nor Riffer believed there would ever be any inspection. Barry shook Simon's hand when he left, looking downcast.

Suddenly Malamut, who had given Barry $1 million just three days ago, remembered that he had the project file from the San Diego job. It was given to him for his lawyer's scrutiny before he put up the money. Everybody drove over to Malamut's office, where Simon eagerly took up the manila folder. As soon as he opened it, he knew it was a fake. It had none of the bulging, dog-eared aspect that a real file gets when it is used over time. Instead the documents were perfectly aligned, the holes clearly punched all at once. There were no carbons, tissue paper or stray notes of the kind found in any normal business file. Everything was too neat. Later, when Jeff Riffer studied the file with an accountant's eye, he found that everything added up to round, even numbers.

Things had begun to spin out of control. On Sunday, Elowsky flew back to New York, puzzling over whether to let Barry have another $225,000. On Monday Barry had to be in Chicago, where he had his hands full. He, Arrington, Moskowitz, Richman and ZZZZ Best board member Harold Lipman met there with officials from both Sears and KeyServ, where the men from ZZZZ Best were grilled about management integrity at their company. The Sears executives knew all about the credit-card allegations, and had even hired a private investigator to do some checking as well. Sears valued its reputation and did not want to be in business with a bunch of crooks.

Barry and the others were dressed respectably and worked hard to persuade Sears that ZZZZ Best was run with absolute propriety. Barry seemed to have an explanation for everything. He didn't mention that the whole discussion was already moot, because he had already begun looting the company. During June, for example, Barry withdrew $3.4 million from the ZZZZ Best account at Lincoln National Bank in Encino and got another $600,000 from Ken Pavia, besides the $1 million from Malamut and the $1,775,000 from Pru-Bache attributable to Shari Elowsky.

Laundering all that money single-handed is a big job. For help, Barry turned to near-identical twins named Jack and Jerry Polevoi. The Polevois are also known as "Big Bucks" and "Little Bucks" for their freewheeling, high-rolling style. Jack Norman Polevoi is "Big Bucks," the faster-talking, higher-rolling twin. He is five feet seven inches tall and about 170 pounds. His brother, Jerry Nathan, is two

inches taller and a good ten pounds heavier, but from their birth on
May 25, 1947, when Jack popped out first, Jerry has tended to follow
his brother's lead.

Jack and his wife, Janet, lived two doors down from Barry, and
when they met him in June of 1986 he invited them to a party at the
Beverly Hilton in celebration of some new ZZZZ Best cleaning outlets. They were so impressed that they bought $10,000 worth of stock
in his company.

Jack could afford it. He owned a landscaping business and a limousine service, and over time the Polevois became Barry's close
friends. As neighbors Jack and Janet assumed a sort of Fred and Ethel
Mertz role; Barry and Joyce were always in and out of their house,
and the Polevois thought nothing of holding on to over $200,000 for
Barry's personal use. Jack and Barry often socialized together: "I liked
his life-style," Polevoi said later. "I got caught up in it."

In March of 1987, Jack Polevoi went to work as president of the
new ZZZZ Best janitorial division, and soon hired Jerry as his West
Coast representative.

Barry must have known the game was up even as he sat in the Sears
meeting in Chicago on Monday, June 29, insisting that ZZZZ Best
was a tower of rectitude with a shining future. In fact the company
was in a state of utter disarray. One sure sign that things were falling
apart was that the Polevoi brothers that very day had sold short 27,500
ZZZZ Best shares at two different brokerage houses.

Why not? Jack Polevoi knew the company was going down the
toilet because Barry had enlisted him to help smuggle out as much
money as possible before the final flush. Jack saw this as a chance to
recoup his earlier losses on 37,000 shares of ZZZZ Best he had purchased around April, only to get slaughtered during the margin calls
following the May 22 *Times* story. Jack and possibly Jerry lost perhaps
$200,000 in that bloodbath. Now Jack knew that Barry was consid-
ering resigning. So what if it was illegal to trade on the basis of this
inside information? "Big Bucks" Polevoi saw a golden opportunity.

Early on Tuesday, June 30, Elowsky called Barry in Reseda, where
somebody said he was traveling. She left a message, and half an hour
later he called back from Chicago, where she told him she was ap-
proving the extra $225,000. That was a good thing, since Barry already
had the money. He somehow got his local Pru-Bache branch to issue
the check the day before. Nevertheless, Barry was delighted.

"I love you," he said. Then the line went dead.

Elowsky didn't know that when Barry got back to Reseda later that day, the $225,000 would be in the hands of "Big Bucks" Polevoi, who, at his twenty-one-year-old boss's behest, was trying in earnest to suck as much cash as possible out of ZZZZ Best.

He wasn't having a great deal of success. At two-thirty P.M. he phoned his old friend Eugene Lasko for help. Lasko, fifty-five, was listed as the owner of Cal-West Services, a landscaping and maintenance concern that really belonged to Jack Polevoi, who owned it secretly because he'd previously sold a similar business and pledged not to compete for five years. Polevoi said he had a cashier's check from Barry and wanted Lasko to cash it at Cal-West's bank. "Meet me at the Bank of America in Woodland Hills," Polevoi said.

Lasko arrived just after three P.M. and knocked on the glass. Polevoi handed a cashier's check through the door. Lasko was stunned by the amount: $240,000.

Lasko took the check to the nearby branch of Great Western Savings, where Cal-West did its banking, and tried to cash it. Lasko was also supposed to get most of the $95,000 Polevoi had deposited into the account the day before. But the people at Great Western said they didn't have that kind of money lying around, and it would take four or five days to get it. Lasko called Big Bucks and told him this. "Well, go back and get travelers checks and cashier's checks," Polevoi said impatiently.

Lasko dutifully requested $320,000 in cashier's checks.

"How big do you want the checks?" the clerk asked.

"I don't know," Lasko said.

"How about ninety-five hundred dollars each?" the clerk asked, explaining that that way they could avoid some unpleasant reporting requirements.

"Fine," said Lasko. He came away with thirty-two cashier's checks for $9,500 each, one for $4,000, and one for $2,500, all payable to himself. He took the remaining $9,500 in cash.

By the time he met Big Bucks and Little Bucks in the ZZZZ Best parking lot, it was four-thirty or five P.M. As Lasko arrived, he saw Barry get into his white BMW and drive off. Barry apparently told the Polevois to head for Las Vegas, where he assumed the casinos were like twenty-four-hour cash-laundromats and bank machines combined.

"Barry, where did all this money come from?" Big Bucks had asked.

"Look, I get paid thirty thousand a month," Barry said. "I just haven't cashed a paycheck for nine months."

Jack Polevoi is not stupid, but he didn't care to question this bizarre explanation because Barry had said the magic words: Las Vegas. Who else but Barry Minkow would send a compulsive gambler to that desert roulette wheel with $700,000 and instructions to bring it all back? Jack had been active in Gamblers Anonymous for years, and had even persuaded Barry to contribute. He had a history of serious gambling binges. Entrusting Jack Polevoi with your money is not like relying on the Bank of England. It's not that Jack is dishonest; he just likes to have a good time. But at the end of June 1987, Barry had a problem. He wanted to steal as much money as he could from ZZZZ Best without writing checks to himself, which would be too easy to trace. He needed somebody to launder the money for him, no questions asked. Presumably he felt the Polevois were the only ones he could entrust with this task. Jack and Janet had already done a good job with Barry's slush fund, keeping careful records and putting in $40,000 or $50,000 at one point when the money ran low.

Thus commenced one of the stranger escapades in ZZZZ Best history. Big Bucks Polevoi gets a rush just from being in Las Vegas, that garish nightmare of orderly capitalist society. Vegas is still America's id in some ways, and for men like Big Bucks, it is the end of all restraint. Worse, Big Bucks soon found himself *forced* to gamble by an almost universal refusal to cash all the checks. The result was a surreal spree during which he "sat at the tables for four solid days," he recalled later, ultimately claiming he lost about $42,000.

What happened was this: Big Bucks, Little Bucks and a couple of attractive women named Kathy flew out and holed up in a lavish suite at the Golden Nugget. Afraid of flying, Lasko arrived at midnight by car, and after everyone ordered up some food, he set to work trying to liquidate ZZZZ Best's assets. Unfortunately, the casinos weren't acting like the money-dispensing, cash-washing machines that Barry had hoped they would. The cashier downstairs wouldn't give Lasko a dime until he could call Great Western in the morning, and even if the bank confirmed that the checks were legit, the casino would only issue chips and markers for the money.

"We're not a bank," said the clerk.

Las Vegas is a stunningly ugly city by day, a municipal hangover crying out for massive aerial administration of aspirin. Wednesday, July 1 dawned hot and bleary for Gene Lasko, who had spent the night on the sofa, his sleep disrupted by all the coming and going and the constant phone calls from Barry. That morning he tried to cash checks at various banks with no success whatsoever, so it was back to the casinos.

Lasko would cash one or two checks somewhere and then bet
or $15 at a time. He drew fishy stares from the pit bosses, and bef
long the word was out.

"After the second one, they sort of caught on," he said later. "
name went across Las Vegas like a house afire. The next hotel I w
to, they didn't want to talk to me."

Lasko found himself trudging from casino to casino in the br
desert heat, carrying a fortune in non-negotiable instruments. At
Hilton, which checked first with Great Western, he managed to
$30,000 worth of chips and decided to walk around with these f
while in order to seem less obvious. When he tried to lay dow
$100 bet, one of the pit bosses threw him out.

It was clear by now that somebody was going to have to do s
serious betting if Barry was ever going to get any cash out of
Vegas. That's when Big Bucks and Little Bucks took over. L
would get some chips and then say loudly, "Jack, play for me.
not a good gambler."

This went on for days. Big Bucks, who was betting $500 a c
at blackjack, had a ball. But he kept careful track of the mo
dividing a bureau drawer in their hotel room into three: one par
Lasko's money, and one part each for the two Kathys, who also
part in the fun. At one point someone from the FBI came up
scared everybody to death. He said he was checking to see if an
the cashier's checks were counterfeit. He looked at them and lef

The Polevois' money-laundering activities weren't entirely
ducted in secret. Bill Davey, an accountant with the Murphy f
was in the basement at ZZZZ Best wading through checks whe
heard a conversation upstairs.

"Murph," he said, calling his office. "You're not going to bel
this, but they're up there bringing money out to Las Vegas."

One of the Kathys, Kathy Carter, helped out. At six A.M., Jul
she was dispatched to a local PaineWebber office to short ZZZZ
using a phony Social Security number to avoid taxes.

"What's shorting?" asked Carter, a former waitress who was am
those paid to cheer at girls' softball games.

"Don't worry," said Little Bucks. "Just bring the money there
I'll take care of everything over the telephone."

At PaineWebber, Carter recalled later, someone went into the o
room and looked at the numbers on the wall. ZZZZ Best was d
¾ of a point and everyone was ecstatic.

25

I no longer liked Barry Minkow, but the timing of his downfall was inconvenient for me. I had a new job and was trying to buy a sixty-five-year-old house, a place so ancient by local standards that a friend suggested I look for the Code of Hammurabi inscribed beneath the paint. When I left the *Times* I left behind all my ZZZZ Best notes and documents, as well as a memo outlining a potentially larger story. In June not much appeared in the papers about Barry, other than news developments, and toward the end of the month I persuaded my editors at the *Journal* that we should do the story ourselves.

After some frantic document-gathering and phone-calling, it was obvious that ZZZZ Best was a major fraud, but proving a negative (that certain jobs don't exist) is difficult, and pinning down all the wild allegations would be time-consuming. Both the *Los Angeles Times* and *BusinessWeek* had stories working, so in order to short-circuit the whole arduous process, I decided to bluff. I told Arthur Barens that ZZZZ Best was a giant Ponzi scheme, and since Padgett would never return my calls, I finally told his secretary: "Tell him it's about the fraud. Tell him I know all about it."

This wasn't strictly true. I only had a hazy outline, and no proof. We were far from publishing a story. But that afternoon, June 29 or 30, someone purporting to be Padgett at last called back.

"You should know that we're about to run a story saying ZZZZ Best and Interstate Appraisal are wholesale frauds," I said. "The insurance contracts you're giving Barry don't exist. I think we better sit down and talk this over."

"You know, this is unbelievable," Padgett said. "Look, since you've

· 232 ·

been after this thing for so long, I'm gonna prove to you these jobs exist. We'll prove the whole thing. This is all supposed to be confidential, but we'll show you documents, checks, contracts, whatever."

"Fine. How about tomorrow morning?"

"Tomorrow? No, I can't tomorrow, I've got to be out of town for the next couple of days. How about Thursday? Come out to the Culver City office Thursday morning at ten. We'll lay out the whole thing for you."

"Thursday morning. Okay. You know, your voice sounds kind of familiar, but I can't quite place it. Where've I heard your voice before?"

"Gee, ah, I don't know—"

"We have spoken before, haven't we?"

"Did we? Uh, I guess to—"

"Remember, when I was with the *Times?*"

"Oh, right, right—"

"But you sound different now, and I'm trying to— Hey, that's it! You sound just like Barry Minkow!"

"Hah hah, yeah, people say that sometimes—"

"Tell you what, give me your number and I'll call you back."

"My number? Uh, hang on a second." There was silence for a moment. Close friends adopt one another's mannerisms and often sound alike, but something told me that's not what had happened in this case. Anyway, Barry never did give me his number. He made some excuse and hung up, promising, as Padgett, to see me on Thursday, July 2.

Late that night the real Tom Padgett was home in Newport Beach, where he had just opened a beer and put a bag of popcorn into the microwave. When the phone rang, he was surprised to find that it was Barry, who was usually early to bed.

"Look, Tom, if something goes wrong and we don't get out of this, the only person I care about is you—"

"Wait a minute, what do you mean?" Padgett had seen Barry virtually walk on water. Now he couldn't credit his ears. "What are you talking about? How are we not going to get out of this?"

"Right, sure," Barry said. "But if we don't, just remember . . ."

Padgett urged him to get some rest.

The next day, Wednesday, as Gene Lasko and the Polevois traipsed all over Las Vegas trying to launder Barry's stolen money, Barry told his loyal lieutenant Mark Morze that he had Prudential-Bache lined up to finance the KeyServ deal and provide working capital.

"This deal is gonna be even bigger than Drexel's," Barry said. "All we need is some money to make payroll in the meantime."

"I've got a couple hundred thousand," Morze offered.

"Give it to me," Barry said.

Morze wrote out a check.

Huge numbers of ZZZZ Best shares were traded the day before, and on Wednesday, as the furious trading continued, Dan Dorfman called Steve Greenberg to ask if it was true that Barry had quit. Dorfman is the sultan of scoop in the world of financial journalism, and Greenberg was patiently explaining that the rumor was absurd, that Barry had just had a great meeting in Chicago with Sears, when Barry called at that very moment on the other line. Greenberg set up a conference call.

"Barry, I have some very definite information that you're resigning," Dorfman said.

"That's ridiculous," Barry scoffed. "I have Price Waterhouse coming in on Friday to meet with Padgett and he's going to divulge the names of all the insurance firms that do business with us. It may jeopardize my business, but I don't care."

Dorfman didn't believe him and reported that same day on Cable News Network that Barry was rumored to have quit.

Shari Elowsky didn't see Dorfman on television, but by then Barry had called saying he would repay Pru-Bache's $2 million on Friday, a week early. He said ZZZZ Best had itself been paid early for one of its insurance jobs.

"Well, I don't want to use the check," Elowsky said. "Can we give you wire instructions? It'll save interest. We're closed that day anyway, but you can just wire it to our bank."

Barry agreed, and said he wanted to see her again. Could Elowsky come to Los Angeles for the upcoming July 4 weekend? Elowsky said she'd already made plans to spend the holiday with friends in upstate New York. Barry said he might come east, then. Elowsky said he would be welcome.

For some reason Barry told Arrington the truth that day. July 1 was Chip Arrington's twenty-seventh birthday, and perhaps even Barry could appreciate loyalty such as his. Arrington had planned to build his future at ZZZZ Best. He had served as Barry's errand boy, bagman and scapegoat for years. He had knowingly broken the law, fought with his wife and sacrificed his good name for Barry. His fealty was complete. Chip was shocked to have Barry walk into his office and say he was quitting over some serious problems with the restoration business.

Sherrie Maloney, Barry's personal secretary, knew something was wrong. Right before Chip's birthday party, Barry called her into his office.

"Close the door," he said. "Sit down."

This was serious. Usually they just shouted across to one another or talked on the phone.

"Sherrie, I've done some things that aren't so good, and I've done some things that are just plain bad. But Tom and Mark have really screwed us. This will be our last day here. Both of us, you and me, are resigning. I want you to take the kids and hide."

That night, Padgett was out with a friend in Hollywood when Roddy, the Ultimate White Man, called on his carphone. "Barry really wants to talk to you," he said. Padgett hated the carphone but used it to talk to Barry, who suddenly sounded more tired than ever.

"Tom, it's over, it's all over. I'm resigning tomorrow."

"Barry, what do you mean? My parents are coming in tomorrow."

"It's no good, it's over. Akst has talked to Travelers, Rothberg opened his big mouth. It's just no good."

The carphone kept fading, and Padgett was feeling desperate. Finally he pulled over to a pay phone. For a half hour, Padgett tried to get Barry to change his mind ("We can say we had foreign insurers," he suggested), but Barry was barely listening. Padgett started to work himself into a frenzy over Rothberg, whom he regarded as an example of why the Jews were always in trouble, and Barry, sensing that his friend was becoming unhinged, interrupted the stream of invective.

"Tom, please, don't go shooting Rothberg or anything," Barry pleaded. "It wasn't really him anyway—it was the press. Look at what brought Richard Nixon down—the press. That's what brought me down. One twerp with a pen."

"Yeah, but—"

"Tom, listen to me. I'm getting my phone number changed, I'll call you with the new number and I'll take care of a lawyer for you. Meanwhile, get out of the house. Right away, tonight, just get out of the house. We're facing criminal charges here."

"What? What am I going to tell Pavia?" Ken Pavia, who had hoped for a romance between Barry and his daughter, lived next door and sometimes worked out with Padgett. It was his house. Barry had never really bought it for Padgett.

"Fuck Pavia. You can get another house. Just get out."

When Padgett got home that night his secretary, Sandra, was there with a waterbed he had sent her out to buy for him. She told him

Debbie—his great love, who always wanted a beach house—had called and wanted to see Tom's place. Padgett broke down and wept.

Mike Malamut wasn't happy either. Just a few hours later, at one or two A.M. on Thursday, he got a call from Jack Polevoi.

"Mike, I'm worried about your investment," said Big Bucks. "I'm cashing a lot of checks up here in Vegas and I'm supposed to turn the money over to Barry. I think some of this cash may be yours."

Thursday came bright and breezy in Los Angeles, and at nine-thirty A.M. I hurried out to Culver City for my meeting with Padgett. He never showed up. The Interstate office in Culver City was suspiciously tidy, and the men who sat at the uncluttered desks looked as if they sold aluminum siding.

Later that day, July 2, Malamut and each of his fellow ZZZZ Best board members received copies of a hand-delivered letter in which Barry said he was resigning for reasons of health.

In the chaos that ensued, Barry himself was nowhere to be found. Arrington, left to maintain order and fend off frantic callers, knew that Barry's resignation was still inside information, so he merely said the chairman wasn't in. But it was difficult to remain calm. The phones wouldn't stop, and everyone was worried and confused. A couple of private investors who had loaned Barry money came in and sat down, determined to wait for him.

Elowsky still didn't know Barry had quit. She tried calling him at first just to provide wire instructions for repaying the $2 million. But suddenly ZZZZ Best stock was falling through the center of the earth, and Elowsky watched in horror as the $2 million loan became partially unsecured (by her company's 30 percent standard) in a matter of just hours. ZZZZ Best stock lost $1.125 on the day to close at $3.50. Wall Street was swept by rumors of Barry's resignation, and ZZZZ Best, with more than two million shares changing hands, was the single most active issue in national over-the-counter trading. Elowsky called Barry five or six times that Thursday, her nerves strung tight as a tennis racket by Diet Cokes and 2 million dollars' worth of bad-loan panic. Each time she called he was out or in a meeting, until finally she tried his house. Who can imagine the despair that smart, sophisticated Shari Elowsky felt when the recording said the number was disconnected?

At seven o'clock that night in Reseda the ZZZZ Best board of directors met in shell-shocked emergency session. All were present except Barry, whose resignation still hadn't been made public. In his absence, kindly old Hal Lipman presided.

The assembled ZZZZ Best directors were never a very inspiring group; now, on the night of Thursday, July 2, they looked absolutely lost. Mike Malamut was worried about his million; he saw a company in total disarray, and wanted badly to restore some order. Hal Berman was worried about $50,000 the company still owed him from previous loans. Dan Krowpman was worried about whether the whole thing was going to unravel, since he was up to his eyeballs in fraud. Perhaps he even regretted putting up the money for Barry to start ZZZZ Best in the first place. Neal Dem and Vera Hojecki were worried too, and Lipman felt a deep personal involvement because his daughter was living with Barry. Attorneys Simon and Riffer, of Kadison, Pfaelzer, were also present, and four Hughes Hubbard lawyers, including Moskowitz, were connected by phone.

First the board accepted Barry's resignation and named chief financial officer Bruce Andersen interim president. Then Simon distributed a draft report of Kadison, Pfaelzer's findings in the independent investigation it had been asked to conduct at ZZZZ Best, adding that the addresses of ZZZZ Best restoration jobs still hadn't been received. By now the Kadison lawyers knew there were no jobs.

Then Andersen came in. Like some financial angel of death, he grimly reported that ZZZZ Best was grossing $200,000 a week from its carpet-cleaning business, but that he couldn't find any of the other funds ZZZZ Best was supposed to have. As far as Andersen could tell, the company had just $68,000 in the bank. The directors were stunned.

"I gave this company one million dollars just a week ago, and you're telling me we have only sixty-eight thousand dollars in the bank!" Malamut said. "Where's my money?"

Andersen didn't know. There was just no sign of it.

"Bruce, you're a CPA," said Malamut. "You're in charge of a multi-million-dollar company. How come you can't tell me where my money is? Don't you have books and records?"

"Barry was always in charge of the checkbook—"

"Barry! I am flabbergasted that you would allow such a lack of controls, to let Barry have the checkbook and not know whether money was coming in or going out," Malamut said heatedly.

"Well, if you know Barry, you don't argue with him," Andersen said. "I take my orders from Mr. Minkow."

"Wait a minute," said Malamut. "I'm getting confused. I have a company smaller than this one. Even when we were very small, I never had the checkbook, and I'm the president and the only stockholder! My accounting department generated all the checks, and any-time I needed a check, I had to leave a copy with my signature. We have controls!"

Malamut knew then that his million dollars, for which he had worked long and hard, for which he had risked and sacrificed, and which included the house his own mother lived in, was gone.

Moskowitz and the others listened in terror. They had all trusted Barry, and even those who were in on the scam probably never imagined they would find themselves raped and abandoned in this way. Rousing itself from its long torpor, the board finally ordered that management change the locks and bank accounts and do whatever else it could to secure the company's assets. Some of the directors apparently still thought there were assets.

Andersen had more bad news: Mark Morze had told him that very morning that much of the insurance restoration business didn't exist. Andersen said ZZZZ Best had paid Marbil Management $18 million in connection with this business, and that Interstate Appraisal owed ZZZZ Best $8.2 million by Monday, July 6. Moskowitz and his colleagues at Hughes Hubbard were instructed to notify the insurer who provided the board's directors and officers liability coverage that claims might soon arise. This step showed how scared everybody was getting, and how paltry their imaginations were compared to Barry's. They all believed there actually was an insurance policy.

Helen Melman, a cool, capable Hughes Hubbard partner who was listening in with Moskowitz, advised all the board members to get their own lawyers. Then Rich Simon, of Kadison, Pfaelzer, called a good bankruptcy lawyer he knew.

The ZZZZ Best board members had been nervous when their meeting got underway that night. When it ended, they were distraught. Barry wasn't in the best frame of mind either. That night he drove over to Richie Schulman's condo in Encino, where he confronted Schulman and Rind.

"You're going to kill me," Barry said. "I resigned, everything was a Ponzi, the whole thing was phony." Rind says he and Schulman were astonished. Certain they were being taped, Moe and Richie wouldn't say anything, and Rind patted Barry down for a body-wire.

The stock market was closed Friday, July 3, in honor of the holiday on Saturday, giving ZZZZ Best a much-needed three-day respite. But investors harbored little hope for a rebound on Monday, and the shorts had long ago smelled blood in the water. Elowsky went to work

Friday morning despite the holiday. She started calling ZZZZ Best as soon as she got there—six A.M. Pacific time—and finally got hold of Arrington three hours later.

"Chip, what's going on? The stock is falling through the floor, I can't reach Barry, and Jimmy Manuel couldn't reach him yesterday either."

Elowsky was stunned to hear that Barry had resigned "for health reasons." Barry had always seemed to her in robust health.

"Well how can I reach him?" she demanded. "I've got this check here for two million that he wrote on ZZZZ Best that's supposed to repay a loan. Is the check still good?"

"A two-million-dollar check?" said Arrington. "I don't know anything about that."

By now the word was out. ZZZZ Best issued a press release saying Barry resigned citing "severe medical problems." The release also said the company probably couldn't complete the KeyServ acquisition. A wave of panic swept through the house of ZZZZ Best, once so solid-looking but now increasingly revealed for the ill-founded structure it truly was. Investors, lenders, stockbrokers, reporters and countless others deluged the company's switchboard. Some came in person; others sent telegrams. Security guards had to be posted. Camera crews camped outside the ZZZZ Best offices in Reseda, and Arrington spent hours on the phone with people who had lost a fortune.

"What resulted was pretty much pandemonium," he said later in court.

Everyone was looking for Barry. Steve Greenberg was among them, and he soon began to see how bad things were. He would lose a chunk of his own money, and investors who had followed him would lose even more. There would be lawsuits; he had touted the stock, and since he had assets, he would be targeted.

The ladies of the luncheon club were thrown into despair. Kay Rozario, who probably made money on ZZZZ Best, talked of suicide. Ada Cohen hyperventilated and later developed a rash. When she broke the news to Suzette Whitmore, "I was devastated," Whitmore says. She drove over to Cohen's house and they cried together. Ann Randall had to be hospitalized. In the months following Barry's resignation, she suffered hepatitis, fever blisters, crippling asthma attacks and Epstein-Barr disease.

Peter Strauss, the Hollywood producer and erstwhile ZZZZ Best joint-venturer, was worried about his and Plushcell's investment. Ken

Pavia had seen a $1.9 million check bounce. Investors big and small were seeing their profit-making idol clearly for the first time and were shocked at the emperor's unsightly nudity.

At five o'clock on the afternoon of July 3, the ZZZZ Best board reconvened. Hal Lipman reported that Kay Rozario called to say that "she had sources of financing available to the Company." Probably no one laughed. Andersen reported that the company was continuing to hemorrhage: revenue was $200,000 a week, but that only covered payroll. Other costs brought total weekly expenses to $350,000.

The board members talked to a bankruptcy lawyer, questioned Arrington about a $50,000 bonus Barry had given him and unanimously agreed to sue Barry, Mark Morze, Tom Padgett, Marbil Management and Interstate Appraisal for fraud. They might just as well have sued themselves.

During the meeting, the board listened on the speakerphone to a call from Elowsky in New York. Elowsky had already seen her professional life flash before her eyes. Canceling her July 4 weekend plans, she stayed behind in the steamy city, where she would lose seven pounds in four days. She made her brother come and stay with her. She didn't sleep, cried on and off and became physically ill. On the phone she rapidly explained that she was holding a $2 million ZZZZ Best corporate check postdated July 10 and given her by Barry for repayment of his debt to Pru-Bache.

"Are you going to honor this check?" she asked.

The board members said they couldn't answer that question just yet, and Elowsky probably guessed that the check would bounce if ever she tried to cash it. Half the ZZZZ Best paychecks had already bounced that day.

Barry wasn't present to preside over his company's death throes or to witness the anguish of all the people like Elowsky, whose hopes were dying with it. He was busy looking out for himself.

In Las Vegas, the Polevoi brothers and Gene Lasko had managed to convert a bunch of the checks into something less than $500,000 cash, which they kept first in a paper shopping bag and then, because it was so heavy they thought it would tear, in a garment bag they bought just for the purpose. On Friday morning, July 3, Janet Polevoi was disturbed to read a front-page article in the *Los Angeles Daily News*, which circulates mainly in the Valley, saying that Barry and his company were under police investigation. The piece, by reporter Patrick Lee, also quoted Barens as saying Barry had told him he planned to quit. Barry Stavro, of the *Los Angeles Times*, quoted Barens the same day as saying Barry already had.

Janet Polevoi was already worried. Her husband, a compulsive gambler, was on the loose in Las Vegas with more than $700,000 from God-knows-where. He had promised to come home by July 2, their daughter's birthday, but hadn't done so. Now the police were involved. Janet Polevoi had been happier. At nine that morning, Gene Lasko dropped off a bag of cash.

There was about $320,000, by Janet's count, which she hid in a closet. Then she and her daughter went to meet her husband at the airport, where they were paged by Mike Malamut's wife. She said Mike wanted to see Jack before he went back home. Janet dropped him off at the Malamuts' and then drove herself and her daughter home. Almost as soon as they got there, Barry and his friend Tony Scamardo showed up. They both wore skin-tight tank tops that showed off their muscles.

"Where's Jack?" Barry asked.

"He's not here," said Janet.

"Well, when's he coming?"

"I know he's due today, but I haven't heard from him yet."

Barry and Tony decided to wait. Barry seemed antsy and paced around, but Janet was a nervous wreck too. What if her daughter should blurt out, "I just saw Daddy?" Finally Janet went upstairs, called the Malamuts' house, and summoned her husband.

A tense confrontation ensued. Polevoi told Barry he had managed to cash most of the checks but not all, and would bring the cash over later, as soon as he and Janet got it all sorted out. He also said he was subtracting $50,000 that Barry owed him.

"Why are you taking it now?" Barry demanded. "You know I'm good for it. Don't you trust me?"

26

ometimes it seems that everybody involved in the ZZZZ Best
fiasco lifted weights, even the prosecutors. James Asperger,
the amiable Assistant U.S. Attorney who first discussed the
case with Rose Schindler, works out regularly at the downtown YMCA, and on weekends looks like a member of the coaching
staff in a small-college football program. He is too boyish to be head
coach, and the resemblance vanishes during the week, when he wears
dark suits. Perhaps reflecting their venue, all the Assistant U.S. Attorneys in Los Angeles look physically fit and mentally alert, without
the hunched, flabby, five-o'clock-shadow look that federal prosecutors
have in some other cities.

Schindler knew Asperger from an earlier case, and liked him. She
also needed him. The SEC can take legal action against miscreants,
but it lacks the power to bring criminal charges. As a result, when
SEC attorneys like Schindler find a really bad actor, they try to get
the local U.S. Attorney's Office interested. In this case the local U.S.
Attorney, Robert C. Bonner, was assumed to be interested. Rudolph
Giuliani, at the time his counterpart in New York City, was domi-
nating the headlines with a spectacular series of prosecutions that had
put several leading mobsters and municipal officials behind bars. Most
of all, Giuliani was in the spotlight for his unrelenting pursuit of
securities fraud on Wall Street, where he had already bagged stock
speculator Ivan Boesky for insider trading. The investigation had
reached deep into Southern California. Boyd L. Jefferies was forced
to quit as chairman of Jefferies & Co., the Los Angeles-based securities
firm that specialized in trading huge blocks of stock, after pleading
guilty to securities violations. More significantly, Giuliani had come

to focus on Drexel Burnham Lambert's fabulously profitable junk-bond operations, based in Beverly Hills and run by Michael Milken, another son of the San Fernando Valley. Drexel eventually pleaded guilty to fraud and paid a record $650 million fine, but Milken was the great white whale to Giuliani's Ahab.

Los Angeles was increasingly a major financial center, yet the regional office of the SEC and the local U.S. Attorney's Office had brought no major securities cases. Bonner was eager to change that.

Knowing this, Schindler and Asperger talked about ZZZZ Best on May 26. The *Los Angeles Times* story about credit-card fraud had just sent the stock into a tailspin, and Schindler knew from her own spadework that something was up. Schindler and Asperger both saw ZZZZ Best as a case of financial fraud and stock manipulation. But the world is full of evil, and law-enforcement resources are limited. Prosecutors must therefore use their judgment in choosing the best cases to pursue. Asperger was already very busy and wasn't sure about the credit-card fraud. He asked Schindler to keep him posted.

But when ZZZZ Best shares jumped on news of the company's glowing earnings report, Asperger was sure there was something wrong, and showed the clippings to Bonner, who was interested. In the weeks that followed, Schindler and Asperger talked about ZZZZ Best almost daily, and before long the FBI was investigating. The case was assigned to Special Agent Bucky Sadler, a lawyer by training who remembered Barry from Sadler's own loansharking investigation of Catain in 1985. Sadler had coincidentally just had a report of possible ZZZZ Best check-kiting at Santa Clarita National Bank, which said that for five days in early June it was exposed to possible losses exceeding $1.2 million. On June 19 Asperger formally requested access to the SEC investigative file on ZZZZ Best. Soon he and other federal authorities were discussing whether FBI agents should go in and seize records. It was becoming evident that ZZZZ Best would warrant some kind of criminal prosecution.

On Thursday, July 2, Schindler and Sadler were among a dozen law-enforcement officials who packed into Asperger's little office in the federal courthouse downtown to talk about Barry Minkow. The FBI, the state Attorney General, the county sheriff and the U.S. Attorney's Office were all represented. The Los Angeles Police were notably absent, even though Mike Brambles was investigating ZZZZ Best full-time and probably knew more than anyone. But Brambles wasn't invited because nobody had any idea the Los Angeles Police were working the case. Brambles had even heard from jailbird Dirk

Summers in early June that he had told Rose Schindler everything, but Brambles didn't call her because of a long-standing animosity between his unit of LAPD and the local office of the FBI, the main federal investigating agency. The two law-enforcement agencies regarded one another with mutual distrust and disdain. FBI agents are generally better educated, consider themselves an elite and sometimes look down on the local police. But the LAPD organized-crime detectives are paid better, and having worked their way up after years as street cops, they know their town and have little patience for snobbery. The two agencies don't cooperate much and share surprisingly little information. As a result, Brambles, feeling burned from past experiences, told federal authorities nothing about his advanced investigation.

At the July 2 meeting, Asperger warned Schindler that Barry had been granted immunity from prosecution in connection with the earlier government investigation of Catain, and that it was therefore crucial to avoid any knowledge of Barry's testimony in that case. If prosecutors were to derive information or even leads from immunized testimony, their charges might become "fruit of the poisoned tree," and be thrown out.

On July 4, Schindler was at home when she got a call from Helen Melman, Moskowitz's colleague at Hughes Hubbard, who gave her some idea of what was going on and requested a meeting. Then she called the various ZZZZ Best board members and obtained permission to talk to the SEC, which could nullify the directors' attorney-client privilege with her firm. Melman was having quite a day. Earlier she had had a terrifying phone conversation with Mark Morze, who told her the restoration business was fake. The following morning, Schindler and her boss, Tom Colthurst, met with Melman, Moskowitz and John Kralik, all of Hughes Hubbard, at the law firm's offices downtown. Schindler and Colthurst were surprised that Kralik, who was only an associate, did most of the talking.

The lawyers met for three solid hours, during which Kralik painted a portrait of a company laid waste by massive wrongdoing. ZZZZ Best's books and records indicated that the company should have lots of money, but virtually none of it could be found. The company's ledgers, which Kralik displayed, showed repeated large payments to a few key vendors, such as Marbil Management, although it now appeared that no restoration work was done. That didn't account for the recently missing money; nobody knew where it was, but signs

pointed to Barry. Kralik said the locks had been changed and that
ZZZZ Best would make some kind of bankruptcy filing in a matter
of days. For Moskowitz, it was the financial equivalent of Edvard
Munch's "The Scream." He had walked the Sacramento job, and now
he was told it didn't exist. Like Catherine the Great, he had toured
a Potemkin village, one of the phony fronts set up to make the countryside look prosperous for the tsarina. Moskowitz had been like an older
brother to this thief, had even exposed his family to Barry, who named
the lawyer's sons in his will. And there was the damned stock! How
would it look that he had accepted the 25,000 shares from Barry? It
wasn't unethical, but some people frown on securities lawyers' taking
equity stakes. ("You want to keep your legal advice and economic
position separate," explains a top Los Angeles securities lawyer.) Always a worrier, Moskowitz had been careful all his life: in school he
had studied hard, and as a lawyer he split hairs that other attorneys
couldn't even see. He had followed the rules as if they were com-
mandments, he had been *good*, and now he was being punished anyway. He had trusted Barry, and now he could *really* worry: that he
had screwed up, that his painstakingly crafted career might be over,
and that his family's well-being might be compromised.
Moskowitz didn't deserve any of this, but at such times it's hard to
say which is worse: to know as much, or to doubt it.

At four P.M. the ZZZZ Best board of directors reconvened and
voted unanimously to file for Chapter 11 protection under the Federal
Bankruptcy Code. Chapter 11 is not strictly what most people understand by the term bankruptcy, which usually means, "I give up,
I'm broke. Please wipe out my debts, take everything but the clothes
off my back, and leave me alone." Chapter 11, by contrast, asks a
judge to hold off the creditors and litigants while the company takes
a breather to reorganize. Chapter 11 presupposes that a business can
be saved.

Andersen proposed jettisoning many of the unprofitable ZZZZ Best
cleaning locations and scaling back to just seven. He said the company
had about $240,000 in receivables, $5,760,000 in heavily mortgaged
assets such as buildings, land and generators, and another $1 million
worth of supplies. The week of July 6 was expected to bring in $67,000
in cash receipts, he said, but there was nothing in the payroll account,
and more checks were due to be issued Tuesday.

The board also ratified Andersen's dismissal of Arrington for taking
"unauthorized payments" from Barry, and authorized the suspension

of Mark Morze. Then the directors approved a press release for the next day, and instructed the lawyers to call Nasdaq to halt trading until the release was issued.

It was a miserable weekend for everyone associated with ZZZZ Best. Shari Elowsky had spent the days and nights in a haze of despair. On Monday morning she arrived at work to find her boss, Robert Bird, leaving for London with a copy of *The Wall Street Journal*. "Look at the article on ZZZZ Best," she told him.

Ninety minutes later Bird was back in her office and Elowsky, in tears, resigned. Headlined ZZZZ BEST IS UNDER SEC INVESTIGATION, MULLS BANKRUPTCY FILING, SOURCES SAY, the *Journal* story said the federal agency was looking into "a wide range of alleged fraudulent practices at ZZZZ Best and believes the company may be forced to file for bankruptcy-law protection shortly." The story also said trading in the stock was expected to be halted, that major contracts now appeared phony and that Barry had resigned.

Elowsky was filled with doom. These events implied that the nearly 1.8 million shares of restricted ZZZZ Best stock P-B had taken from Barry as collateral weren't likely to hold their value. Sure enough, ZZZZ Best stock didn't open that morning. Nasdaq delayed trading pending a news announcement, and when ZZZZ Best finally opened at ten-thirty AM it immediately headed south.

The ZZZZ Best news announcement said that "the Company has discovered facts which appear to substantiate allegations of fraud associated with the Company's restoration business and which disclose possible misappropriation of significant assets." The press release, which filled short-sellers with glee, went on to say that, "The apparent misappropriation of corporate funds has substantially depleted the Company's liquid assets" and made it tough to stay in business. ZZZZ Best would file for Chapter 11 protection.

Monday, July 6, was a busy day all around. ZZZZ Best filed a lawsuit in Los Angeles Superior Court accusing Barry, Morze, Padgett, Interstate and Marbil of fraud, conversion and breach of fiduciary duty for paying out $18 million in company funds for non-existent restoration work. The suit claimed Barry withdrew more than $3 million in corporate funds in June alone, and requested an injunction to prevent him from disposing of any ZZZZ Best assets. Arthur Barens, Barry's lawyer, proclaimed the suit to be without merit, adding that "none of those monies were taken from the company."

Also on Monday, Moskowitz spent five anguished hours with Asperger. Melman, also present, said Mark Morze had told her the restoration business was fake. The same day, Schindler's Order of Investigation finally came through from Washington, granting her subpoena power in the case of ZZZZ Best. The only question now was whether there would be anything left to subpoena. Some ZZZZ Best insiders were already taking steps to get rid of incriminating evidence: Barry had Scamardo burn two boxes of documents, and a whole truckload was lost from 4Z Equipment. Whether the SEC ever unraveled the tangled mess might be small consolation to investors anyway. When the markets closed, ZZZZ Best stock could be had for only 75 cents a share—down $2.75 from before the holiday week-end—and once again it was the day's most active over-the-counter issue. The company's market valuation—number of shares times price per share—had plummeted from more than $210 million in April to less than $9 million, and on Monday, July 6, nobody was lining up to pay that much.

Back in Reseda, things were getting ugly. ZZZZ Best corporate headquarters was in chaos, and the place was besieged by irate employees pounding at the locked door, demanding to be paid. At other ZZZZ Best facilities, workers were stealing equipment and supplies, following in the footsteps of an inspirational leader who had set new standards for looters.

At seven P.M., a group of frightened individuals sat down in yet another meeting of the ZZZZ Best board of directors. Hal Lipman and Dan Krowpman were absent, but Malamut, Dem, Berman and Hojecki made a quorum. Also attending were Andersen, now the interim president; Dennis Harris, the in-house accountant; and attorney Melman. Melman said Krowpman still hadn't resigned, even though several directors had suggested he should because of payments to Cornwell that had come to light. Andersen reported that fifteen of the twenty-one ZZZZ Best locations were still open and that the company had $15,000 in cash receipts on the day. But he said phone equipment and other materials were missing from some ZZZZ Best facilities. Perhaps feeling things were too far out of control, the board voted to seek a court-appointed trustee to take over the company. The ZZZZ Best directors never convened again, and the investigations by Kadison, Pfaelzer and John Murphy & Associates ended. There was no money to pay them, and the lawyers had been authorized by the ZZZZ Best board to cooperate with law-enforcement authorities.

At this point I knew that Barry was a fraud, the insurance jobs were fake, the generators were junk and shady characters such as Rind and Victor were involved. I'd been working day and night to get a

front-page story ready on ZZZZ Best, but the company was a moving
target, and I was sickened to see stories on the subject starting to
appear over the hot July 4 weekend (the *Journal* doesn't publish on
weekends or holidays). On Sunday I wrote the story about the SEC
probe that Elowsky and her boss saw on Monday, July 6. The front-
page story was ready later that day, but the need for careful editing
and lawyerly review, as well as the bicoastal time difference and the
priorities of page one, kept it out of Tuesday's paper, for which I had
written a smaller piece about the ZZZZ Best lawsuit against Barry,
Padgett and Morze. The big story didn't make Wednesday's paper
either, and by now I was practically frantic to get the thing into print.
Predictably, on Wednesday ZZZZ Best exploded.

Armed with warrants, Brambles and other officers of the LAPD
Organized Crime Intelligence Division searched Barry's house, ZZZZ
Best headquarters and fourteen other locations connected with the
company. They did so despite a last-minute call from the FBI, which
asked that the searches be delayed. The FBI had heard what Brambles
was up to and had even gained consent from some of the search
subjects, but Brambles wasn't about to wait for the feds. The same
day, ZZZZ Best filed for Chapter 11 protection. And that afternoon
Los Angeles' ambitious and freewheeling chief of police, Daryl F.
Gates, held an amazing press conference at which he announced that
ZZZZ Best was suspected of "laundering huge profits from narcotics
trafficking" for organized crime. He went on to name names and tell
the whole story, with the emphasis firmly on drug money. Gates said
the insurance restoration business was a scam designed to boost ZZZZ
Best stock and to provide a front for laundering the dough.

Gates is a controversial figure in Los Angeles, and people were
pretty much horrified by his press conference. The crooks didn't like
it because it blew their cover, and there was much injured denial:
there may have been financial shenanigans, but drugs? Never! Civil
libertarians were appalled that Gates could make such devastating
allegations without filing a single charge. Federal authorities—including Asperger and Schindler—were incensed at Gates's grandstanding,
which they knew was designed to assure that the police got the glory.
The press conference could hurt only when it came time to actually
press charges, and Gates had also backed his own officers into a corner.
They had just executed the search warrants. What if the evidence
they found pointed in a different direction?

I was practically apoplectic. The chief of police had just given away
most of what I had developed on my own, so that when our front-

page story ran on Thursday, July 9, everybody else had at least some kind of ZZZZ Best story as well. The following afternoon, a Friday, ZZZZ Best stock closed out the week at 69 cents a share.

Barry's downfall brought forth an outpouring of headlines that seemed to surpass even those that heralded his rise. On July 13, for example, *USA Today* ran a multipage spread with several stories, pictures, a chronology and thumbnail biographies on the major players. Eventually a Congressional subcommittee held hearings, and the ZZZZ Best debacle contributed to a major change in accounting rules requiring auditors to look for fraud. In September of 1988 Barry finally made Johnny Carson, although not in person.

"I know this is going to be a great audience tonight," Carson began his monologue. "But of course I'm an optimist. I'm still waiting for Barry Minkow to clean my carpets."

27

Things slowed down considerably for Barry once ZZZZ Best collapsed. In the second half of 1987 he spent a good deal of time around the house, lounging with Joyce and their friends beside the pool with the giant Zs on the bottom. He had a new phone number that hardly anyone knew, and even though he lived in a gated, guarded community, he had a plainclothes security guard at his house.

Despite his high legal bills—Barry said later, in court, that he paid Barens about $400,000—things weren't altogether terrible for him. The sun was shining, the birds sang and despite the collapse of ZZZZ Best, life went on. Occasionally there was some unpleasantness. Elaine Orlando and her youthful boyfriend came by one day, breezing right past the gatehouse with a smile and a wave. They parked around the corner and came up to the house on foot.

"Joyce, I need to see Barry," Orlando said.

"He's not here," Joyce replied.

"I don't think you understand," Orlando said, beginning to weep. "I need to see him."

"He's not here. You can go inside and look for yourself."

Orlando was unconvinced. Barry's white BMW and red Ferrari (with the ZZZZBST plates) were parked out front, and Elaine carried on so much that Joyce finally went inside and dialed Jack Polevoi.

"Jack, put him on the phone," she said. Then, to Barry, she said, "Elaine Orlando is here and she's crying." She listened for a moment and then hung up. "He can't see you," she told Orlando.

"I'm not leaving until I see him," Orlando insisted. She was out $350,000 and was becoming hysterical.

Joyce called Barry again and was more insistent: "Elaine is crying and she's not going to leave!"

Barry finally came walking up the block, looking casual and fit in shorts and the inevitable tank top. They talked near the pool.

"Barry, what's happening? What's going on?"

"They think I stole from my own company, but I didn't."

"Does this mean I've lost my money?"

"No," said Barry. "Just wait for the dust to settle."

"How long will that be?"

"Just a couple of weeks."

"You mean—I'll get my money back then?"

"Yes."

But Elaine was now more nervous than ever. Barry's manner did it. He wasn't friendly and warm the way he'd been in the past. Now he was cold, remote, uncaring. He actually seemed annoyed.

"Elaine, you made a lot of money with me."

"How could I?" Orlando asked, still weeping. "I don't have my money back."

"If you want your money back, ask Kay Rozario."

"Kay doesn't have any money."

"Yes she does, she has two million."

"That's ridiculous."

"She does, and you got usurious interest out of me."

"That's ridiculous."

"I shouldn't even be talking to you, Elaine. Don't tell anyone we talked. My lawyer told me I could get in a lot of trouble for this."

When they were done they hugged, almost as a reflex. Orlando went away weeping.

Mike Malamut had a similar experience. Unable to reach Barry any other way, he got Rob Byers to help with a visit on Sunday, July 12. Byers lived in the Westchester County compound. When Malamut got there he was astonished to see Barry frolicking in the sunshine with several young men and women.

"How are you feeling, Barry?" Malamut asked.

"Fine," Barry said, wearing shorts and a tan.

Mike Malamut is not a violent man. When he and Barry got down to business in private, he simply explained the situation.

"I put up my house, my mother's house, some pieces of property I worked over fifteen years to get, and now it's all in jeopardy."

"Mike, you have nothing to worry about."

"Barry, my mother is crying because she's afraid she's going to lose her house!"

"Tell her she's got nothing to worry about," Barry insisted.

"Really? Why?"

"I'm going to pay you back personally."

"I don't understand."

"You were a board member and you didn't get anything. You're the only person connected with this company that got nothing out of it, that isn't dirty. And I feel bad. These others, they invested, but they were working on the house's money. They put money in, got money out and reinvested, but I don't feel sorry for those people."

Of course Barry exaggerated. Some people profited, but the losses swamped any gains.

"How are you going to pay me back?" Malamut asked in wonder.

"Don't worry. I got plenty of money outside the country, and I'm going to bring it in and pay you."

Malamut, who hadn't slept in a week, felt better for an instant, until Barry hastened to add, "Now this is going to take some time. It's expensive to bring the money back in and it'll take a couple of weeks."

"Barry, my money was supposed to go for materials," Malamut said. "Can't I go and get the materials and return them and get some money back that way?"

Barry must have been stunned by Malamut's credulity.

"Mike," he said. "There are no materials."

"What do you mean? What about the restoration job in Texas?"

"There is no Texas job."

Despite all he had heard and read, Malamut was flabbergasted.

"What did you need the money for if there was no Texas job?"

"We were just trying to show better profits," Barry said.

"I don't understand."

"We'd show money going in and money going out—to raise the stock price," Barry explained quietly.

"What about Sacramento? What about the lawyers who visited? Was there any Sacramento restoration project?"

"No," Barry said. "We just set that up. That was just a big scam. We staged it. They bought the program hook, line and sinker."

"Barry, this is just shocking. I can't believe this."

"Mike, the biggest job we ever had was maybe a fifty-thousand-dollar restoration."

"Barry, you can get in a lot of trouble here—"

"No I won't," Barry said. "I'm going to come out of this smelling like a rose."

"What do you mean?"

"Do you think anyone's gonna believe a twenty-one-year-old engineered all this? The rest of the guys are going to take the hit, guys like Krowpman and Morze. Not me. Nobody's gonna believe that a twenty-one-year-old could have pulled something like this off."

Malamut sat utterly stupefied. He wanted to smash Barry's brains in with a baseball bat, but he also felt like an idiot. "How could I be such a sucker?" he wondered. When he left, Barry promised to pay a large portion of the $1 million Malamut was owed within two weeks.

A couple of weeks later, Barry told Malamut that he was being watched and couldn't bring the money into the country. Perhaps, Barry said, he could make interest payments in the interim.

Nothing happened, so Malamut went to see Barry again, this time at a crowded Belgian waffle restaurant in Encino that Barry was supposed to have an interest in. Barry was frying eggs, wearing a chef's uniform.

"Hey, Mike," he said cheerfully. "Can I make you some eggs?"

"No," Malamut said. "But I'd like to talk."

Barry spoke enthusiastically of his budding business empire. He said he owned the waffle place in the name of a relative—"I'm going to learn this business from start to finish," he told Malamut—and owned a couple of other businesses in the Valley as well, including a pest-control service that he claimed would soon be the biggest in the industry. (Barry's parents and Sherrie Maloney worked there; Scamardo was Barry's front man as owner.)

"Just sit tight," Barry said. "I'm going to have some money for you. Just give me some more time."

Barry filed for personal bankruptcy on August 7, 1987. As well as I can make out, his assets were $1,069,300, not counting his new business ventures and the sale of his Testarossa, which he fraudulently failed to disclose. His known liabilities were about $20 million, but that doesn't include any of the unknown liabilities, which would probably run to another $100 million if anyone could ever sort them out. The financial picture was such that Malamut's friends told him to give up, the cause was lost. But he was a desperately unhappy man, and he still wanted to believe. At one point Barry sent him $1,200. Another time, Barry called and asked him to release the lien on his—Barry's—house. That way, Barry said, he could transfer it to Arthur Barens and keep it away from the bankruptcy court. Malamut wouldn't go along unless he got his share of the home equity in advance.

"What do you mean?" Barry demanded. "Are you going to play hardball with me over this?"

"Hardball?!" Malamut was almost speechless. "You sting me for a million dollars and I'm playing hardball with you?"

"Okay, look, maybe I can give you twenty-five thousand—"

Malamut hung up. Not long after, he got on an airplane bound for Las Vegas to attend a Honda Motors car show. Suddenly, Barry came aboard.

"Hi, Mike," he called cheerily. "How ya doin'?"

Barry liked going to Las Vegas. Janet Polevoi says he went twice with her husband (Janet went along once) and bet heavily, using black chips worth $1,000 each. Once in late October or early November, while checking on her cigarette concession at Bally's Grand Hotel in Las Vegas, Suzette Whitmore couldn't believe her eyes. One of her saleswomen was selling a cigar to Barry Minkow at the 21 table. As the woman came away, Whitmore stopped her.

"Go tell him here's one cigar compliments of Suzette."

"What? What if he asks—"

"Go do it! I'll be right behind you."

The cigar woman went back to Barry and said, "Here's a cigar compliments of Suzette."

It's against the rules for someone like Suzette to take a gambler away from the table, but Barry spoke momentarily to the pit boss, left perhaps $2,500 worth of chips on the table and walked a few feet away with Suzette, who was out $59,600. He gave her a kiss on the cheek and leaned against an empty crap table.

"So how are the kids?" he asked.

"Barry, I trusted you, I believed in you. I'm broke now, I'm an old lady. What am I going to do?"

"Suzette, I can't talk to you about the case," Barry said apologetically. "My lawyer told me not to talk to any of you."

"Please, I'm not trying to do anything else. Please just give me some of my money back."

Finally, as if he would do something for her at last, Barry wrote two phone numbers down for her on a napkin. Suzette was ecstatic until she got into her car. Then she realized, "That little bastard, he's done it to me again." She ran back inside and paged him, but he was gone, and later, when she called the numbers again and again, someone always said Barry would be back in an hour. She never heard from him again.

As a company, ZZZZ Best expired soon after Barry's resignation. Herb Wolas, a hard-nosed, Bronx-born member of the local bankruptcy bar, was named the court-appointed trustee in charge of the company, and he shut it down almost immediately. At that point, July 16, ZZZZ Best had $30,000 in cash on hand. Ten days later, to Wolas's disappointment, two former ZZZZ Best executives and a third man paid just $62,000 at auction for the company's name and portable assets. (Much later Wolas managed to recoup about $800,000 by selling assets and pursuing people who had received some of the company's ill-gotten gains. He got $109,000 for the 4Z generators, for example, and $105,000 plus a fur coat from Candi Apple, Mark Morze's girlfriend.) On July 21 Nasdaq delisted ZZZZ Best stock, at this point really a formality, since the shares had already ceased being securities and commenced a life as artifacts.

Lawsuits flourished in the wake of ZZZZ Best. Numerous shareholder actions were filed against anybody and everybody who had anything to do with the fiasco; since all the suits were class actions, a federal judge mercifully consolidated them into a single case. People like Barry Minkow usually do not have to worry about such lawsuits. Barry was sued, all right, but if he had any money it was safely offshore, and the irate investors, lenders and creditors would have to wait until the criminal authorities got done with him anyway.

When such litigation arises, the wronged parties typically look around to see who's got money. These monied targets are known as "deep-pocket parties," and plaintiffs make sure to include them as defendants. Rooney, Pace was out of business, and getting money out of the conspirators seemed unlikely. But Ernst & Whinney, the accounting firm, and Hughes Hubbard & Reed, the law firm, have pockets that go way, way down. Besides their own great wherewithal, these two esteemed firms have insurance, although ZZZZ Best–watchers are betting that the firms themselves, if they lose, will still end up writing some big checks.

All of that is likely to take years to work its way through the courts. The devastation that Barry Minkow brought to his human victims is more immediate. The worst sufferers—Elowsky, Malamut, Gray, Moskowitz, Randall, Orlando and Marchese, just to name a few—felt themselves fall as if through a trapdoor from security and affluence to humiliation and in some cases impoverishment. All had huge chunks of their peace, faith and wealth torn away by the seductive young man who knew the secret of their vulnerability. Many of Barry's victims have since been sleepless and depressed, filled with doubt about themselves and the world they were once so comfortable in. Some suffered physical illnesses, and one or two thought briefly of suicide.

"It was a nightmare," says Whitmore. "I just want to forget."

Like others who find themselves victimized in some way, many of the people Barry robbed felt a horrible sense of shame. Some blame themselves, even though at most they share only a part of the responsibility, or could only be blamed for being human. They kick themselves for their stupidity, their naïveté, their greed. They excoriate themselves for hurting their families, and they worry about their own future.

Shari Elowsky couldn't face her parents for six weeks following the July 4 weekend, when ZZZZ Best collapsed. She cried a lot, and lost a couple of her best friends, who were connected in some way to Prudential-Bache. Jobless, she had to sell her apartment, and eventually she moved far away from New York.

Mike Malamut suffered more than a staggering financial loss. People keep asking him how he got mixed up in such a sleazy mess, and the credit unions and others that his business deals with want explanations as well. The large loss and ensuing litigation will be with him for years. "I don't really feel I've been myself since this happened to me," he said in court, citing insomnia and depression.

Larry Gray of Ernst & Whinney and Mark Moskowitz of Hughes Hubbard are still partners at their firms, but their reputations and careers probably were severely damaged. Neither man would be interviewed for this book.

Ann Randall moved in with her mother. Barry's betrayal left her broke, ailing and afraid to trust her own judgment.

Adman David Marchese saw his firm break up, in part because of its ZZZZ Best losses. Barry left Pearlman Wohl Olshever Marchese holding the bag for $900,000.

Countless others suffered milder losses that still hurt, and Ladenburg, Thalmann clients are prominent on this list. Jenny Raphael, a funny and philosophical New York businesswoman, bought ZZZZ Best stock on the recommendation of her Ladenburg broker and ended up losing $50,000. Like many others, she initially made money in the stock and reinvested. Ladenburg chairman Ronald Koenig, who believed in the stock and the entrepreneur his own company was touting, was among the losers. He bought 15,000 shares of ZZZZ Best at $7 and watched $105,000 disappear.

Others bought ZZZZ Best because of Rooney, Pace. Kay Woodfin, a loan officer in the private banking division of Citibank, had a Rooney, Pace broker who'd met Barry. She lost about $23,000. "It's criminal," she says. "It's like being robbed from your own home." No babe in the financial woods, Woodfin holds an MBA from New York University and has invested in the stock market for more than twelve years.

St. Louis attorney Mark Goodman has one client who lost $155,000 in ZZZZ Best. Another bought it—at his broker's suggestion—for his pension plan and lost about $40,000.

It is easy to call many of these people stupid, but that misses the point. Stupidity is not a moral failing, nor is any one of us immune to it. To dismiss the misery of the foolish or misguided is to turn a cold shoulder to perhaps the majority of human suffering.

Around July 20, 1987, I received a handwritten letter from Joan Bachetti in Cypress, Texas, whose husband had died the year before after a long, painful battle with cancer. Bachetti has a limited income, and for some reason she decided to invest $11,800 in ZZZZ Best. "I saw this as a good chance to make some money for my future," she explained.

Predictably, Mrs. Bachetti lost it all.

"Do you know of any way I can get my money back?" she asked. "I don't know how Barry can live with himself, when he can do things like this to people that had such faith in him."

Barry was just doing what he did best. One of his post-ZZZZ Best investments was in a company called Novelty Carpet Cleaning, and maybe because someone figured it would look good later at trial, Barry put on dark glasses and went out to clean a few carpets himself.

28

It was October, a glorious time of year in New York. The two detectives from out west hadn't arrived on horseback, but they were still having a difficult time in the city. They had come east in the fall of 1987 to question potential witnesses in the ZZZZ Best investigation, and on their first morning in town they were looking for a place to park. They buttonholed one of the city's brown-uniformed, civilian parking enforcement officers.

"We're police officers from Los Angeles. Can we park here?"

"Sure," the brownie said cheerfully.

Pleased at such intramural cooperation, the Angelenos parked and went about their business. When they got back, their car was gone.

First they figured it was stolen, and after a frantic minute or two they waved down a couple of New York cops, who were busy berating an Iranian cab driver for double-parking. The cops explained that the missing car was just the brownies' idea of fun; the local police and the civilian parking agents were always at each other's throats, and the brownies liked nothing better than to tow a cop's car. The visitors listened and had the kind of feeling Americans sometimes get in Rome, or in Cairo.

The two detectives from Los Angeles were Mike Brambles and Jeff Redman. Brambles is well-traveled and approaches the world with a certain wonder; he liked New York. Redman, who is not well-traveled and would prefer to have a beer, wasn't exactly prepared for the city, and he hated it. On Columbus Day he climbed all 354 steps to the top of the Statue of Liberty in pointy-toed cowboy boots, so his feet were killing him, and it was already obvious that a car was of little use in the city. One of the cops they met didn't even have a driver's license. Redman thought he must be from Mars.

The two detectives were in New York partly because Brambles was still convinced ZZZZ Best was laundering drug money, and that the company was heavily infiltrated by organized crime. But by now he and Asperger had threshed out an agreement to share information with federal prosecutors, and from July on Brambles, Schindler and Asperger worked closely on the case.

Asperger, however, didn't share Brambles' conviction about the drug profits or the mob infiltration, and wasn't bound by anything the police chief had said in the glare of the klieg lights. Working with FBI agents Bucky Sadler and John Orr, IRS agent Paul Davis and some of Brambles' information, Asperger put together a powerful fraud case. In January, when the federal grand jury finally handed up its indictment, Rind, Schulman and Victor were left out. Despite Brambles' vehement insistence, Asperger had decided that there wasn't enough evidence against them, at least not yet. They would be prosecuted separately, if at all. First and foremost, there would be Barry.

On January 14, Barry Minkow and ten others were charged with a variety of federal offenses stemming from their involvement in ZZZZ Best. Gene Lasko was charged separately in an "information," meaning he waived indictment. Since all twelve defendants were as guilty as anyone could possibly be, ten of them pleaded guilty to reduced charges during the ensuing months in exchange for their cooperation against Barry. Krowpman, Arrington, Padgett, Roddy, the Morze brothers, the Polevoi twins, Lasko and Edward Krivda all entered guilty pleas and provided evidence. Barry and Rothberg were the lone holdouts. There would have to be a trial.

Swamped, Asperger asked his superiors to assign a second prosecutor to the case. He had already talked about it with his friend Gordon Greenberg, chief of the office's financial investigations unit, who was considering going into private practice. Greenberg agreed to stay for the ZZZZ Best case and was assigned to work on it with Asperger.

Both men are straight enough to make arrows jealous. Asperger, thirty-five when the trial commenced, grew up in Fresno and studied political science and philosophy at the University of California–Davis. By the time he came to the U.S. Attorney's Office in Los Angeles, he had acquired a set of glittering legal credentials, including editorship of the law review at UCLA and clerkships with conservative Supreme Court Justice William Rehnquist (now Chief Justice) and liberal California Supreme Court Justice Stanley Mosk. Asperger had also worked in the top-flight law firm of Latham & Watkins in Washington, D.C.

Greenberg, thirty-four, brought tremendous criminal experience to the case. A tall, powerfully built Chicagoan, his black beard and whimsical smile make him look just a little like a rabbinical student on steroids, but he had the perfect background for prosecuting Barry Minkow. He studied psychology and finance at the University of Illinois, graduated from law school at the Illinois Institute of Technology and immediately went to work as an assistant state's attorney in Chicago, where he prosecuted murders and gang violence. Greenberg scored a coup after coming to the U.S. Attorney's Office in Los Angeles by convicting Oscar Fernando Cuevas on charges of conspiring to aid narcotics organizations by laundering money. Cuevas was a Harvard-educated Colombian who, from Europe, supervised the laundering of more than $100 million in the United States, authorities say. After a huge legal battle that went all the way to the Swiss Supreme Court, Cuevas became the first money-laundering suspect extradited from the land of financial secrecy. Greenberg's courtroom victory was doubly sweet because Cuevas' lawyer was Don Re, who with Howard Weitzman defeated federal prosecutors in Los Angeles to gain acquittal for John De Lorean, the maverick auto executive arrested on drug-trafficking charges. Cuevas even got Harvard legal scholar Alan Dershowitz to appeal, without success. By the time Greenberg was assigned to ZZZZ Best, he had prosecuted more than fifty-five different criminal cases, and ZZZZ Best had begun to seem his destiny. How many other prosecutors have ever bench-pressed 315 pounds? How many could say that Barry Minkow, who quit July 2, had resigned on their birthday?

It didn't take long for Asperger and Greenberg to realize that this was a pretty important case. Their names were in the newspapers, their mothers were excited and their boss in the office's criminal division went out of his way to avoid pressuring them, except to say that if they lost they would have to jump off the top of nearby City Hall. Apparently he didn't consider the seventeen-story federal courthouse high enough.

The two prosecutors remained calm, putting Barry out of their minds for minutes every day. Greenberg and Asperger are probably the only people in the world who were even more obsessed with ZZZZ Best than Barry. They made Robin Swanson look like a hobbyist.

Asperger and Greenberg have a lot in common. Close in age and temperament, they both started work at the U.S. Attorney's Office around June of 1983, and were both married to fellow Assistant U.S. Attorneys (Greenberg's wife is now a Los Angeles municipal court judge). They had always been reasonably friendly, but their joint assignment on the ZZZZ Best case made them practically into a chain gang. Together they worked seven days a week, devoting all their waking hours to the case. They exercised together at the Y, and when their wives wanted to take a long weekend, they vacationed together. On a skiing trip to Mammoth Lakes, California, Greenberg and Asperger drove up in one car and their wives took another. For most of 1988 these bright, attractive women were ZZZZ Best widows, and by the beginning of 1989 just the word carpet was enough to make their eyes glaze.

Soon after his indictment, Barry got rid of Arthur Barens and interviewed a series of prospective replacements before settling on David Kenner, then forty-six, one of the best-known criminal lawyers in Los Angeles. Quick-witted, combative and flamboyant, Kenner is a sole practitioner who had defended many narcotics and white-collar suspects. He reportedly took on the frustrating task of defending Barry Minkow without pay, merely for the challenge, the publicity and the prospect of selling a book or movie that might bring some money later.

Barry's stance at first was one of shock. He claimed to be just as amazed as anyone else to learn that the big ZZZZ Best insurance contracts weren't real. Barry soon recognized that that story wouldn't hold water, and finally admitted everything. But he insisted he had no choice: he was acting under duress the whole time, forced into a life of crime by people who beat him, held his head underwater and threatened to kill his family. "It was my parents I was worried about," Barry said.

This defense was no less preposterous than claiming ignorance, but was somewhat more troubling for Asperger and Greenberg. For one thing, the Los Angeles Police had made such a big deal about the Mafia at ZZZZ Best that they had given unwitting credibility, however slight, to Barry's claims of duress. Brambles' furious efforts to link Barry and his company to mob families in the East looked like they might backfire in the short run. Barry's lawyer would call Brambles, Victor and Rind (Rind took the Fifth Amendment ninety-two times) as witnesses. And Barry had thoughtfully faked a shooting episode to make it look like someone had tried to kill him. On August 10, 1987, he got Scamardo to shoot a couple of holes in the side of his truck. The next day Barry told police that a white Lincoln Continental had pulled up beside them as they were driving along Santa Susanna Pass Road and fired four shots. The news even made *The Washington Post*. Scamardo disposed of the weapon—Robert Minkow's handgun—in the Pacific Ocean.

In June of 1988, Asperger and Greenberg got the grand jury to issue a superseding indictment from which they dropped the racketeering charges but added credit-card fraud and Barry's earliest restoration-loan scam, which predated his involvement with Catain. This time, instead of a potential sentence totaling 350 years, Barry faced 403.

As with Drexel, Barry was once again sunk by his own big mouth. The prosecution had videotapes of him on "The Oprah Winfrey Show," as master of ceremonies at a big ZZZZ Best awards banquet, and in various news interviews in which he was clearly in command. Barry's ease in those tapes bordered on arrogance, and his eyes, in retrospect, seemed to hold a secret.

Even more ironically, Barry was sunk by a taped forty-minute conversation between him and Dan Krowpman Sr., who called Barry in cooperation with police. The detectives kept passing Krowpman notes telling him to ask about various alleged mobsters, and Barry continually scoffed. Krowpman sounded frantic. Barry couldn't have been calmer.

"Danny, take the Fifth Amendment," he urged. "Don't say a fucking word."

Barry's trial before Judge Dickran Tevrizian commenced on August 24, 1988, and dragged on for nearly sixteen weeks. It would have been hard to find a more fitting judge than Dick Tevrizian. The son of Armenian immigrants, he was born in 1940, studied business and then law at the University of Southern California, and worked briefly for the Big Eight accounting firm of Arthur Andersen & Co. before becoming a business litigator. A staunch Republican whose career has been marked by bipartisan advancement, he was first a municipal and then a superior court judge before moving up to the federal judiciary, where the cases are more important, the judges and lawyers more accomplished and the all-around level of law higher. Tevrizian is short and bald and seems a little dour at first, but soon reveals himself to be a warm man with a jolly sense of humor. As a jurist he is known as tough but extremely fair, and willing to give the defense much latitude in introducing evidence. During the ZZZZ Best trial he revealed a profound knowledge of finance, accounting, securities law and business in general. Despite his relatively modest judge's salary (compared to what he could make in private practice), in Los Angeles legal circles Tevrizian is rumored to have grown wealthy as the result of shrewd investing. Judge Tevrizian embodies some very old-fashioned values: family, hard work, honesty and opportunity. He particularly relishes swearing in new citizens, whom he urges to vote and help keep their country clean and graffiti-free.

Kenner did not have an easy time. Between Barry and Tevrizian, he gained thirty pounds during the course of the trial, exacerbating the problem of his physical appearance in the courtroom. Asperger and Greenberg, with their ramrod posture and their tasteful suits and ties, were the picture of what jurors might expect to see in a prose-cutor. Kenner looked fat and flashy, with his cuff links and graying pompadour, and his battles with Tevrizian only made him look worse, since the judge quickly established himself for the jurors as a regular guy who could joke about his baldness and was solicitous of their well-being.

The prosecution put on a parade of witnesses who testified vividly to Barry's extraordinary wrongdoing. Malamut, whose hands were clean, was particularly devastating, as was Arrington, who wept in sorrow at his own foolishness. Except for canny Suzette Whitmore (who isn't really destitute), the ladies of the luncheon club seemed sad, frightened and confused. Rozario wasn't called because of her connection to Catain and questions about how much money she got as an intermediary. But Elaine Orlando was very sad. Sharon Elowsky might have been just a little too cute, but she was the most articulate of the lot by far, and did Barry much harm. No one could recall Barry ever showing signs of being beaten, of taking orders from anyone or of missing a day's work. Dr. Lovitz, his physician, testified that except for stomach troubles and stress, Barry was unscathed. Dr. Lovitz knew whereof he spoke: he used to treat prizefighters.

When the prosecution rested, Asperger, Greenberg and Kenner worked out a possible plea bargain. Barry could admit to a bunch of charges, and the trial would be over. Kenner asked Judge Tevrizian what sentence he would give Barry under those circumstances, and Tevrizian said twelve years.

Kenner went back to Barry. Throughout the government's case, Kenner had tried to make the prosecution's witnesses look greedy and negligent, but had succeeded mostly in blaming the victim and trying the judge's patience. It had been a struggle every step of the way with Tevrizian, who said pointedly that the greed or stupidity of the witnesses had little to do with Barry's innocence or guilt. Kenner had prolonged the trial for weeks with tedious cross-examinations and confusing check-by-check analysis, only to be reminded again and again by an increasingly irritable judge that he had presented not one shred of evidence for duress. Kenner's father had died during the summer, and he was working himself to exhaustion gathering material, preparing for court and keeping track of tens of thousands of documents in what was beginning to look like a sure loser of a case.

"Barry, I strongly advise you to accept the plea agreement," Kenner reportedly said.

Barry refused. He had fooled so many people so often before, he apparently couldn't see that it might not work this time, when the stakes were so much higher for himself. Perhaps he was no longer able to distinguish the truth from his own imaginings. Maybe by now he was convinced of his own lies. Personally, I would have been disappointed if he had accepted. It would have been un-Barrylike.

Kenner had no other choice but to put his own client on the stand. Characteristically, Barry had long ago mastered the mechanics of the stylized ritual going on around him. Emphasizing his youth, he dressed like Dobie Gillis in unfashionable sweaters instead of jacket and tie, and while the jurors were in the room he strained every fiber of himself to appear clean and honest. When they filed out for a break, though, he would put his feet up and lock his hands behind his head, chatting amiably with whoever was around. Once, before the day's proceedings commenced, he advised the judge's clerk on how to get a stain out of her carpet.

Barry had spent hours and hours studying documents in the case, and in court would sometimes nudge his attorney to object on grounds of striking subtlety. By the time he took the stand, Barry had an explanation ready for virtually everything.

As a witness, Barry's genius was probably his own undoing. He looked just like a worried defendant, with dark circles under his eyes complementing the faint mustache that always seemed left after he shaved, making him look that much more like a frightened teenager. He had an odd twitch, too, a sudden blink and nod that I hadn't seen before. His performance was extraordinary. He managed to appear penitent, open and honest, like one with nothing to hide. Faced with a question from his own lawyer, which he certainly must have expected, Barry would sometimes screw up his face, frown or even look up at the ceiling for a moment, as if searching, searching for the truth. He was magnificent, amazing, and in a subtle sort of way, dreadful, because his performance was recognizable for just what it was—a very fine performance whose utter falseness was beyond doubt. When he answered a question, he turned his whole body toward the jury, adopting a pleading expression, and when the judge and lawyers held one of their innumerable sidebar conferences, he once or twice lowered his head onto his arms, as if in despair. The air was soon heavy with Barry's dramatic sighing.

Also, his lies were too outlandish. Despite a mountain of evidence—including videotapes—attesting to his obsession with ZZZZ Best, he insisted he had wanted to abandon the company while in high school, but was forced to keep it going by Krowpman and the others.

"I wanted to be a foot doctor," he said, as the courtroom erupted in guffaws.

Barry's performance had to be given against the backdrop of Judge Tevrizian, whose boiling demeanor broadcast pure contempt for the witness. Tevrizian was infuriated by the wonder boy's testimony, and wouldn't even look at Barry as he admonished him again and again through clenched teeth to answer the question and not editorialize. Tevrizian has no patience with dishonesty and especially hates financial chicanery. Most of all, he prides himself on clearing cases swiftly. I swear I saw steam coming out of his ears.

When Barry contended that he couldn't turn to the police because the mobsters said they had friends there and would know about it, the judge disgustedly interceded.

"Ever heard of the FBI?" he demanded.

"Yes, I have, your honor."

"Ever heard of the sheriff—the Los Angeles County Sheriff?"

"Yes, I have, your honor."

"Ever heard of the state Attorney General?"

"Yes."

"Ever heard of the county marshal?"

"I have."

"Did you ever attempt to contact any of those individuals regarding threats against you?"

"Didn't matter," Barry answered calmly. "They told me that no matter where I went . . . it would be found out."

Later, Barry was asked about Sharon Elowsky and the $2 million from Prudential-Bache.

"Shari Elowsky came out to California and I had one goal in mind. I had to get that money. I had to," Barry said. "I took her to dinner. I took her to her hotel . . . and at that hotel, we did more than what she testified to."

"Are you proud of that?" Tevrizian interrupted.

"No I'm not, your honor, at all, but I'm telling you the truth," said Barry.

"All right, then be a gentleman about it," the judge said curtly.

It was the ruthlessness which came across in his own testimony that probably had as much as anything to do with Barry's failure as a witness. He never seemed even remotely sorry. Under a withering cross-examination by Greenberg, Barry's heedless mendacity was unmasked. If he committed what Greenberg called "this 1,825 days of crime" out of fear for himself and his family, wasn't he worried now that he was coming clean? Wouldn't the mobsters get him this time for sure? Barry answered with emotion: "I'll be damned if I'm going to let another nineteen-year-old kid get swelled up as an entrepreneur with these sharks that are out there."

Barry's eagerness to manipulate the system was naked. When he detected that the judge was trying to keep something from the jury as irrelevant or prejudicial, he would find a way to blurt it out. Tevrizian wouldn't allow Barry's wild allegations that Krowpman had sexually abused him. When Kenner asked the next question about Krowpman, Barry replied, "After he made his attempted rape or before?" Toward the end of his testimony it began to seem that Tevrizian would send him to Devil's Island.

On December 14, 1988, the beleaguered jury of six men and six women found Barry guilty on all fifty-seven counts after less than four days of deliberations and a weekend of rumination. There were so many charges that it took more than twenty minutes just to read the verdict. Five days later the jurors convicted Rothberg on all counts as well.

Barry amazed everybody right up until the end. Some of his lieutenants have felt remorse, or shame, or the need to rationalize. Barry's personality, by contrast, appears seamlessly, coherently false, free of guilt or worry over what he has done. Even at the end, his insincerity was utter. After the verdict, he sent out handwritten Christmas greetings, including one to Asperger and Greenberg, his prosecutors. All the misspellings are Barry's.

Dear Jim and Gordon,

Just a brief note to wish you both a wonderful holiday season. You guys truely are the best at what you do. I wouldn't of wanted anyone else up there making me look soooo bad. I am *really* sorry for all the trouble I've caused you and your staff. But the real tragidy would of been if I haven't learned anything through all of this. But I have! God bless you both and I wish you all the best in the future.

All my best wishes,
Barry

At the bottom of the card were printed the words, "Remembering you is one of the special joys of the season."

29

On March 27, Barry Minkow was sentenced to twenty-five years in federal prison. To this day it's not clear how much money he made from his crimes. The government estimated at his trial that he got more than $3 million in benefits from January 1, 1985, to October of 1987, but that doesn't count cash. The truth is probably millions higher. Whether Barry stashed any money overseas will probably never be known. He will be eligible for parole after about eight years, but he's likely to serve perhaps ten, in which case he would be thirty-two.

Federal authorities were still investigating Maurice Rind, Richard Schulman and Robert Victor as this book was completed, but they hadn't been charged with anything. Asperger said in court that Rind and Schulman probably made more than $1 million each on ZZZZ Best. Victor, he said, probably made "a couple hundred thousand."

Mark Morze got an estimated $2.25 million, most of it spent on cars, houses, jewelry, furs and the like for himself and Candi Apple. He pleaded guilty to fraud and tax evasion and got eight years; like the other defendants, he will probably have to serve between one-third and two-thirds of that term.

Brian Morze, who probably got $125,000, pleaded guilty to fraud and got three years. Minta Morze wasn't charged.

Dan Krowpman Sr., who got about $600,000, pleaded guilty to fraud and filing a false tax return. He was sentenced to three years.

Tom Padgett probably got several hundred thousand dollars, although when the scam collapsed he was left penniless. He pleaded guilty to four counts of fraud and was sentenced to eight years. Padgett seemed mainly upset about the drug allegations, vehemently denying any involvement in such things. I believe him. He plans to do a lot of reading—I gave him Robert Hughes' *The Fatal Shore* as a going-away present—and to be more careful the next time around. "I'd really have to think twice before going into business with Barry again," he says sensibly.

The Ultimate White Man, Mark Roddy, pleaded to four counts of fraud and got five years, on top of the four-year sentence arising from his New Mexico drug arrest.

Chip Arrington, Barry's chief operating officer and all-around gofer, pleaded guilty to two fraud counts. He was sentenced to six months in a halfway house and five years' probation.

Jack and Jerry Polevoi both pleaded guilty to two counts of conspiracy and two counts of filing a false tax return, and they were sentenced to eighteen months each.

Eugene Lasko pleaded guilty to conspiracy and obstructing the IRS in connection with money laundering. He was sentenced to thirty days in a halfway house, 300 hours community service and a $1,000 fine.

Edward Krivda, who sold carpet to ZZZZ Best and verified fictitious invoices for Price Waterhouse just two days before Barry resigned, pleaded guilty to lying to the SEC and was sentenced to sixty days in a halfway house.

Norman Rothberg, ever ill-starred, rejected a plea-bargain that would have averted incarceration, because it would have cost him his CPA license. He was convicted of conspiracy and fraud, sentenced to a year and a day in prison and will lose his license anyway. He got perhaps $27,000 from the scheme.

The victims far outnumbered the perpetrators. There were 715 shareholders of record when ZZZZ Best collapsed, but the actual number was substantially higher, since trust companies or other nominees acted as stand-ins for many but were counted as one. There were about 3,000 creditors in the company's bankruptcy.

The biggest losers financially include Union Bank, out $7 million, and First Interstate, out $1.8 million or more. Prudential-Bache lost $2 million. Steve Greenberg seems to have dropped about $1 million, as did Malamut. Plushcell, whose agent was Peter Strauss, appears to have lost $5 or $6 million.

Calculating total losses in the ZZZZ Best affair is tricky because so much was lost in the stock market. Although ZZZZ Best shares peaked at more than $18 and then plummeted to zero, many stockholders bought for less, and some bailed out on the way down, so it's not just a matter of multiplying $18 by half of 11.6 million (the approximate number of shares in public hands at the collapse). Information about actual trading wasn't publicly available as this book was completed. Nevertheless, it seems clear that shareholders, banks, private investors and creditors lost a total of at least $100 million because of Barry Minkow.

As this book was completed, the ZZZZ Best case was far from over. Many of those associated with the company faced possible legal action from the SEC, although the Los Angeles police had yet to bring any charges in connection with the allegations Chief Gates made at his press conference. Certainly ZZZZ Best was not primarily a laundering operation for mob drug money, as Brambles for so long insisted. Beyond the criminal, the civil litigation flowing from ZZZZ Best is likely to last for years. In the words of Stuart D. Wechsler, one of the lawyers trying to recoup investor losses, "It's astounding that a fellow who's hardly shaving could cause a financial debacle of this kind."

The term psychopath is out of favor with the mental-health establishment. Like "sociopath," it has been succeeded by the more clinical-sounding "antisocial personality disorder," which means the same thing and applies to Barry Minkow just as well. A psychopath is someone who can act without regard to conscience, victimizing people again and again without remorse. Psychopaths are charming, intelligent and make superb liars. They are unreliable and tend not to learn from experience. Amoral, they are often criminals; although many killers are psychopaths, there are far more psychopaths who never take a human life. Yet most do use people as disposable objects, and the true psychopath is probably incapable of love. The late Dr. Hervey Cleckley, who spent a lifetime studying the subject, said that unlike the psychotic, who is patently crazy, the psychopath usually wears "a convincing mask of sanity." Cleckley described the psychopath as a sad and dangerous creature, "a subtly constructed reflex machine which can mimic the human personality perfectly," yet lacks the deepest and most important characteristics of humanity.

Most psychopaths are men, and many were hyperactive children who felt helpless and inferior. Often they lacked a parent or strong parental discipline. In later life they frequently turn to alcohol or drugs, are wildly impulsive, boastful, irritable and aggressive to the point of belligerence. Yet psychopaths are superficially winning and—sometimes—strangely kind. They routinely bounce checks, default on debts and break the law. They have terrible driving records.

Dr. Ethel Spector Person, a Columbia University psychiatrist whose patients have included many in business, has drawn some similarities between psychopaths and entrepreneurs. "We usually reserve the term psychopath for the 'unsuccessful' psychopath," she writes, adding: "Some successful entrepreneurs might also be 'successful' psychopaths."

That seems to stretch the definition a bit, but some of the psychopath's traits would suit him to business, politics or other leadership roles. Often charismatic, psychopaths tend to be manic and adept at attracting others to themselves or their ideas. They are good at going their own way, but bad at being alone. Perspective and guilt aren't very helpful to them, they can easily justify hurting others, and they welcome risk. They also excel at manipulating people.

No one knows why there are psychopaths. Heredity plays a role, and there are signs that the basis of psychopathy is physiological— that this sickness of the soul is really a sickness of the body, some blind biochemical glut or deficiency that we can't yet understand. Psychopaths are promiscuous and tend to reproduce themselves. There is evidence that their proportion in society is growing.

These things imply evil as a natural, random, self-perpetuating force that is no less puzzling for its physical basis. The ZZZZ Best fiasco can be seen the same way. Changing the accounting rules and securities laws will help, but every now and then a Barry Minkow will come along, and ZZZZ Best will happen again. Such frauds are in the natural order of things, I suspect, as old and enduring as human needs.

Yet Barry was so young, it's hard not to think of him as uniquely a product of his own time. He was sentenced in 1989, and to those of us cursed with an apocalyptic perspective about the giddy prosperity of the decade and its flimsy financial and moral underpinnings, his story feels like a requiem. Before the eighties were out, Ronald Reagan had left office, Ivan Boesky was behind bars, Drexel had pleaded guilty to securities charges and Michael Milken was indicted. What with the federal, trade and typical household deficits, America was bathing in red ink as if it were champagne. Charles Ponzi would have been proud.

As for Barry himself, there may be hope for him yet. The psychopath's worst symptoms tend to wane once he passes age thirty (just as the hyperactive's subside past age nine), and Barry will be in prison until then. Meanwhile, despite bouts of depression and consultations with an unidentified spiritual adviser, he remains irrepressible. When Assistant U.S. Attorney Maury Leiter, a colleague of Asperger and Greenberg, was touring the new federal detention center in downtown Los Angeles, he heard someone calling his name. It was Barry.

"Hey, Mr. Leiter—how do you like the place?"

It seems very nice, the prosecutor said.

"It's real nice," Barry agreed. "The carpets are real clean, too. And they're gonna stay that way, for a long, long time."

Index